PUTIN'S

ASYMMETRIC ASSAULT ON DEMOCRACY

IN RUSSIA AND EUROPE

IMPLICATIONS FOR U.S. NATIONAL SECURITY

INTRODUCTION BY CHRIS SAMPSON

SKYHORSE PUBLISHING

First published by the 115th US Congress in 2018.
Introduction Copyright © 2018 by Chris Sampson

All rights reserved. No part of this book may be reproduced in any manner without the express written consent of the publisher, except in the case of brief excerpts in critical reviews or articles. All inquiries should be addressed to Skyhorse Publishing, 307 West 36th Street, 11th Floor, New York, NY 10018.

Skyhorse Publishing books may be purchased in bulk at special discounts for sales promotion, corporate gifts, fund-raising, or educational purposes. Special editions can also be created to specifications. For details, contact the Special Sales Department, Skyhorse Publishing, 307 West 36th Street, 11th Floor, New York, NY 10018 or info@skyhorsepublishing.com.

Skyhorse® and Skyhorse Publishing® are registered trademarks of Skyhorse Publishing, Inc.®, a Delaware corporation.

Visit our website at www.skyhorsepublishing.com.

10 9 8 7 6 5 4 3 2 1

Cover design by Brian Peterson

Print ISBN: 978-1-5107-3987-1
Ebook ISBN: 978-1-5107-3988-8

Printed in the United States of America

PUTIN'S ASYMMETRIC ASSAULT ON DEMOCRACY IN RUSSIA AND EUROPE: IMPLICATIONS FOR U.S. NATIONAL SECURITY

A MINORITY STAFF REPORT

PREPARED FOR THE USE OF THE

COMMITTEE ON FOREIGN RELATIONS

UNITED STATES SENATE

ONE HUNDRED FIFTEENTH CONGRESS

SECOND SESSION

JANUARY 10, 2018

Printed for the use of the Committee on Foreign Relations

Available via World Wide Web:
http://www.gpoaccess.gov/congress/index.html

U.S. GOVERNMENT PUBLISHING OFFICE

28–110 PDF   WASHINGTON : 2018

For sale by the Superintendent of Documents, U.S. Government Publishing Office
Internet: bookstore.gpo.gov   Phone: toll free (866) 512–1800; DC area (202) 512–1800
Fax: (202) 512–2104   Mail: Stop IDCC, Washington, DC 20402–0001

COMMITTEE ON FOREIGN RELATIONS

BOB CORKER, Tennessee, *Chairman*

JAMES E. RISCH, Idaho	BENJAMIN L. CARDIN, Maryland
MARCO RUBIO, Florida	ROBERT MENENDEZ, New Jersey
RON JOHNSON, Wisconsin	JEANNE SHAHEEN, New Hampshire
JEFF FLAKE, Arizona	CHRISTOPHER A. COONS, Delaware
CORY GARDNER, Colorado	TOM UDALL, New Mexico
TODD YOUNG, Indiana	CHRISTOPHER MURPHY, Connecticut
JOHN BARRASSO, Wyoming	TIM KAINE, Virginia
JOHNNY ISAKSON, Georgia	EDWARD J. MARKEY, Massachusetts
ROB PORTMAN, Ohio	JEFF MERKLEY, Oregon
RAND PAUL, Kentucky	CORY A. BOOKER, New Jersey

TODD WOMACK, *Staff Director*
JESSICA LEWIS, *Democratic Staff Director*
JOHN DUTTON, *Chief Clerk*

CONTENTS

Introduction vii
Letter of Transmittal xi
Executive Summary 1
Chapter 1: Putin's Rise and Motivations 7
    Ascent to the Top 8
    Return of the Security Services 10
    The Kremlin's Paranoid Pathology 13
Chapter 2: Manipulation and Repression Inside Russia 15
    Influencing Ideology, Politics, and Culture 17
    Controlling the Public Narrative 24
    Corrupting Economic Activity 31
Chapter 3: Old Active Measures and Modern Malign Influence Operations 35
    A Brief History of Soviet Active Measures 35
    Modern Malign Influence Operations 37
    The Kremlin's Disinformation Platforms 40
Chapter 4: Weaponization of Civil Society, Ideology, Culture, Crime, and
    Energy 47
    The Role of State Foundations, GONGOs, NGOs, and Think Tanks 47
    The Kremlin's Cultivation of Political Extremes 50
    The Use of the Russian Orthodox Church 53
    The Nationalization of Organized Crime 54
    The Export of Corruption 57
    The Leveraging of Energy Supplies for Influence 58
Chapter 5: Kremlin Interference in Semi-Consolidated Democracies and Tran-
    sitional Governments 65
    Ukraine 67
    Georgia 73
    Montenegro 77
    Serbia 81
    Bulgaria 89
    Hungary 94
Chapter 6: Kremlin Interference in Consolidated Democracies 99
    Baltic States: Latvia, Lithuania, and Estonia 100
    Nordic States: Denmark, Finland, Norway, and Sweden 109
    The Netherlands 113
    United Kingdom 116
    France 121
    Germany 127
    Spain 133
    Italy 137
Chapter 7: Multilateral & U.S. Efforts to Counter the Kremlin's Asymmetric
    Arsenal 141
    Collective Defenses Against Disinformation and Cyber Attacks 141
    European Energy Diversification and Integration 144
    EU and U.S. Efforts to Sanction Malicious Actors 145
    U.S. Efforts to Create Alternative and Accurate Quality Programming 148
    Assessing the State Department's Global Engagement Center 149
Chapter 8: Conclusions and Recommendations 153

APPENDICES

Appendix A: 1999 Apartment Building Bombings 165
Appendix B: Alleged Political Assassinations 171
Appendix C: Russian Government's Olympic Cheating Scheme 175
Appendix D: Russia's Security Services and Cyber Hackers 181
Appendix E: Attacks and Harassment Against Human Rights Activists and
Journalists Inside Russia 187
Appendix F: Flawed Elections in the Russian Federation Since 1999 191
Appendix G: Harsh Treatment of LGBT Individuals and Women in the Rus-
sian Federation 193
Appendix H: Disinformation Narratives, Themes, and Techniques 195
Appendix I: Letter from Senator Cardin to European Ambassadors 199

INTRODUCTION

ON JANUARY 10, 2018, the Minority Staff for the Committee on Foreign Relations in the United States Senate released the official report on the efforts by Russian President Vladimir Putin to undermine the United States and its democratic allies in Europe. The timely report detailed the Russian campaign to increase nationalist sentiments, erode confidence in democracy, and chip away at the NATO alliances of the post–World War II era. The targets, goals, and toolkits have been updated for the twenty-first century, but the mission to destroy longstanding international partnerships has roots since before the 1917 Russian Revolution. In the early days of the Soviet Union, the ideology-driven operations aimed to spread the Marxist ideals across the globe. But by the twenty-first century the ideology of old was gone, and the Kremlin's ambitions became apparent, intertwined with the rise of the Russian oligarchs.

In the early 1980s, Americans first became aware of the finer details of the hybrid warfare method used by the Soviet bloc countries to manipulate public opinion to attain the Kremlin's objectives. In congressional testimony, former KGB officers like Stanislav Levchenko, who had defected to the west, shared details on how they engaged in operations to recruit sources, spread disinformation, and gain the upper hand on the global stage without firing a single shot. They called these influence operations "active measures." Active measures during the Cold War were aimed to confuse the West about Soviet activities and capabilities, including military power, technological development, and economic standing. Though the Soviet Union collapsed by the early

1990s, Russia's intelligence service never disappeared. The Russian government rebranded these spy agencies—the KGB became the FSB (Federal Security Service) as well as the SVR (External Intelligence Service). And just as these spy agencies never disappeared, neither did their methods. The influence operations called "active measures" became "methods of support."

While the FSB and SVR now used many of the KGB's old influence operations methods around the world, they also developed new tools found in the cyber world, providing a global reach mixed with the ability to disguise the origin of operations. The use of disinformation and agents of influence were still an old reliable method, but now they use updated methods on modern platforms of social and broadcast media. Perhaps most notably, these updated methods include powerful new cyber tools, including computer hacking and troll armies (known in Russia as web brigades), who are groups of people paid to go online and harass for or against a position, candidate, or social movement.

Though the re-emergence of active measures was exposed again in the 2016 United States presidential campaign, they had never truly ceased with the fall of the Soviet Union. A criminal class of wealthy oligarchs had stolen the ambitions of Russian democracy in the 1990s, and now sought to capitalize on their control of resources. Over the two decades since the collapse of the U.S.S.R., these campaigns were aimed to control and manipulate the former Soviet satellite states. During the Cold War of the twentieth century, intelligence services in Soviet-controlled countries aided in attacking the West, but now those countries had their own ambitions and residual memories of Soviet occupation. The Kremlin targeted neighboring countries, including Ukraine and Georgia, with cyber-attacks, propaganda campaigns, and seizure of territory. In addition, the Kremlin had its sights on other countries in the West.

Outside the neighbor states bordering Russia, operations aimed at Western democracies now seek to give rise to nationalist movements that resist involvement in NATO efforts that have long kept Russian power confined. This included meddling in the United Kingdom, France, Germany, Spain, and the United States. Where once the Soviets worked to fuel left wing and Marxist groups, the Russians now are playing to the extremes that feed right wing movements.

This report gives a new overview of the history, current goals, targets, and the methods Russian President Vladimir Putin now uses as part of a hybrid warfare arsenal. More importantly, it recommends sensible countermeasures to curtail these operations and to defend democracies targeted by the Kremlin. As all citizens of the world are affected by the consequences of these global influence operations, we would be well advised to recognize the historical dangers the report documents, heed its consequential warnings, and implement its recommendations.

Chris Sampson

January 19, 2018

Co-Author of *Hacking ISIS: How to Destroy the Cyber-Jihad*

with Malcolm Nance

LETTER OF TRANSMITTAL

UNITED STATES SENATE,
COMMITTEE ON FOREIGN RELATIONS,
Washington, DC, January 10, 2018

DEAR COLLEAGUES: For years, Vladimir Putin's government has engaged in a relentless assault to undermine democracy and the rule of law in Europe and the United States. Mr. Putin's Kremlin employs an asymmetric arsenal that includes military invasions, cyberattacks, disinformation, support for fringe political groups, and the weaponization of energy resources, organized crime, and corruption. The Kremlin has refined the use of these tools over time and these attacks have intensified in scale and complexity across Europe. If the United States fails to work with urgency to address this complex and growing threat, the regime in Moscow will become further emboldened. It will continue to develop and refine its arsenal to use on democracies around the world, including against U.S. elections in 2018 and 2020.

Following attacks like Pearl Harbor and 9/11, U.S. presidents have rallied the country and the world to address the challenges facing the nation. Yet the current President of the United States has barely acknowledged the threat posed by Mr. Putin's repeated attacks on democratic governments and institutions, let alone exercised the kind of leadership history has shown is necessary to effectively counter this kind of aggression. Never before in American history has so clear a threat to national security been so clearly ignored by a U.S. president.

The threat posed by Mr. Putin's meddling existed before the current U.S. Administration, and may well extend beyond it. Yet, as this report will demonstrate, the Russian government's malign influence operations can be deterred. Several countries in Europe took notice of the Kremlin's efforts to interfere in the 2016 U.S. election and realized the danger posed to their democracies. They have taken steps to build resilience against Mr. Putin's aggression and interference, and the range of effective measures implemented by European countries provide valuable lessons for the United States.

To that end, this report recommends a series of actions that the United States should take across government, civil society, and the private sector—and in cooperation with our allies—to push back against the Kremlin's aggression and establish a set of long-term norms that can neutralize such efforts to undermine democracy. Yet it must be noted that without leadership from the President, any attempt to marshal such a response will be inherently weakened at the outset.

In addition, it is important to draw a distinction between Mr. Putin's corrupt regime and the people of Russia. Many Russian citizens strive for a transparent, accountable government that operates under the democratic rule of law, and we hold hope for better relations in the future with a Russian government that reflects these demands. In the meantime, the United States must work with our allies to build defenses against Mr. Putin's asymmetric arsenal, and strengthen international norms and values to deter such behavior by Russia or any other country.

The events discussed in this report are illustrative, not exhaustive, and cover a period ending on December 31, 2017. There are several important geographic areas that remain beyond the scope of this report, including the Russian government's role in the Syria conflict, its complicated relationship with Turkey, or its involvement in places like Central Asia and Latin America. The Russian government's use of corruption and money laundering also merit additional examination by relevant committees in Congress, as well as the Executive Branch. Given the ongoing investigations by the Senate Intelligence and Judiciary Committees, this report does not delve into Russia's interference in the 2016 U.S. election. Furthermore, U.S. election infrastructure, electrical grids, and information systems are outside the jurisdiction of the Senate Foreign Relations Committee and therefore beyond the scope of the recommendations in this report, but certainly warrant further study.

Finally, there must be a bipartisan sense of urgency so the United States immediately begins taking the steps necessary to fortify and protect our democracy from Mr. Putin's malicious meddling. There is a long bipartisan tradition in Congress in support of firm policies to counter Russian government aggression and abuse against its own citizens, our allies, and universal values. This report seeks to continue that tradition.

Sincerely,

BENJAMIN L. CARDIN,
Ranking Member.

PUTIN'S ASYMMETRIC ASSAULT ON DEMOCRACY IN RUSSIA AND EUROPE: IMPLICATIONS FOR U.S. NATIONAL SECURITY

Executive Summary

Nearly 20 years ago, Vladimir Putin gained and solidified power by exploiting blackmail, fears of terrorism, and war. Since then, he has combined military adventurism and aggression abroad with propaganda and political repression at home, to persuade a domestic audience that he is restoring Russia to greatness and a respected position on the world stage. All the while, he has empowered the state security services and employed them to consolidate his hold on the levers of political, social, and economic power, which he has used to make himself and a circle of loyalists extraordinarily wealthy.

Democracies like the United States and those in Europe present three distinct challenges to Mr. Putin. First, the sanctions they have collectively placed on his regime for its illegal occupation of Crimea and invasion of eastern Ukraine threaten the ill-gotten wealth of his loyalists and hamper their extravagant lifestyles. Second, Mr. Putin sees successful democracies, especially those along Russia's periphery, as threats to his regime because they present an attractive alternative to his corrupt and criminal rule. Third, democracies with transparent governments, the rule of law, a free media, and engaged citizens are naturally more resilient to the spread of corruption beyond Russia's borders, thereby limiting the opportunities for the further enrichment of Putin and his chosen elite.

Mr. Putin has thus made it a priority of his regime to attack the democracies of Europe and the United States and undermine the transatlantic alliance upon which Europe's peace and prosperity have depended upon for over 70 years. He has used the security services, the media, public and private companies, organized criminal groups, and social and religious organizations to spread malicious disinformation, interfere in elections, fuel corruption, threaten energy security, and more. At their most extreme, the Russian government's security services have been used to harass and even assassinate political enemies at home and abroad; cheat at the Olympic Games; and protect and exploit cybercriminals in Russia who attack American businesses and steal the financial information of American consumers. Mr. Putin resorts to the use of these asymmetric tools to achieve his goals because he is operating from a position of weakness—hobbled by a faltering economy, a substandard military, and few followers on the world stage.

The tactics that Putin has deployed to undermine democracies abroad were developed at home, and over nearly two decades he has used them against the Russian people with increased impunity. The result has been hundreds of billions of dollars stolen and spirited away abroad, all while independent media and civil society, elections, political parties, and cultural institutions have been manipulated and suppressed, significantly hindering effective domestic opposition to Putin's regime.

While consolidating his grip on power at home, Mr. Putin oversaw an opportunistic expansion of malign influence operations abroad, targeting vulnerable states on Russia's periphery, as well as countries in Western institutions like the European Union (EU) and the North Atlantic Treaty Organization (NATO). The Kremlin has substantially increased its investments in propaganda outlets beyond Russia's borders, funded and supported nongovernmental organizations and political parties that advanced Mr. Putin's anti-EU and anti-NATO agenda, nationalized mafia groups to help launder money and commit other crimes for the state abroad, and used its near-monopoly over energy supplies in some countries to exert influence and spread corruption.

In semi-consolidated democracies and transitional governments on Russia's periphery, the Kremlin most aggressively targets states that seek to integrate with the EU and NATO or present an opportunity to weaken those institutions from within. For example, as Georgia and Ukraine moved closer to these institutions, the Russian government attacked them with cyberwarfare, disinformation campaigns, and military force. When the Kremlin's attempt to politically influence Montenegro's election failed, its security services allegedly tried to launch a coup. In Serbia, the Kremlin exploits cultural connections and leverages its near monopoly on energy supplies to attempt to slow down or derail the country's Western integration efforts. And though they are in the EU and NATO, countries like Hungary and Bulgaria face acute challenges from the Russian government, which exerts significant influence in politics, business, and the energy sector. Despite some efforts to counter Russian malign influence, these countries remain significantly vulnerable to the Kremlin's corrupt agenda.

In consolidated democracies within the EU and NATO, the Russian government seeks to undermine support for sanctions against Russia, interfere in elections through overt or covert support of sympathetic political parties and the spread of disinformation, and sow discord and confusion by exacerbating existing social and political divisions through disinformation and cultivated ideological groups. This group of countries has developed several effective countermeasures that both deter Russian government behavior and build societal resilience. As it crafts its response, the United States should look to these lessons learned:

- The United Kingdom has made a point to publicly chastise the Russian government for its meddling in democracies, and moved to strengthen cybersecurity and electoral processes.

- Germany pre-empted Kremlin interference in its national election with a strong warning of consequences, an agreement among political parties not to use bots or paid trolls, and close cyber cooperation between the government and political campaigns.
- Spain has led Europe in cracking down on Russia-based organized crime groups that use the country as an operational base and node for money laundering and other crimes.
- France has fostered strong cooperation between government, political, and media actors to blunt the impact of the Kremlin's cyber-hacking and smear campaigns.
- The Nordic states have largely adopted a "whole of society" approach against Mr. Putin's malign influence operations, involving the government, civil society, the media, and the private sector, with an emphasis on teaching critical thinking and media literacy.
- The Baltic states have kept their publics well-informed of the malicious activities of Russia's security services, strengthened defenses against cyberattacks and disinformation, and diversified energy supplies to reduce dependence on Russia.

While the countries of Europe have each had unique responses to the Kremlin's aggression, they have also begun to use regional institutions to knit together their efforts and develop best practices. NATO and the EU have launched centers focused on strategic communications and cyber defense, and Finland's government hosts a joint EU/NATO center for countering hybrid threats. A number of independent think tanks and non-governmental organizations (NGOs) have also launched regional disinformation monitoring and fact-checking operations, and European governments are supporting regional programs to strengthen independent journalism and media literacy. Some of these initiatives are relatively new, but several have already begun to bear fruit and warrant continued investment and broader expansion. Through the adoption of the Third Energy Package, which promotes energy diversification and integration, as well as a growing resistance to the Nord Stream 2 pipeline, many European countries are reducing their dependence on Russian energy supplies, though much remains to be done.

Despite the clear assaults on our democracy and our allies in Europe, the U.S. government still does not have a coherent, comprehensive, and coordinated approach to the Kremlin's malign influence operations, either abroad or at home. Although the U.S. government has for years had a patchwork of offices and programs supporting independent journalism, cyber security, and the countering of disinformation, the lack of presidential leadership in addressing the threat Putin poses has hampered a strong U.S. response. In early 2017, Congress provided the State Department's Global Engagement Center the resources and mandate to address Kremlin disinformation campaigns, but operations have been stymied by the Department's hiring freeze and unnecessarily long delays by its senior leadership in transferring authorized funds to the office. While many mid-level and some senior-level officials throughout the State Department and U.S. government are cognizant of the threat posed by Mr. Putin's asymmetric arsenal, the

U.S. President continues to deny that any such threat exists, creating a leadership vacuum in our own government and among our European partners and allies.

KEY RECOMMENDATIONS

The recommendations below are based on a review of Mr. Putin's efforts to undermine democracy in Europe and effective responses to date. By implementing these recommendations, the United States can better defend against and deter the Kremlin's malign influence operations, and strengthen international norms and values to prevent such behavior by Russia and other states. A more comprehensive list of recommendations can be found in Chapter Eight.

1. *Assert Presidential Leadership and Launch a National Response:* President Trump has been negligent in acknowledging and responding to the threat to U.S. national security posed by Mr. Putin's meddling. The President should immediately declare that it is U.S. policy to counter and deter all forms of Russian hybrid threats against the United States and around the world. The President should establish a high-level interagency fusion cell, modeled on the National Counterterrorism Center (NCTC), to coordinate all elements of U.S. policy and programming in response to the Russian government's malign influence operations. And the President should present to Congress a comprehensive national strategy to counter these grave national security threats and work with the Congress and our allies to get this strategy implemented and funded.

2. *Support Democratic Institution Building and Values Abroad and with a Stronger Congressional Voice:* Democracies with transparent governments, the rule of law, a free media, and engaged citizens are naturally more resilient to Mr. Putin's asymmetric arsenal. The U.S. government should provide assistance, in concert with allies in Europe, to build democratic institutions within the European and Eurasian states most vulnerable to Russian government interference. Using the funding authorization outlined in the Countering America's Adversaries Through Sanctions Act as policy guidance, the U.S. government should increase this spending in Europe and Eurasia to at least $250 million over the next two fiscal years. To reinforce these efforts, the U.S. government should demonstrate clear and sustained diplomatic leadership in support of individual human rights that form the backbone of democratic systems. Members in the U.S. Congress have a responsibility to show U.S. leadership on values by making democracy and human rights a central part of their agendas. They should conduct committee hearings and use other platforms and opportunities to publicly advance these issues.

3. *Expose and Freeze Kremlin-Linked Dirty Money:* Corruption provides the motivation and the means for many of the Kremlin's malign influence operations. The U.S. Treasury Department should make public any intelligence related to Mr. Putin's personal corruption and wealth stored abroad, and take steps with our European allies to cut off Mr. Putin and his inner circle from the international financial system. The U.S.

government should also expose corrupt and criminal activities associated with Russia's state-owned energy sector. Furthermore, it should robustly implement the Global Magnitsky Human Rights Accountability Act and the Countering America's Adversaries Through Sanctions Act, which allow for sanctions against corrupt actors in Russia and abroad. In addition, the U.S. government should issue yearly reports that assign tiered classifications based on objective third-party corruption indicators, as well as governmental efforts to combat corruption.

4. *Subject State Hybrid Threat Actors to an Escalatory Sanctions Regime:* The Kremlin and other regimes hostile to democracy must know that there will be consequences for their actions. The U.S. government should designate countries that employ malign influence operations to assault democracies as State Hybrid Threat Actors. Countries that are designated as such would fall under a preemptive and escalatory sanctions regime that would be applied whenever the state uses asymmetric weapons like cyberattacks to interfere with a democratic election or disrupt a country's critical infrastructure. The U.S. government should work with the EU to ensure that these sanctions are coordinated and effective.

5. *Publicize the Kremlin's Global Malign Influence Efforts:* Exposing and publicizing the nature of the threat of Russian malign influence activities, as the U.S. intelligence community did in January 2017, can be an action-forcing event that not only boosts public awareness, but also drives effective responses from the private sector, especially social media platforms, as well as civil society and independent media, who can use the information to pursue their own investigations. The U.S. government should produce yearly public reports that detail the Russian government's malign influence operations in the United States and around the world.

6. *Build an International Coalition to Counter Hybrid Threats:* The United States is stronger and more effective when we work with our partners and allies abroad. The U.S. government should lead an international effort of like-minded democracies to build awareness of and resilience to the Kremlin's malign influence operations. Specifically, the President should convene an annual global summit on hybrid threats, modeled on the Global Coalition to Counter ISIL or the Countering Violent Extremism (CVE) summits that have taken place since 2015. Civil society and the private sector should participate in the summits and follow-on activities.

7. *Uncover Foreign Funding that Erodes Democracy:* Foreign illicit money corrupts the political, social, and economic systems of democracies. The United States and European countries must make it more difficult for foreign actors to use financial resources to interfere in democratic systems, specifically by passing legislation to require full disclosure of shell company owners and improve transparency for funding of political parties, campaigns, and advocacy groups.

8. *Build Global Cyber Defenses and Norms:* The United States and our European allies remain woefully vulnerable to cyberattacks, which are a preferred asymmetric weapon of state hybrid threat actors. The U.S. government and NATO should lead a coalition of countries committed to mutual defense against cyberattacks, to include the establishment of rapid reaction teams to defend allies under attack. The U.S. government should also call a special meeting of the NATO heads of state to review the extent of Russian government-sponsored cyberattacks among member states and develop formal guidelines on how the Alliance will consider such attacks in the context of NATO's Article 5 collective defense provision. Furthermore, the U.S. government should lead an effort to establish an international treaty on the use of cyber tools in peace time, modeled on international arms control treaties.

9. *Hold Social Media Companies Accountable:* Social media platforms are a key conduit of disinformation campaigns that undermine democracies. U.S. and European governments should mandate that social media companies make public the sources of funding for political advertisements, along the same lines as TV channels and print media. Social media companies should conduct comprehensive audits on how their platforms may have been used by Kremlin-linked entities to influence elections occurring over the past several years, and should establish civil society advisory councils to provide input and warnings about emerging disinformation trends and government suppression. In addition, they should work with philanthropies, governments, and civil society to promote media literacy and reduce the presence of disinformation on their platforms.

10. *Reduce European Dependence on Russian Energy Sources:* Payments to state-owned Russian energy companies fund the Kremlin's military aggression abroad, as well as overt and covert activities that undermine democratic institutions and social cohesion in Europe and the United States. The U.S. government should use its trade and development agencies to support strategically important energy diversification and integration projects in Europe. In addition, the U.S. government should continue to oppose the construction of Nord Stream 2, a project which significantly undermines the long-term energy security of Europe and the economic prospects of Ukraine.

Chapter 1: Putin's Rise and Motivations

A Russian interior minister once remarked that "we are on the eve of a revolution" and "to avert a revolution, we need a small victorious war" to "distract the attention of the masses."[1] While he made the comment in 1903, the year before the Russian Empire entered a disastrous war with Imperial Japan, he could also have been speaking before Russian forces invaded Chechnya in 1999, Georgia in 2008, Ukraine in 2014, or Syria in 2015. Those conflicts reflect a nearly twenty-year pattern of the Kremlin prosecuting similar "small" wars to achieve internal political objectives, revealing a direct link between the Russian government's external aggression and its internal oppression.[2]

President Vladimir Putin's Kremlin has used a sophisticated combination of propaganda and suppression to keep the Russian public supportive of wars abroad and distracted from the regime's criminality and corruption at home. Putin's overarching domestic objectives are to preserve his power and increase his net worth, and he appears to have calculated that his regime can best do so by inflating his approval ratings with aggressive behavior abroad.[3] While the first-order effect of Putin's survival methodology poses a serious threat to global peace and stability, it has also created a profound series of second-order effects that threaten to corrode democratic institutions and open economies around the world, including here in the United States. It is not enough to sell the necessity of Russia's foreign interventions to only a domestic audience and to delegitimize or silence any Russian voices that rise in opposition. For Putin to succeed, he also requires a divided opposition abroad.

To that end, the Kremlin has honed its arsenal of malign influence operations at home and taken it global. And while the methods used may differ across countries, the goals are the same: sow distrust and confusion, promote radical voices on divisive political

---

[1] Simon Montefiore, *The Romanovs*, Alfred A. Knopf, at 514 (2016). When he made the remark, Vyacheslav Plehve, Tsar Nicholas's interior minister, had just put down a strike in Odessa. He had also turned the Ohkrana, the nickname for the Security Bureau, into "the world's most sophisticated secret police." *Ibid.* at 510. Lenin adopted the Ohkrana's methods when he formed the Cheka, predecessor of Stalin's NKVD, which became the KGB and, in its current incarnation, the FSB. Ben Fischer, *Okhrana: The Paris Operations of the Russian Imperial Police,* Diane Publishing, at 10 (1999).

[2] *See* Statement of Daniel B. Baer, *The European Union as a Partner Against Russian Aggression: Sanctions, Security, Democratic Institutions and the Way Forward,* Hearing before the U.S. Senate Committee on Foreign Relations, Apr. 4, 2017.

[3] Putin's net worth is estimated at between $40 billion and $200 billion (at the low end, making him the wealthiest person in Europe and, at the high end, in the world) and, as some believe, is held partly by a group of proxies. Samantha Karas, "Vladimir Putin Net Worth 2017: Russia's Leader May Be One of the Richest Men in the World," *International Business Times,* Feb. 15, 2017; Organized Crime and Corruption Reporting Project and Novaya Gazeta, *Putin and the Proxies,* https://www.occrp.org/en/putinandtheproxies, Oct. 24, 2017.

issues, and gain economic leverage, all while eroding support for the democratic process and rules-based institutions created in the aftermath of the Second World War. These efforts are largely led by the government's security services and buttressed by state-owned enterprises, Kremlin-aligned oligarchs, and Russian criminal groups that have effectively been nationalized by the state. The length and intensity of these operations emanate out in geographic concentric circles: they began in Russia, expanded to its periphery, then into the rest of Europe, and finally to the United States. The United States must now assume that the Kremlin will deploy in America the more dangerous tactics used successfully in Russia's periphery and the rest of Europe. This includes, for example, support for extremist and far-right groups that oppose democratic ideals, as well as attempts to co-opt politicians through economic corruption.

Putin's regime appears intent on using almost any means possible to undermine the democratic institutions and transatlantic alliances that have underwritten peace and prosperity in Europe for the past 70-plus years. To understand the nature of this threat, it is important to first look at who is responsible for it, their motivations, and what they are willing and capable of doing to achieve their objectives. To that end, the rest of this chapter will detail how Putin rose to power by exploiting blackmail, the fear of terrorism, and war, and subsequently used the security services to consolidate political and economic power. The motivations and methods behind Putin's rise help explain how he views the role of the security services and his willingness to use them to do the regime's dirty work, including assaulting democratic institutions and values in Europe and the United States.

ASCENT TO THE TOP

In 1999, Russian president Boris Yeltsin faced a problem. His second presidential term would end the following year, and his political rivals appeared positioned to take power. Russians at the time were not happy with Yeltsin's tenure: hyperinflation, austerity, debt, and a disastrous privatization scheme combined to decrease GDP by over 40 percent between 1990 and 1998, a collapse that was twice as large and lasted three times longer than the Great Depression in the United States.[4] The health and mortality crises that resulted from this economic disaster are estimated to have caused at least three million "excess deaths."[5] Yeltsin's approval ratings had also cratered amid allegations of rampant corruption, which also touched his family members. He needed a successor who could protect him and his family after he left office, but no one in his inner circle was nearly popular enough to secure victory.[6] He finally settled on a relatively unknown bureaucrat to serve as his sixth prime minister in less than a year and a half: Vladimir Vladimirovich Putin, who was then director of the Federal Security Service (or FSB, the KGB's successor). Why Putin? In the

---

[4] Robert English, "Russia, Trump, and a New Detente," *Foreign Affairs*, Mar. 10, 2017.
[5] *Ibid.*
[6] Mikhail Zygar, *All the Kremlin's Men*, PublicAffairs, at 9 (2016).

words of one Russia expert, "it was like spin the bottle, and the bottle stopped spinning at Putin."[7]

Putin had also shown that he was willing to protect Yeltsin and his family. In 1999, Russia's prosecutor general, Yury Skuratov, was conducting an investigation into high-level corruption in the Kremlin, including among Yeltsin's family members.[8] As Skuratov was pursuing his investigation, Yeltsin's chief of staff summoned him to the Kremlin and showed him a grainy videotape that purported to show him with two prostitutes in a hotel room. Skuratov submitted his resignation, though he later insisted that the tape was a fabrication.[9] But the resignation had to be approved by the upper chamber of Russia's parliament, the Federation Council, which insisted that Skuratov testify first. The day before his scheduled testimony, the sex tape was played on a television station after reportedly being personally delivered by Putin.[10] When showing the tape on TV did not prove enough to push the Federation Council into action, Putin went on TV himself and told the Russian public that the man in the tape was indeed Skuratov.[11] A former KGB general, Oleg Kalugin, maintains that the whole episode "was a special FSB operation to discredit an official with the help of a video featuring a person who resembled the prosecutor-general."[12] The "special operation" succeeded, and Yeltsin chose Putin to succeed him.[13]

Putin's confirmation vote for prime minister was called during Parliament's August recess, when legislators were distracted by upcoming parliamentary elections in four months.[14] There was not much debate about Putin's promise to "strengthen the executive vertical of power" or to do away with direct elections of regional governors.[15] The leader of the centrist group Regions of Russia, Oleg Morozov, reflected the overall mood of the legislature when he said, "I don't think we should torment ourselves with this decision .... We should vote, forget about it, and get on with business. We all have things to do."[16] Some in parliament were said to have supported Putin "mainly because he will be yet another 'technical' prime minister" and would have "no real political role."[17]

---

[7] Eleanor Clift, "Blame This Drunken Bear for Vladimir Putin," *The Daily Beast,* Apr. 22, 2014 (quoting Russian expert Strobe Talbott).

[8] Sharon LaFraniere, "Yeltsin Linked to Bribe Scheme," *The Washington Post,* Sept. 8, 1999. A Swiss construction company, Mabetex, which had won renovation contracts at the Kremlin, was found to have spent between $10-15 million on bribes for Russian officials, including President Yeltsin and his two daughters. *Ibid.*

[9] Julia Ioffe, "How State-Sponsored Blackmail Works in Russia," *The Atlantic,* Jan. 11, 2017; "World: Europe Kremlin Corruption Battle," *BBC News,* Apr. 2, 1999.

[10] Julia Ioffe, "How State-Sponsored Blackmail Works in Russia," *The Atlantic,* Jan. 11, 2017. The tape was "rumored to have been delivered personally to the head of RTR by 'a man who looked like the head of the FSB,' who at the time was none other than Vladimir Putin." *Ibid.*

[11] *Ibid.* The tape was also reportedly authenticated by Yuri Chaika, who succeeded Skuratov as Russia's prosecutor general. Andrew E. Kramer, "The Master of 'Kompromat' Believed to Be Behind Trump Jr.'s Meeting," *The New York Times,* July 17, 2017.

[12] Anastasia Kirilenk & Claire Bigg, "Ex-KGB Agent Kalugin: Putin Was 'Only a Major,'" *Radio Free Europe/RadioLiberty,* Mar. 31 2015.

[13] Celestine Bohlen, "Yeltsin Resigns, Naming Putin as Acting President To Run in March Election," *The New York Times,* Jan. 1, 2000.

[14] Vladimir Kura-Murza, "The August Vote That Changed Russia's History," *World Affairs,* Aug. 16, 2017.

[15] *Ibid.*

[16] *Ibid.*

[17] Floriana Fossato, "Russia: Duma Approves Putin as Prime Minister," *Radio Free Europe/Radio Liberty,* Aug. 9, 1999.

A poll taken at the same time of the confirmation vote showed that just two percent of Russia's population favored Putin for the presidency.[18] But it did not take long for Putin to seize on an opportunity—though a tragic one—to increase his public profile and strengthen his position to succeed Yeltsin. In early September 1999, less than three weeks after Putin was installed as prime minister, a series of large bombs destroyed apartment buildings in Dagestan, Volgodonsk, and Moscow, killing hundreds of people as they slept.

Prime Minister Putin reacted fiercely and promised to hunt down the terrorists and even "wipe them out in the outhouse," if that was where they chose to hide.[19] Despite no clear evidence or claims of responsibility linking the bombings to "Chechen terrorists," within days of the last explosion, Russian warplanes started a bombing campaign in Chechnya that the Russian defense minister claimed would "eliminate the bandits," and within a week, Russian troops crossed Chechnya's border.[20] As the war progressed, so did Putin's popularity, and the number of voters who said they would choose him for president increased sharply: from just two percent in August 1999 (before the bombings), to 21 percent in October, then nearly doubling to 40 percent in November, and reaching 55 percent in December.[21]

Yet even though Russian authorities said that there was a "Chechen trail" leading to the bombings, no Chechen claimed responsibility.[22] In February 2000, the U.S. Senate Foreign Relations Committee asked then Secretary of State Madeleine Albright if she believed that "the Russian government is justified when it accuses Chechen groups as responsible for the bombings." Secretary Albright responded: "We have not seen evidence that ties the bombings to Chechnya."[23] To this day, no credible source has ever claimed credit for the bombings and no credible evidence has been presented by the Russian authorities linking Chechen terrorists, or anyone else, to the Moscow bombings (for more information on the 1999 apartment building bombings, see Appendix A).

RETURN OF THE SECURITY SERVICES

On December 31, 1999, President Yeltsin resigned, making Putin acting president and pushing forward the date of the presidential election from June to March—effectively cutting the remaining campaign period in half. With the advantage of incumbency, a short campaign period, a large amount of monetary support from business interests (the average check from oligarchs to the cam-

---

[18] International Republican Institute, *Russia Presidential Pre-Election Assessment Report,* at 7 (Mar. 20, 2000).

[19] Sergei Karpov, "Putin Vows to Annihilate 'Terrorists' after Suicide Bombings," *Reuters,* Dec. 31, 2013.

[20] David Satter, *The Less You Know, the Better You Sleep: Russia's Road to Terror and Dictatorship under Yeltsin and Putin,* Yale University Press, at 11 (2016); Ruslan Musayev, "Russia Prepared for Ground War Against Chechnya," *Associated Press,* Sept. 27, 1999.

[21] International Republican Institute, *Russia Presidential Pre-Election Assessment Report,* at 7 (Mar. 20, 2000).

[22] Satter, *The Less You Know, the Better You Sleep,* at 2 (citing Ilyas Akhmadov & Miriam Lansky, *The Chechen Struggle: Independence Won and Lost,* Palgrave Macmillan, at 162 (2010)).

[23] Responses of Secretary of State Madeleine K. Albright to Additional Questions Submitted by Senator Jesse Helms, *2000 Foreign Policy Overview and the President's Fiscal Year 2001 Foreign Affairs Budget Request,* Hearing before the U.S. Senate Committee on Foreign Relations, Feb. 8, 2000, S. Hrg. 106-599 at 70.

paign was about $10 million), and rising popularity from the pros-
ecution of the war in Chechnya, Putin won the presidency at the
ballot box with 53 percent of the vote.[24] For his first act as president, he guaranteed Yeltsin immunity from prosecution.[25] He was
now the most powerful man in Russia; yet even before his election,
he had already been hard at work extending his influence throughout the government. Yeltsin would recall later in his memoirs that,
after he appointed Putin as prime minister, "[he] turned to me and
requested absolute power ... to coordinate all power structures."[26]

And so he did. Putin eliminated independent centers of power by
redistributing resources from oligarchs to security officers, absorb-
ing oligarch-controlled media empires, and neutering regional
power centers that did not respect Moscow's orders.[27] He began to
install former colleagues into positions of power, drawing from his
contacts both in the security services and from his time working in
the mayor's office in St. Petersburg in the 1990s.[28] By 2004, former
security services personnel reportedly occupied all of the top federal
ministerial posts and 70 percent of senior regional posts.[29] A 2006
analysis by the director of the Center for the Study of Elites at the
Russian Academy of Sciences estimated that those with back-
grounds affiliated with the military or security services composed
78 percent of Russia's leading political figures.[30]

Some experts maintain that there is no precise "vertical of
power" in the Russian government, with everything controlled by
one man. Rather, they describe Russian power as "a conglomerate
of clans and groups that compete with one another over resources,"
with Putin acting as a powerful arbiter and moderator who has the
last word.[31] His power comes from his office, his relations with the
elites, his high approval ratings among the public, as well as his
control over much of the energy sector and major state-owned
banks and, especially, the security services.[32]

As Putin's power increased, so did that of the security services,
which, according to independent journalists Andrei Soldatov and
Irina Borogan, Putin invited "to take their place at the head table
of power and prestige in Russia" as he "opened the door to many
dozens of security service agents to move up in the main institutions of the country."[33] Russia's security services are aggressive,
well-funded by the state, and operate without any legislative oversight. They conduct not just espionage, but also "active measures
aimed at subverting and destabilizing European governments, operations in support of Russian economic interests, and attacks on

[24] Zygar, *All the Kremlin's Men*, at 11; Michael Wines, "Putin Wins Russia Vote in First Round, But His Majority Is Less Than Expected," *The New York Times*, Mar. 27, 2000.
[25] Statement of David Satter, Senior Fellow, Hudson Institute, *Russia: Rebuilding the Iron Curtain*, Hearing before the U.S. House Committee on Foreign Affairs, May 17, 2007.
[26] Amy Knight, "Finally, We Know About the Moscow Bombings," *The New York Review of Books*, Nov. 22, 2012.
[27] Minchenko Consulting Communication Group (Russia), *Vladimir Putin's Big Government and the "Politburo 2.0.,"* Jan. 14, 2016.
[28] Satter, *The Less You Know, The Better You Sleep*, at 79; Damien Sharkov, "'Putin Involved in Drug Smuggling Ring', Says Ex-KGB Officer," *Newsweek*, Mar. 3, 2015.
[29] Satter, *The Less You Know, The Better You Sleep*, at 79.
[30] Peter Finn, "In Russia, A Secretive Force Widens," *The Washington Post*, Dec. 12, 2006.
[31] Minchenko Consulting, *Vladimir Putin's Big Government and the "Politburo 2.0."*
[32] *Ibid.*
[33] Andrei Soldatov & Irina Borogan, *The New Nobility: The Restoration of Russia's Security State and the Enduring Legacy of the KGB*, PublicAffairs, at 241 (2010).

political enemies." [34] Some analysts assert that the security services are divided internally, compete in bureaucratic turf wars, and
make intelligence products of questionable quality. Nonetheless,
they are extremely active and, since returning to the presidency in
2012, Putin has "unleashed increasingly powerful intelligence agencies in campaigns of domestic repression and external destabiliza-
tion." [35] Similar to his predecessors, Putin believes that he can best
hold together Russia, with its variety of ethnicities and disparate
regions, by using the security services to concentrate economic resources and political power.[36]

The most powerful of Russia's four main intelligence agencies is
the FSB, which reports to Putin indirectly through the head of the
Presidential Administration (the executive office of the president)
and directly through informal channels built on long-standing relationships.[37] The FSB's mindset is described as "shaped by Soviet
and Tsarist history: it is suspicious, inward looking, and clan-
nish." [38] While its predecessor, the KGB, was controlled by the Soviet Politburo, the FSB is a "self-contained, closed system" that is
"personally overseen by Putin." [39] The FSB also controls the Investigative Committee, Russia's equivalent to the FBI, meaning that
no prosecutor's office has independent oversight over it and the
courts defer to it when making judgements. To monitor the private
and public sector, all large Russian firms and institutions reportedly have FSB officers assigned to them, a practice carried over
from the Soviet Union.[40] According to scholars of the FSB, "Putin's
offer to the generation of security service veterans was a chance to
move to the top echelons of power. Their reach now extends from
television to university faculties, from banks to government ministries, but they are not always visible as men in epaulets ... .
Many officers, supposedly retired, were put in place as active
agents in business, media, and the public sector while still subordinated to the FSB." [41] And, according to Vladimir Kara-Murza, the
twice-poisoned Russian opposition activist, the FSB "doesn't just
rule Russia, it owns it." [42]

The security services have grown accustomed to operating with
impunity inside Russia's borders. More alarmingly, over the past
decade they have applied this mentality beyond Russia's borders
with measurable success. They have been accused of assassinating
Putin's political opponents abroad (see Appendix B), conspiring to
cheat doping standards to win more Olympic medals (see Appendix
C), and protecting cybercriminals who steal credit card and online
account information from U.S. consumers (see Appendix D).

[34] Mark Galeotti, "Putin's Hydra: Inside Russia's Intelligence Services," *European Council on Foreign Relations*, at 1 (May 2016).
[35] *Ibid.*
[36] "Take Care of Russia," *The Economist*, Oct. 22, 2016.
[37] Galeotti, "Putin's Hydra: Inside Russia's Intelligence Services," at 12.
[38] Soldatov & Borogan, *The New Nobility: The Restoration of Russia's Security State and the Enduring Legacy of the KGB*, at 242.
[39] "Wheels Within Wheels: How Mr. Putin Keeps the Country Under Control," *The Economist*, 22 Oct. 2016.
[40] *Ibid.*
[41] Andrei Soldatov & Irina Borogan, *The New Nobility: The Restoration of Russia's Security State and the Enduring Legacy of the KGB*, PublicAffairs, at 27, 28 (2010).
[42] Committee Staff Discussion with Vladimir Kara-Murza.

THE KREMLIN'S PARANOID PATHOLOGY

Despite the Kremlin's increasingly aggressive tactics beyond Russia's borders, the United States and its partners and allies should not conflate the Russian people with the Russian regime. The Russian people have the same hopes and aspirations as any other country's citizens: a government that is accountable to the people for providing safe streets and good jobs, schools, and hospitals. But they are ruled by a regime that has a very different set of priorities, focused primarily on the maintenance of Putin's power and wealth. Free, fair, and open elections are a threat to his grip on power and to the enormous wealth he has stolen from Russia's people. If Putin can demonstrate to the Russian people that elections everywhere are tainted and fraudulent, that liberal democracy is a dysfunctional and dying form of government, then their own system of "sovereign democracy"—authoritarianism secured by corruption, apathy, and an iron fist—does not look so bad after all. As the National Intelligence Council put it, Putin's "amalgam of authoritarianism, corruption, and nationalism represents an alternative to Western liberalism ... [which] is synonymous with disorder and moral decay, and pro-democracy movements and electoral experiments are Western plots to weaken traditional bulwarks of order and the Russian state." [43]

In dealing with Putin and his regime, the United States and its partners and allies should not assume that they are working with a government that is operating with the best interests of its country in mind. Rather, according to a former British ambassador to Moscow, Putin's "overriding aim appears to be to retain power for himself and his associates. He has no perceptible exit strategy." [44] Furthermore, Putin's regime and most of the Russian people view the history of the late 20th century and early 21st century in a starkly different light than most of the West does. The historical narrative popular in Russia paints this period as one of repeated attempts by the West to undermine and humiliate Russia. In reality, the perceived aggression of the United States and the West against Russia allows Putin to ignore his domestic failures and present himself as the leader of a wartime nation: a "Fortress Russia." This narrative repeatedly flogs core themes like enemy encirclement, conspiracy, and struggle, and portrays the United States, NATO, and Europe as conspiring to encircle Russia and make it subservient to the West.

As part of this supposed conspiracy, the EU goes after former Soviet lands like Ukraine, and Western spies use civil society groups to meddle in and interfere with Russian affairs. [45] A good example of this narrative at work was Putin's remarks after terrorists attacked a school in Beslan, Russia, in 2004, killing hundreds, many of whom were children. Putin's response ignored the failure of his own security services, and pointed the finger outward, declaring "we live in a time that follows the collapse of a vast and great state, a state that, unfortunately, proved unable to survive in a

---

[43] National Intelligence Council, *Global Trends: Paradox of Progress* at 125 (Jan. 2017).
[44] Sir Roderic Lyne, Former British Ambassador to the Russian Federation, Memorandum to the UK Parliament Foreign Affairs Committee, Nov. 22, 2016.
[45] Monitor 360, *Master Narrative Country Report: Russia* (Feb. 2012).

rapidly changing world ... . Some would like to tear from us a
'juicy piece of pie.' Others help them." [46] Putin's reaction to that
tragic event demonstrates the reasoning behind analysts' observa-
tions that he embodies a "combustible combination of grievance
and insecurity" and that "Russian belligerence is not a sign of resurgence, but of a chronic, debilitating weakness." [47]

Despite Russia's weakness, however, Putin's regime has developed a formidable set of tools to exert influence abroad. According
to a study by The Jamestown Foundation, these tools include "cap-
turing important sectors of local economies, subverting vulnerable
political systems, corrupting national leaders, penetrating key security institutions, undermining national and territorial unity, conducting propaganda offensives through a spectrum of media and social outlets, and deploying a host of other tools to weaken obstinate
governments that resist Moscow." [48]

On the foreign policy front, Vladimir Putin's fortunes improved
in 2015. His military intervention in Syria reestablished Russia as
a geopolitical player in the Middle East. In 2016, the UK voted to
leave the European Union and the United States elected Donald
Trump, who had warmly praised Putin's leadership. Pro-Russia
candidates won elections in Bulgaria and Moldova. But as Western
democracies woke up to the Kremlin's interference efforts to destabilize democratic processes and international institutions, the pen-
dulum has begun to swing back in defense of democracy. Emmanuel Macron won a resounding victory in France's presidential elections last spring against a field of candidates with pro-Russian
sympathies. In Germany, Putin's critic Angela Merkel won a plurality of votes in the September elections. And countries throughout Europe, increasingly vigilant, are dedicating increased resources and coordinating efforts to counter Russian malign influence.

Nonetheless, the United States and Europe can and should expect Putin to continue to use all the tools at his disposal to assault
democratic institutions and progress around the world, just as he
has done so successfully inside Russia over nearly two decades.

[46] Mikhail Zygar, *All the Kremlin's Men*, PublicAffairs, at 79 (2016).
[47] William Burns, "How We Fool Ourselves on Russia," *The New York Times*, Jan. 7, 2017;
"The Threat from Russia," *The Economist*, Oct. 22, 2016.
[48] Janusz Bugajski & Margarita Assenova, *Eurasian Disunion: Russia's Vulnerable Flanks*,
The Jamestown Foundation, at 6 (June 2016).

Chapter 2: Manipulation and Repression Inside Russia

Many of the tactics that Vladimir Putin's Kremlin has deployed abroad to undermine democracy were first used domestically, and their brazenness and brutality have grown over time. To effectively understand and respond to the Russian government's malign influence operations around the world, then, requires starting at the Kremlin's own gates. Within Russia, Putin's regime has harassed and killed whistleblowers and human rights activists; crafted laws to hamstring democratic institutions; honed and amplified anti-Western propaganda; curbed media that deviate from a pro-government line; beefed up internal security agencies to surveil and harass human rights activists and journalists; directed judicial prosecutions and verdicts; cultivated the loyalties of oligarchs through corrupt handouts; and ordered violent crackdowns against protesters and purported enemies. This laundry list reflects not just governance tactics in the abstract, but tangible, regrettable impacts on lives and prosperity. Some cases in point: an estimated $24 billion dollars has been amassed by Putin's inner circle through the pilfering of state resources.[49] At least 28 journalists have been killed for their reporting inside Russia since Putin took office in December 1999.[50] The pro-Putin United Russia party's hold on seats in the Russian Duma grew to 76 percent in the 2016 elections, and the number of seats currently held by liberal opposition has been reduced to zero.[51] This chapter illustrates in more detail the Kremlin's manipulation and repression within its own borders, later deployed or mimicked abroad, in three areas: ideological, political, and cultural influence; controlling the public narrative; and corrupting economic activity.

In October 2014, Putin's then-first deputy chief of staff, Vyacheslav Volodin, famously quipped that "there is no Russia today if there is no Putin."[52] The statement encapsulated a consolidation of power in Russia over nearly 15 years into a "highly centralized, authoritarian political system dominated by President Vladimir Putin."[53] By equating Putin with the Russian state,

---

[49] The Organized Crime and Corruption Reporting Project, *Putin and the Proxies,* https://www.occrp.org/en/putinandtheproxies, Oct. 24, 2017.

[50] Committee to Protect Journalists, "58 Journalists Killed in Russia/Motive Confirmed," https://cpj.org/killed/europe/russia (visited Dec. 5, 2017).

[51] Andrew Osborn & Maria Tsvetkova, "Putin Firms Control With Big Win For Russia's Ruling Party," *Reuters,* Sept. 17, 2016.

[52] "'No Putin, No Russia,' Says Kremlin Deputy Chief of Staff," *The Moscow Times,* Oct. 23, 2014.

[53] U.S. Department of State, *Country Reports on Human Rights Practices for 2015: Russia,* at 1.

Volodin's assertion—just months after Russia's invasion of Crimea that brought on international sanctions—linked the fate of the Russian people with Putin's own. For Putin and his advisors, the move to co-opt the identity of an entire nation was no doubt fueled by his soaring popularity among Russians—from a "slumping" 61 percent prior to the Sochi Winter Olympics in February 2014 to above 80 percent in the months after.[54] Yet Volodin's statement also marked a break from the Kremlin's attempts to maintain a semblance of democratic institutions and processes—it revealed that these institutions and processes, which became increasingly subordinated to the needs and interests of Putin's ruling clique, now existed only to prop it up.

Volodin's predecessor as first deputy chief of staff, Vladislav Surkov, had been credited with developing a policy of "sovereign democracy," an oxymoronic term explained by writer Masha Lipman as a "Kremlin coinage that conveys two messages: first, that Russia's regime is democratic and, second, that this claim must be accepted, period. Any attempt at verification will be regarded as unfriendly and as meddling in Russia's domestic affairs."[55] As described in a 2016 profile, Surkov maneuvered through a complex Russian political system to implement this vision, "cultivating fake opposition parties and funding pro-Kremlin youth groups. He personally curated what was allowed on to Russia's television screens, and was seen as the architect of 'post-truth politics' where facts are relative, a version of which some have suggested has now taken hold in the west."[56]

The Kremlin's concept of a "sovereign democracy" was intended to serve not just as a mechanism for domestic governance in Russia, but also as a model to other countries. The more that Russia's sovereign democratic model could appeal to and be replicated elsewhere as "a style of government that corresponds with the needs and interests of the power elites," the more Russia would be able to extend its diplomatic reach and provide a counterpoint to the democratic principles that the United States has long championed.[57]

The trajectory of Russia's "sovereign democracy" experiment has unfolded along a spectrum ranging from deft manipulation to outright oppression of the media, civil society, elections, political parties, and cultural activities. All the while, the Kremlin's sustained and global effort to undermine human rights and the governments, alliances, and multilateral institutions that champion them has sought to reduce outside scrutiny of the anti-democratic abuses that are core to its "sovereign democratic" system. And similar to Putin's capitalizing on the 1999 apartment bombings to galvanize his own standing (see Chapter 1 and Appendix A), he has used other hardships befalling the Russian people as justification for tightening his grip on power. Such punctuating moments include the Kursk submarine disaster in 2000, which prefaced a crackdown

[54] Michael Birnbaum, "How to Understand Putin's Jaw-droppingly High Approval Ratings," *The Washington Post*, Mar. 6, 2016.
[55] Masha Lipman, "Putin's 'Sovereign Democracy,'" *The Washington Post*, July 15, 2006.
[56] Shaun Walker, "Kremlin Puppet Master's Leaked Emails Are Price of Return to Political Frontline," *The Guardian*, Oct. 26, 2016.
[57] David Clark, "Putin Is Exporting 'Sovereign Democracy' To New EM Allies," *The Financial Times*, Dec. 20, 2016.

on media critical of the government's response; the 2004 terrorist siege of a school in Beslan, after which Putin moved to replace a system of popularly-elected regional governors with centrally-appointed ones; and international sanctions resulting from the 2014 Russian military invasion of Ukraine, upon which Putin has amplified the narrative of Russia as a besieged fortress requiring his strong hand to defend.[58]

Another key opportunity he seized was to bring a face-saving close to the conflict in Chechnya—a major element of the Putin founding narrative, as discussed in Chapter 1—by supporting strongman Ramzan Kadyrov's effort to stamp out rivals in Chechnya who were fueling the insurgency against Moscow and effectively establish his own fiefdom in the Chechen republic.[59] Observers have noted that the brutal Kadyrov is "essentially employed by Putin to stop Chechens from killing Russians, but he has also been linked to a long list of killings" and human rights abuses in the North Caucasus region and elsewhere in the country.[60] Moscow has provided subsidies to cover an estimated 81 percent of the Chechen Republic's budget.[61] In exchange, Putin relies on Kadyrov and his security services to keep a lid on the Chechen conflict, deploys them as needed for hybrid operations in Ukraine and Syria, and uses the threat of terrorism in Chechnya as justification for restricting civic freedoms throughout the country.[62] The outsized power Putin has afforded to internal security services (in both Moscow and Grozny) has proven useful to him, but has also placed the Kremlin atop a figurative tiger that it must ride in an inherently corrupt, brittle system fraught with risk.

INFLUENCING IDEOLOGY, POLITICS, AND CULTURE

Independent Civil Society

Soviet-era dissidents who monitored and exposed state repression provided the main blueprint for a modern-day independent and activist civil society in Russia. And much like their Soviet prede-

---

[58] The Russian navy submarine Kursk sank in the Barents Sea on August 12, 2000 after multiple explosions onboard, resulting in the deaths of 118 Russian seamen. In the aftermath of the disaster, reports revealed that 23 crewmen had survived the initial explosion, but likely died several hours later in an escape compartment that filled with water, raising questions of whether the individuals could have been rescued in the interim. Government officials first claimed that the sinking was caused by a collision with a Western submarine, disputing assertions that faulty onboard equipment led to the disaster, and initially rejected foreign offers of assistance with the rescue effort. See "What Really Happened to Russia's 'Unsinkable' Sub," *The Guardian,* Aug. 4, 2001. In 2004, a group of Chechen rebels besieged a school in Beslan, North Ossetia, taking more than 1,000 individuals hostage, many of whom were children. Russian security services stormed the facility in an operation to end the standoff, during which approximately 330 individuals were killed. The European Court of Human Rights recently ruled in a complaint case brought by 409 Russian nationals that their government failed to prevent, and then overreacted in responding to, the attack, leading to inordinate loss of life. See European Court of Human Rights, "Serious Failings in the Response of the Russian Authorities to the Beslan Attack," Apr. 13, 2017.

[59] Ekaterina Sokirianskaia, "Is Chechnya Taking Over Russia?" *The New York Times,* Aug. 17, 2017.

[60] Oliver Bullough, "Putin's Closest Ally—And His Biggest Liability," *The Guardian,* Sept. 23, 2015. In December 2017, Kadyrov was sanctioned by the U.S. government for gross violations of human rights under the Sergei Magnitsky Rule of Law Accountability Act. U.S. Department of the Treasury, Office of Foreign Assets Control, "Publication of Magnitsky Act Sanctions Regulations; Magnitsky Act-Related Designations," Dec. 20, 2017.

[61] Anna Arutunyan, "Why Putin Won't Get Tough on Kadyrov," *European Council on Foreign Relations,* Apr. 25, 2017.

[62] Ekaterina Sokirianskaia, "Is Chechnya Taking Over Russia?" *The New York Times,* Aug. 17, 2017.

cessors, Putin's Kremlin has suppressed independent civil society and human rights activists through a variety of means, including legal restrictions and administrative burdens, the creation of government-sponsored civil society groups to counter independent organizations, and violent attacks.

Russia's restrictive legal framework for civil society was designed and refined over many years. In December 2005, the Duma passed amendments that increased scrutiny and bureaucratic reporting requirements of NGO finances and operations, used vaguely defined provisions to prohibit foreign NGO programming, barred foreign nationals or those deemed "undesirable" from founding NGOs inside the country, and prohibited any NGO deemed a threat to Russian national interests.[63] Surkov argued that the amendments were a needed defense against the specter of Western countries and organizations set on fomenting regime change in Russia. In 2012, after Putin's re-election to the presidency, the Kremlin shepherded through new legislation that further tightened the operating climate for NGOs: any group receiving foreign funding and engaged in political activities had to self-report as a "foreign agent"—a Soviet-era term used to describe spies and traitors.[64] Observers widely saw the foreign agent law as an attempt to stigmatize and deny funding to NGOs working on human rights and democracy.[65] In May 2014, the law was amended to enable Russia's Justice Ministry to directly register groups as foreign agents without their consent, and authorities have since expanded the definition of "political activities" to include possible aspects of NGO work and fined or closed organizations for violations of the law.[66]

Russia's restrictive NGO laws have had a significant effect. Human Rights Watch reported in September 2017 that "Russia's Justice Ministry has designated 158 groups as 'foreign agents,' courts have levied staggering fines on many groups for failing to comply with the law, and about 30 groups have shut down rather than wear the 'foreign agent' label."[67] Other laws—relating to extremism, anti-terrorism, libel, and public gatherings—have also been selectively utilized by Russian officials to repress independent NGOs and human rights activists, among other targets. The hostile environment for domestic NGOs also fueled a blowback against foreign entities who sought to support them. The United States Agency for International Development (USAID), which for two decades had supported democracy and rule of law promotion in Russia, as well as health and education, announced in October 2012 that it

---

[63] Katherin Machalek, "Factsheet: Russia's NGO Laws" in *Contending With Putin's Russia: A Call for U.S. Leadership*, at 10-13, Freedom House, Feb. 6, 2013; "Russian Duma Passes Controversial NGO Bill," *Radio Free Europe/Radio Liberty*, Dec. 23, 2005.

[64] *Ibid.* This term connotes a different meaning than the Foreign Agents Registration Act in U.S. law, in which it is defined in part as "any person who acts as an agent, representative, employee, or servant, or any person who acts in any other capacity at the order, request, or under the direction or control, of a foreign principal or of a person any of whose activities are directly or indirectly supervised, directed, controlled, financed, or subsidized in whole or in major part by a foreign principal" and which, most significantly, does not constrain activities of the agent but merely requires registration. 22 U.S.C. § 611(c).

[65] U.S. Department of State, *Country Reports on Human Rights Practices for 2012: Russia*, at 25.

[66] U.S. Department of State, *Country Reports on Human Rights Practices for 2016: Russia*, at 2.

[67] Human Rights Watch, "Russia: Government vs. Rights Groups," Sept. 8, 2017.

19

would shut down its mission amidst pressure from the Kremlin.[68] USAID was not alone: by December of that year, the International Republican Institute (IRI) announced it was closing its office on orders from the Russian government, and the National Democratic Institute (NDI) closed its office in Russia and moved its staff out of the country.[69] In January 2015, the Chicago-based MacArthur Foundation announced it was closing its Moscow office after the Duma asked the Justice Ministry to investigate whether a select group of organizations, including MacArthur as well as the U.S.-based Open Society Foundations (OSF) and Freedom House, should be declared "undesirable" and banned from the country.[70] By June 2017, the Russian government had listed OSF, NDI, IRI, and eight other organizations as "undesirable."[71]

Legal and administrative tactics used during Putin's tenure to create headwinds against the work of independent civil society organizations have not only muted criticism of his own regime at home and abroad, but have afforded other governments a roadmap to similarly deflect criticism. Research by Human Rights First published in February 2016 cites at least fourteen countries where Russia has provided a "bad example" that may have inspired other governments to introduce or pass restrictive NGO laws; this includes countries like Azerbaijan and Kazakhstan traditionally viewed by Russia as within its geographic sphere of influence, as well as countries further afield such as Ethiopia, Cambodia, Egypt, and Ecuador.[72]

The Kremlin has also sought to co-opt civil society by "devot[ing] massive resources to the creation and activities of state-sponsored and state-controlled NGOs."[73] Commonly referred to as "GONGOs" (Government Organized Non-Governmental Organizations), such groups are used to toe a government-friendly line or to promote alternative narratives to counter the work of legitimate Russian and international human rights NGOs. As one former U.S. ambassador to the OSCE described it, "GONGOs are nothing more than the real-world equivalent of the Internet troll armies that insecure, authoritarian, repressive regimes have unleashed on Twitter. They use essentially the same tactics as their online counterparts—creating noise and confusion, flooding the space, using vulgarity, intimidating those with dissenting views, and crowding out legitimate voices."[74] An expert from the National Endowment for Democracy has noted that "Russia sinks extensive resources into

[68] Arshad Mohammed, "USAID Mission In Russia To Close Following Moscow Decision," *Reuters*, Sept. 18, 2012.
[69] "U.S. Pro-Democracy Groups Pulling Out Of Russia," *Reuters*, Dec. 14, 2012; National Democratic Institute, Russia: Overview, https://www.ndi.org/eurasia/russia (visited Dec. 11, 2017).
[70] Alec Luhn, "American Ngo to Withdraw From Russia After Being Put on 'Patriotic Stop List,'" *The Guardian*, Jul 22, 2015.
[71] The International Center for Not-for-Profit Law, *Civic Freedom Monitor: Russia*, http://www.icnl.org/research/monitor/russia.html, (updated Sept. 8, 2017).
[72] Melissa Hooper & Grigory Frolov, *Russia's Bad Example*, Free Russia Foundation, Human Rights First, Feb. 2016.
[73] Statement of Michael McFaul, Senior Associate, Carnegie Endowment for International Peace, *Russia: Rebuilding the Iron Curtain*, Hearing before the U.S. House Committee on Foreign Affairs, May 17, 2007. McFaul became U.S. Ambassador to the Russian Federation in 2012.
[74] Ambassador Daniel B. Baer, U.S. Permanent Representative to the OSCE, "Mind the GONGOs: How Government Organized NGOs Troll Europe's Largest Human Rights Conference," U.S. Mission to the Organization for Security and Cooperation in Europe, Sept. 30, 2016.

GONGOs in countries on its periphery and beyond," where it can "eagerly exploit" the relatively free operating space for civil society to maximize their impact.[75] He also notes that, similar to Russia, "leading authoritarian governments have established a wide constellation of regime-friendly GONGOs, including think tanks and policy institutes, that operate at home and abroad."[76]

The Kremlin has also focused on cultivating youth activism to serve its own purposes. In 2005, after youth activists fueled protests in Ukraine that ultimately toppled the government, Surkov sought a buffer against such upheaval in Russia. Seizing on the anxieties of a nascent youth group in St. Petersburg, he helped develop it into the Nashi ("Ours") youth organization and recruited participants, particularly from Russia's poorer regions, who could be readily mobilized as a counter-force to pro-democracy demonstrations.[77] The group's first summit was held at a Kremlin-owned facility outside Moscow and included pro-Kremlin activists.[78] Within months, Nashi held a rally in Moscow in which thousands of activists were bussed in to celebrate Russia's World War II victory over Germany.[79] Nashi and its projects were funded by both the state and pro-Kremlin oligarchs and focused on pro-Putin gatherings and the political "training" of youth in summer camp-style gatherings, which included posters demeaning Kremlin critics and human rights activists as liars and Nazis.[80] More recently, a "military-patriotic movement" of 11- to 18-year-olds known as Yunarmiya ("Youth Army") has been promulgated in schools across Russia, a project of Russian Defense Minister Sergei Shoigu endorsed by Putin and enjoying sponsorship from four state-owned banks.[81] Its ranks swelled from 100 members in 2016 to more than 30,000 a year later, and Yunarmiya was prominently featured in the Kremlin's annual World War II Victory Day parade in May 2017—just weeks after a large number of Russian youth turned out at opposition-organized anti-corruption protests around the country.[82]

Finally, the Kremlin has created a climate where physical attacks against civil society activists, as well as political opponents and independent journalists, occur regularly and often with impunity (see Appendix E). While such attacks are not exclusively part of the Russian "sovereign democracy" toolkit, the impunity with which they have been perpetrated in Russia has provided comforting company to other authoritarian governments who use similar tactics.

Political Processes, Parties, and Opposition

Russia's "sovereign democracy" relies on democratic structures, albeit largely hollow ones, to give a sheen of legitimacy to a regime

[75] Christopher Walker, "Dealing with the Authoritarian Resurgence," *Authoritarianism Goes Global*, Larry Diamond et al. eds. at 226 (2016).
[76] *Ibid.* at 218.
[77] Eva Hartog, "A Kremlin Youth Movement Goes Rogue," *The Moscow Times*, Apr. 8, 2016.
[78] Mikhail Zygar, *All the Kremlin's Men*, PublicAffairs at 98 (2016).
[79] *Ibid.* at 99.
[80] Julia Ioffe, "Russia's Nationalist Summer Camp," *The New Yorker*, Aug. 16, 2010; Eva Hartog, "A Kremlin Youth Movement Goes Rogue," *The Moscow Times*, Apr. 8, 2016.
[81] Ilnur Sharafiyev, "Making Real Men Out of Schoolchildren," *Meduza*, Oct. 6, 2017.
[82] Daniel Schearf, "Putin's Youth Army Debuts on Red Square for 'Victory Day,'" *Voice of America*, May 8, 2017.

that puts its own interests before those of its citizens. Under
Putin's leadership, the Russian government has undermined political processes, parties, and opposition that present a meaningful
check on the Kremlin's power.[83]

Putin and his allies have neutered political competition by creating rubber-stamp opposition parties and harassing legitimate opposition. For example, Mikhail Khodorkovsky, the founder of the
Russian oil company Yukos, was imprisoned for more than a decade on a spate of charges deemed to be politically motivated.[84] His
prosecution could be broadly interpreted as a signal to other powerful oligarchs that supporting independent or anti-Putin parties car-
ries great risk to one's personal wealth and well-being. Genuine opposition party candidates have also been blocked from registering
or participating in elections.[85] At the same time, parties invented
by the Kremlin to take away votes from the real opposition have
received resources and support from the state and the private sector. Yet when these co-opted parties have asserted a degree of independence, they have had their leadership and resources gutted.[86]
More recently, opposition activists attempting to join forces through
the Khodorkovsky-supported Open Russia platform have been
blocked from using hotels and conference facilities to hold gatherings, and some have even had their homes raided.[87] And the
Kremlin appears set on quashing the 2018 electoral aspirations of
anti-corruption activist and presidential hopeful Alexey Navalny,
as the Central Election Commission declared him ineligible to run
because of an embezzlement conviction, which international observers and his supporters allege was politically motivated.[88]

Putin has also sought to centralize institutional power in Moscow
and weaken the parliament as a check on presidential authority.
Early in his first term, he undermined the authority of elected regional governors by creating seven supra-regional districts, to
which he appointed mainly former generals and KGB officers.[89] By
acquiring greater control over media resources, he achieved electoral victories for a growing swath of United Russia candidates and
thereby reduced parliamentary autonomy.[90] In 2004, Putin "radi-
cally restructured" the Russian political system by eliminating the
election of regional governors by popular vote in favor of centrally-
directed appointments, characterizing this significant power grab

[83] Statement of Michael McFaul, Senior Associate, Carnegie Endowment for International Peace, *Russia: Rebuilding the Iron Curtain,* Hearing before the U.S. House Committee on Foreign Affairs, May 17, 2007.
[84] Tom Parfitt, "Mikhail Khodorkovsky Sentenced to 14 years in Prison," *The Guardian,* Dec. 30, 2010; David M. Herszenhorn & Steven Lee Myers, "Freed Abruptly by Putin, Khodorkovsky Arrives in Germany," *The New York Times,* Dec. 20, 2013.
[85] Statement of Michael McFaul, Senior Associate, Carnegie Endowment for International Peace, *Russia: Rebuilding the Iron Curtain,* Hearing before the U.S. House Committee on Foreign Affairs, May 17, 2007.
[86] *Ibid.*
[87] "Russian Law Enforcement Raid Homes of Khodorkovsky's Open Russia Employees," *The Moscow Times,* Oct. 5, 2017; Anna Liesowska, "Online Democracy Group Open Russia Refused Entry to Major Hotels," *The Siberian Times,* Mar. 27, 2015.
[88] Vladimir Soldatkin & Andrew Osborn, "Putin Critic Navalny Barred from Russian Presidential Election," *Reuters,* Dec. 25, 2017.
[89] Statement of Michael McFaul, Senior Associate, Carnegie Endowment for International Peace, *Russia: Rebuilding the Iron Curtain,* Hearing before the U.S. House Committee on Foreign Affairs, May 17, 2007.
[90] Peter Baker, "Putin Moves to Centralize Authority," *The Washington Post,* Sept. 14, 2004.

as an effort to forge "national cohesion" in the wake of the terrorist attack at a school in Beslan in North Ossetia.[91]

The erosion of democratic processes in Russia's elections has directly corresponded to Putin's efforts to secure a mandate and tighten his grip on power (see Appendix F for a summary of flawed elections in Russia since 1999). Around the most recent presidential election in 2012, in which Putin returned to power amidst credible allegations of fraud, tens of thousands of Russian citizens joined large-scale demonstrations in Moscow in late 2011 and early 2012, chanting "Russia without Putin!"[92] The Kremlin's response ranged from coalescing support to cracking down on criticism. Throngs of pro-government supporters were bussed in to participate in campaign rallies expressing support for Putin in a "battle" for Russia that painted any opposition as traitorous.[93] Following the protests that tarnished Putin's inauguration, the government fast-tracked passage of a law that increased administrative penalties by a factor of one hundred for unsanctioned protests and other violations of the law on public assembly.[94] Working through the Investigative Committee, a beefed-up internal security service that then-President Dmitry Medvedev established in 2011 and which reports directly to the president, the Kremlin carried out smear campaigns and discredited opposition figures through dubious charges and flawed legal proceedings.[95] The backlash against political competition reached alarming levels in February 2015, when opposition leader Boris Nemtsov was murdered just steps from the Kremlin.[96] Nemtsov was to participate two days later in a protest he organized against the Kremlin's economic mismanagement and interference in Ukraine. He was also planning to release a report on Russia's role in Ukraine.[97] Observers alleged that the demonization in pro-government media of opposition figures as traitors had contributed to his death.[98] In June 2017, a Russian court convicted five Chechen men of Nemtsov's killing. While the verdict was welcomed by the United States and other governments, Nemtsov's supporters charged that the masterminds behind the killing remained at large, and Nemtsov's family has called for Ramzan Kadyrov to be interrogated in the case.[99]

Notably, despite this hostile climate, large-scale opposition protests have continued each year on the anniversary of Nemtsov's death. In addition, presidential hopeful Alexey Navalny spearheaded several anti-corruption protests in cities across Russia in 2017. Using social media, Navalny's Anti-Corruption Fund has broadly circulated the results of its investigative work into alleged

[91] *Ibid.*

[92] Ellen Barry & Michael Schwirtz, "After Election, Putin Faces Challenges to Legitimacy," *The New York Times*, Mar. 5, 2012.

[93] Marc Bennetts, "How Putin Tried and Failed To Crush Dissent in Russia," *Newsweek*, Feb. 26, 2016.

[94] U.S. Department of State, *Country Reports on Human Rights Practices for 2012: Russia*, at 24.

[95] Nastassia Astrasheuskaya & Steve Gutterman, "Putin Foe Charged, Russian Opposition Fear KGB Tactics," *Reuters*, July 31, 2012.

[96] "Russian Opposition Politician Boris Nemtsov Shot Dead," *BBC*, Feb. 28, 2015.

[97] Alec Lunh, "Boris Nemtsov Report on Ukraine to be Released by Dead Politician's Allies," *The Guardian*, May 12, 2015.

[98] "Russian Opposition: Critics or Traitors?" *Al Jazeera*, Mar. 2, 2015.

[99] Ivan Nechepurenko, "5 Who Killed Boris Nemtsov, Putin Foe, Sentenced in Russia," *The New York Times*, July 13, 2017; "Nemtsov's Daughter Requests Questioning Of Kadyrov," *Radio Free Europe/Radio Liberty*, Apr. 28, 2016.

corruption by Prime Minister Dmitry Medvedev and other high-ranking officials. At least 1,750 Russian citizens were detained after June 2017 anti-corruption protests, according to the Russian monitoring group OVD-Info.[100]

Cultural Forces and Religious Institutions

Under Putin, the Kremlin has engaged and boosted cultural forces and religious institutions inside Russia to provide an additional bulwark against the democratic values and actors it paints as anathema to the country's interests. One prominent example is the strong ties that Putin and his inner circle have forged with the Russian Orthodox Church and its affiliates.[101] The Russian Orthodox Church enjoys special recognition under Russian law, while in contrast, laws such as the 2006 NGO laws and the 2016 "Yarovaya" package of counterterrorism laws have enabled pressure against non-Russian Orthodox religious entities through cumbersome registration processes and administrative constraints, restrictions on proselytizing, and expanded surveillance.[102] Additionally, the U.S. State Department has reported that the Russian state has provided security and official vehicles to the Russian Orthodox patriarch (but not to other religious leaders) and noted reports that the Russian Orthodox Church has been a "primary beneficiary" of presidential grants ostensibly designed to reduce NGO dependence on foreign funding.[103]

In return for the state's favor, the Russian Orthodox Church has promoted Putin and the state's policies at multiple turns. A former editor of the official journal of the Moscow Patriarchate (the seat of the Russian Orthodox Church and its affiliated churches outside the country) told *The New York Times* in 2016 that "The [Russian Orthodox] church has become an instrument of the Russian state. It is used to extend and legitimize the interests of the Kremlin."[104] This is noteworthy given Putin's roots in the KGB—the tip of the Soviet spear in restricting religious activity during the Communist era—and it reflects a careful cultivation of his identity as a man of faith and a defender of the Orthodox faithful. The image of Putin as defender of traditional religious and cultural values has also been leveraged by the Kremlin "as both an ideology and a source of influence abroad."[105] In projecting itself as "the natural ally of those who pine for a more secure, illiberal world free from the tradition-crushing rush of globalization, multiculturalism and women's and gay rights," the Russian government has been able to mobilize

---

[100] Marc Bennetts, "'There Are Better Things Than Turnips:' Navalny Plans Putin Birthday Protests," *The Guardian*, Oct. 5, 2017.

[101] See Chapter 4 for more information on the Russian Orthodox Church's role in promoting Kremlin objectives abroad.

[102] U.S. Department of State, *International Religious Freedom Report for 2006, Russia;* U.S. Department of State, *International Religious Freedom Report for 2016: Russia,* at 1.

[103] U.S. Department of State, *International Religious Freedom Report for 2016: Russia,* at 23-24; U.S. Department of State, *Country Reports on Human Rights Practices for 2016: Russia,* at 53 (citing report published in the *Moscow Times.*

[104] Andrew Higgins, "In Expanding Russian Influence, Faith Combines With Firepower," *The New York Times*, Sept. 13, 2016.

[105] Simon Shuster, "Russia's President Putin Casts Himself as Protector of the Faith," *TIME*, Sept. 12, 2016.

some Orthodox actors in places like Moldova and Montenegro to vigorously oppose integration with the West.[106]

The Kremlin's cultivation of the Russian Orthodox Church intensified following the massive 2011-12 street protests opposing Putin's return to the presidency. Patriarch Kirill, who assumed leadership of the Russian Orthodox Church in 2009, endorsed Putin's long rule as a "miracle of God" on February 8, 2012, weeks before the presidential election. He praised Putin for "correcting [the] crooked twist" of Russia's tumultuous democratic transition in the 1990s, and derided Putin's opponents as materialistic and a threat to Russia.[107] Eleven days later, members of the rock group Pussy Riot performed a protest song, "Virgin Mary, Redeem Us of Putin" in Moscow's Cathedral of Christ the Savior. In a high-profile and widely criticized prosecution, three Pussy Riot members were later sentenced to two years' imprisonment for "hooliganism motivated by religious hatred."[108] In a December 2012 speech, Putin invoked traditional and spiritual values as the antidote to Russian decline and criticized foreign influences, defining Russia's democracy as "the power of the Russian people with their traditions" and "absolutely not the realization of standards imposed on us from outside."[109] And in January 2013, Putin signed a law criminalizing "insulting religious believers' feelings" which enabled fines and prison time of up to three years.[110] The Kremlin's fueling of culture wars has also provided context for the passage of laws criminalizing "gay propaganda" and decriminalizing first instances of domestic violence.[111] The effects of these laws on the security of LGBT persons and women in Russia is discussed in more detail in Appendix G.

CONTROLLING THE PUBLIC NARRATIVE

Media Capture

Throughout Putin's tenure in Russia, the Kremlin has pressured independent media outlets to prevent them from being a meaningful check on his power. From the early days of Putin's first term, the U.S. State Department noted the threats to editorial independence posed by an increasing concentration of media ownership in Russia and news organizations' heavy reliance on financial sponsors or federal and local government support to operate.[112] Print media required the services of state-owned printing and distribution companies, while broadcast media relied on the government for access to airwaves and accreditation to cover news. Kremlin favoritism, then, played heavily in determining which outlets survived.

---

[106] Andrew Higgins, "In Expanding Russian Influence, Faith Combines With Firepower," *The New York Times*, Sept. 13, 2016.

[107] Gleb Bryanski, "Russian Patriarch Calls Putin Era 'Miracle Of God,'" *Reuters*, Feb. 8, 2012.

[108] U.S. Department of State, *International Religious Freedom Report for 2012, Russia*, at 9.

[109] Ellen Barry, "Russia's History Should Guide Its Future, Putin Says," *The New York Times*, Dec. 12, 2012.

[110] Carl Schreck, "Holy Slight: How Russia Prosecutes For 'Insulting Religious Feelings,'" *Radio Free Europe/Radio Liberty*, Aug. 15, 2017.

[111] Lucian Kim, "Russian President Signs Law to Decriminalize Domestic Violence," *National Public Radio*, Feb. 16, 2017.

[112] U.S. Department of State, *Country Reports on Human Rights Practices for 2001, Russia*.

Conversely, media outlets that criticized President Putin or his actions risked retaliation.[113]

A seminal moment in the Kremlin's efforts to capture the media in Russia came after the August 2000 Kursk submarine disaster that killed 118 Russian seamen. Questions swirled about how much the government knew about the accident and whether it had done enough to mitigate it.[114] Putin, who had been vacationing in Sochi when the Kursk disaster unfolded and did not speak about it until days later, held a town hall with families of the dead, in which several relatives excoriated him for incompetence. Despite Kremlin efforts to limit media access to one Russian state broadcaster and to heavily edit the footage that was aired, international and Russian print media released details of the meeting and interviews with family members that cast Putin's young government in a harsh light.[115] In a secretly taped record of the meeting by a journalist from Kommersant, a national Russian newspaper, Putin fumed that national television channels were lying about the Kursk events and accused them of destroying the Russian military through their corruption and efforts to discredit the government.[116] The independent channel NTV, founded by oligarch Vladimir Gusinsky, had swiftly challenged the government's explanation of the Kursk tragedy and criticized its refusal of foreign assistance for the first five days following the initial explosion.[117] (NTV had also aired a piece in 1999 asserting an FSB role in the failed apartment bombing in Ryazan, after which the Kremlin informed Gusinsky he had "crossed the line." In 2000, Gusinsky was briefly jailed, exiled, and pressured to sell his stake in NTV to the state energy company Gazprom.)[118] In October 2000, a critical one-hour TV special aired about the Kursk disaster on ORT, a public television channel partly owned by oligarch Boris Berezovsky, who had helped to execute the smooth transfer of power from Yeltsin to Putin a year earlier but subsequently fell out of favor with the Kremlin and announced his opposition.[119]

The Kremlin took steps thereafter to further rein in both NTV and ORT, and then other media outlets over which it lacked effective or editorial control. Beyond targeting its patron Gusinsky, the Kremlin began after Kursk to target NTV's investigative journalists and editorial infrastructure. A popular NTV presenter was questioned by prosecutors early in 2001, and the phone line of NTV managing director Evgeniy Kiselev was reportedly tapped.[120] Gazprom undertook a "corporate coup" of the channel in an early

[113] U.S. Department of State, *Country Reports on Human Rights Practices for 2001, Russia.*
[114] Michael Wines, "'None of Us Can Get Out' Kursk Sailor Wrote," *The New York Times*, Oct. 27, 2000.
[115] Ian Traynor, "Putin Faces Families' Fury," *The Guardian*, Aug. 22, 2000.
[116] Arkady Ostrovsky, *The Invention of Russia: The Journey from Gorbachev's Freedom to Putin's War*, Atlantic Books, at 277-78 (2015).
[117] *See* Jonathan Steele, "Fury Over Putin's Secrets and Lies," *The Guardian*, Aug. 21, 2000.
[118] Robert Coalson, "Ten Years Ago, Russia's Independent NTV, The Talk Of The Nation, Fell Silent," *Radio Free Europe/Radio Liberty*, Apr. 14, 2011. NTV was founded by opposition oligarch Vladimir Gusinsky and was known for its popular satirical puppet show called Kukly ("Dolls") that lampooned Putin and other politicians.
[119] Inna Denisova & Robert Coalson, "Kursk Anniversary: Submarine Disaster Was Putin's 'First Lie,'" *Radio Free Europe/Radio Liberty*, Aug. 12, 2015; "Oligarch Who Angered Putin: Rise and Fall of Boris Berezovsky," *CNN*, Mar. 25, 2013.
[120] Ostrovsky, *The Invention of Russia*, at 281.

morning office raid in April 2001, installing a new editorial staff.[121] NTV was subsequently transformed into largely an entertainment channel, focused on "pulp crime reporting and low-brow action series instead of critical political coverage." [122] Meanwhile, the Kremlin reportedly delivered a message to Berezovsky after the Kursk disaster that he would no longer be permitted to control ORT's editorial policy; Berezovsky subsequently sold his stake in ORT to oligarch Roman Abramovich, who asserted years later in UK court proceedings that Putin and his chief of staff had directed him to make the purchase.[123] ORT was subsequently transformed into Perviy Kanal ("Channel One"), which has become Russia's largest state-controlled national television network.[124]

The Kremlin's early efforts to neutralize independent or critical national media and consolidate state ownership of media outlets had a chilling effect on the development of independent journalism in the country, and both official and unofficial pressure have continued against TV, print, and online media outlets that challenge the Kremlin line. Since Putin's return to the presidency in 2012, a spate of firings, resignations, and closures among numerous media outlets suggest that the Kremlin under Putin has no intention of reversing its longstanding trend of controlling the media space. For example, a high-ranking executive and editor of the Kommersant-Vlast news magazine was fired in late 2011 after publishing allegations of fraud in the parliamentary elections that year and a photo of a ballot with an expletive regarding Putin written on it.[125] RIA-Novosti, Russia's state-run international news agency, was liquidated in December 2013 on a decree from Putin and refashioned into Russiya Segodnya ("Russia Today") under the helm of an unabashedly pro-Kremlin commentator, Dmitry Kiselev.[126] In 2014, opposition channel Dozhd ("Rain") was dropped from several cable providers and evicted from its Moscow studio space.[127] The U.S. State Department has noted that "significant government pressure" continues on Russian independent media, limiting coverage of Ukraine, Syria, elections, and other sensitive topics and prompting "widespread" self-censorship.[128] Meanwhile, state-controlled media regularly slander opposition views as traitorous or foreign, which has engendered "a climate intolerant of dissent" in which a spate of violent attacks and criminal prosecutions of journalists have occurred (see Appendix E).[129] Most recently, on November 25, 2017, Putin signed a bill enabling Russian authorities to list and scrutinize media outlets as "foreign agents"and requir-

[121] *Ibid.* at 280-81.
[122] "Takeover Not Celebrated," *The Moscow Times*, Apr. 14, 2011.
[123] Zygar, *All the Kremlin's Men*, at 29.
[124] Joshua Yaffa, "Putin's Master of Ceremonies," *The New Yorker*, Feb. 5, 2014.
[125] Michael Schwirtz, "2 Leaders in Russian Media Are Fired After Election Articles," *The New York Times*, Dec. 13, 2011.
[126] Daniel Sandford, "Russian News Agency RIA Novosti Closed Down," *BBC News*, Dec. 9, 2013; Rossiya Segodnya, which translates to "Russia Today," is distinct from RT, the international television network supported by the Russian government. Dmitry Kiselev is unrelated to Evgeniy Kiselev, mentioned previously in this section.
[127] Benyumov, "How Russia's Independent Media Was Dismantled Piece by Piece," *The Guardian*, May 25, 2016.
[128] U.S. Department of State, *Country Reports on Human Rights Practices for 2016: Russia*, at 23.
[129] *Ibid.*

ing their content to be branded as such as well as their foreign funding sources to be disclosed.[130]

Disinformation and Propaganda

The use of disinformation and propaganda has long been a hallmark of the Kremlin's toolbox to manipulate its own citizens. The historical precedent for these tactics stem from the Soviet era, when the government routinely utilized propaganda to "suppress any suggestion of the unpleasant and reassure the viewer that life in the communist empire was peaceful and optimistic."[131] While propaganda inside Russia has long cast aspersions on the Western democratic model as a counterpoint to Russia's own, the Kremlin's use of disinformation and propaganda under Putin has not sought simply to keep a lid on unpleasantness at home, but rather to whip up anxieties and generate fevered sentiment in support of its policies and actions.

To implement its propaganda, Putin's deputies reportedly summon chief editors on a regular basis to coordinate the Kremlin line on various news and policy items and distribute it throughout mainstream media outlets in Moscow.[132] Driving the narrative often requires media partners who have "created myths and explained reality" in the production of news as well as entertainment—often blurring lines between the two to ensure that media content fuels enthusiasm for the Kremlin's overall narrative.[133] Russian journalist Arkady Ostrovsky quotes one such partner at the helm of leading Russian television channel Perviy Kanal, Konstantin Ernst on this imperative: "Our task number two is to inform the country about what is going on. Today the main task of television is to mobilize the country."[134]

Propaganda under Putin has played up examples of Western failures in an attempt to undermine the credibility of a Western-style alternative system of government to Russia's corrupt, authoritarian state. Founder of independent television outlet Dozhd, Mikhail Zygar, summarizes it this way:

> Russian television doesn't suggest that Russian leaders are any better or less corrupt, or more honest and just, than Western leaders. Rather, it says that everything is the same everywhere. All the world's politicians are corrupt—just look at the revelations in the Panama Papers. Everywhere, human rights are being violated—just look at what American cops do to black people. All athletes dope. All elections are falsified. Democracy doesn't exist anywhere, so give it up.[135]

Ginning up cynicism among the Russian population about democratic nations also provides a convenient brush with which to tar Russia's democratic opposition at home. As Ostrovsky notes:

---

[130] "Russia's Putin Signs Foreign Agents Media Law," *Reuters*, Nov. 25, 2017.
[131] Joshua Yaffa, "Dmitry Kiselev Is Redefining the Art of Russian Propaganda," *New Republic*, July 1, 2014.
[132] Bill Powell, "Pushing The Kremlin Line," *Newsweek*, May 20, 2014.
[133] Ostrovsky, *The Invention of Russia*, at 297.
[134] *Ibid.* at 297.
[135] Mikhail Zygar, "Why Putin Prefers Trump," *Politico*, July 27, 2016.

In the weeks before his death, [opposition leader Boris Nemtsov] was demonized on television," to great effect. In Moscow street protests at that time, "hate banners carrying his image were hung on building facades with the words 'Fifth column—aliens among us' ... [marchers] carried signs proclaiming PUTIN AND KADYROV PREVENT MAIDAN IN RUSSIA alongside photographs of Nemtsov identifying him as 'the organizer of Maidan.'" This climate led Nemtsov to assert in an interview hours before his death that Russia was turning into a "fascist state" with "propaganda modeled on Nazi Germany's.[136]

Putin's propaganda machine has asserted a "moral superiority" over the West, bolstered by a focus on traditional values of the state and the Russian Orthodox Church.[137] This was especially useful at home as the 2011-2012 protests against Putin's return to the presidency gained steam, particularly among a relatively secular and urban middle class, forcing the Kremlin to appeal to its "core paternalistic and traditionalist electorate."[138] As such, state-sponsored media outlets have displayed an unforgiving tone for members of Russian society who buck traditional or religious mores. In April 2012, for example, the popular, pro-Kremlin "News of the Week" presenter Dmitry Kiselev said that gays and lesbians "should be prohibited from donating blood, sperm, and in the case of a road accident, their hearts should be either buried or cremated as unsuitable for the prolongation of life."[139]

State-sponsored media have also doctored the Kremlin's image to help justify Russian military incursions into Georgia, Ukraine, and Syria to the Russian population. During the 2008 invasion of Georgia, Ostrovsky notes that "television channels were part of the military operation, waging an essential propaganda campaign, spreading disinformation and demonizing the country Russia was about to attack."[140] Russian television inflated figures of civilian deaths and refugees in South Ossetia by the thousands. Alleging genocide, the picture that media painted was of the Kremlin "fighting not a tiny, poor country that used to be its vassal but a dangerous and powerful aggressor backed by the imperialist West."[141] Six years later, these tactics would be taken to new extremes during the so-called Euromaidan protests in Ukraine in which pro-European protesters railed against the pro-Russian government in Kiev, and the subsequent illegal Russian occupation of Crimea in 2014. Russian media painted the Euromaidan protesters as a collection of "neo-Nazis, anti-Semites, and radicals" staging an American-sponsored coup in Kiev.[142] "Pass this Oscar to the Russian Channel and to Dmitry Kiselev for the lies and nonsense you are telling people about Maidan," one protester said to a Russian state television

---

[136] Ostrovsky, *The Invention of Russia*, at 2; the name "Maidan," a borrowed word in the Russian and Ukrainian languages that refers to an open public space or town square, has been frequently used to refer to popular protests and street revolutions in the former Soviet space.
[137] Chapter 4 for more information on the Russian Orthodox Church's role in promoting traditional values abroad.
[138] Ostrovsky, *The Invention of Russia*, at 312.
[139] Joshua Yaffa, "Dmitry Kiselev Is Redefining the Art of Russian Propaganda," *New Republic*, July 1, 2014.
[140] Ostrovsky, *The Invention of Russia*, at 298.
[141] *Ibid.* at 298-99.
[142] *Ibid.* at 315.

broadcaster reporting from the Kyiv square, handing him a small statue.[143] The Kremlin's portrayal of its September 2015 involvement in the Syria conflict followed a similar pattern—a carefully-constructed narrative of Putin as the responsible and humanitarian actor who was intervening to stop U.S.-generated chaos in the Middle East.[144] State-sponsored media painted it as a successful fight against ISIS, though facts on the ground indicated that Russian bombs were in fact targeting the Syrian opposition to Bashar al-Assad.[145]

Russian security services have long collected compromising material known as "kompromat" on their own citizens and disseminated it through friendly, pro-Kremlin media. This tactic was instrumental in Putin's 1999 rise to power (see Chapter 1) and has continued to be deployed brazenly during his tenure to smear opposition activists. For example, the Nashi youth group, with Kremlin support, was reportedly behind the release of a 2010 video reel showing Victor Shenderovich, a prominent satirist and popular host of a television show that lampooned Russian officials, having sex with a woman suspected to be a Kremlin "honey trap." [146] The scandal prompted the release of information from other liberal media and opposition figures who said they had been entrapped by the same woman.[147] In 2016, grainy footage aired on pro-Kremlin channel NTV showing former Prime Minister and head of the PARNAS liberal opposition party, Mikhail Kasyanov, and another Russian opposition activist, Natalia Pelevina, in bed in a room together and exchanging criticisms about other members of the opposition.[148] Pelevina claimed that the video must have been compiled at Putin's direction to "destroy" Kasyanov, whose party was contending upcoming parliamentary elections, describing it as spliced together from perhaps six months' worth of secret footage and edited for maximum effect.[149]

Fake news and internet trolling have been used by the Kremlin against Russian citizens and were ramped up considerably after the 2011-2012 anti-Putin protests, according to investigative reporting by *The New York Times*. Set on reining in social media and online platforms, which were used by the opposition to disseminate electoral fraud allegations and mobilize protesters, the Kremlin used software to monitor public sentiment online and flooded social media with its own content, "paying fashion and fitness bloggers to place pro-Kremlin material among innocuous posts about shoes and diets." [150] Representatives of Alexey Navalny's Anti-Corruption Fund lamented to a *New York Times* journalist about the "atmosphere of hate" and the proliferation of pro-Kremlin hashtags that permeated Russia's Internet space after the protests, which clouded

---

[143] A.O. "Russia's Chief Propagandist," *The Economist*, Dec. 10, 2013.
[144] Ostrovsky, *The Invention of Russia*, at 324.
[145] Zygar, *All the Kremlin's Men*, at 337.
[146] Julia Ioffe, "Bears in a Honey Trap," *Foreign Policy*, Apr. 28, 2010.
[147] *Ibid.*
[148] Susan Ormiston, "Sex Tape Scandal Was Work of Putin, Says Russian Political Activist Exposed in Video," *CBC News*, Apr. 9, 2016.
[149] *Ibid.*
[150] Adrian Chen, "The Agency," *The New York Times*, June 2, 2015.

their messages with "so much garbage from trolls" that they became less effective.[151]

Efforts to crack down on free expression online and via social media also picked up renewed steam after Putin's return to the presidency. For example, a 2014 law enabled Russian authorities to block websites deemed extremist or a threat to public order without a court order, resulting in the blockage of three major opposition news sites and activist Alexey Navalny's blog.[152] Later that year, in September, Putin signed a law requiring non-Russian companies to store all domestic data on servers within the Russian Federation, ostensibly for data protection, but many observers saw it as an effort to tighten control over email and social media networks.[153] When the law took effect in 2015, some foreign companies refused to immediately comply. In response, Russian authorities ordered internet service providers in the country to block LinkedIn for non-compliance and threatened to shut down Facebook in 2018 if it did not comply.[154] Russian security services also ratcheted up influence over widely used Russian social media platform VKontakte—which has a broad user base in Russia as well as in Ukraine and other parts of the former Soviet space—pressuring its chief executive to reveal information on Euromaidan protesters in Ukraine and anti-corruption activists in Russia. Upon refusal, the CEO was fired, leaving the company in the control of Kremlin-friendly oligarchs.[155]

In addition, the Kremlin has, though at times clumsily, sought greater control of the internet space inside Russia as another way to surveil and restrict potential threats to its power. In the late 1990s, during Putin's FSB tenure, the government reportedly took steps to reinvigorate a Soviet-era surveillance mechanism called the System of Operative Search Measures (SORM) for the internet era. This SORM-2 aimed to intercept email, internet traffic, mobile calls, and voice-over internet protocols.[156] The new system required Russian Internet service providers to "install a device on their lines, a black box that would connect the internet provider to the FSB. It would allow the FSB to silently and effortlessly eavesdrop on emails, which had become the main method of communication on the internet by 1998."[157] Despite initial resistance from some service providers when news of the plan was leaked, ultimately most companies complied with its provisions.[158] Observers have noted that SORM-2 also expanded Kremlin capacity to surveil financial transactions, providing Putin "with a complete view of what the Russian political and economic elite was doing with its

[151] Ibid.
[152] "Russia Censors Media By Blocking Websites and Popular Blog," The Guardian, Mar. 14, 2014.
[153] U.S. Department of State, Country Reports on Human Rights Practices for 2014: Russia, at 33; Alexei Anishchuk, "Russia Passes Law to Force Websites onto Russian Servers," Reuters, July 4, 2014; Glenn Kates, "Russia's 'Cheburashka' Internet? Probably Not, But Here Are Some Other Options," Radio Free Europe/Radio Liberty, May 6, 2014.
[154] Ilya Khrennikov, "Russia Threatens to Shut Facebook Over Local Data Storage Laws," Bloomberg Technology, Sept. 26, 2017.
[155] Andrei Soldatov & Irina Borogan, The Red Web: The Kremlin's War on the Internet, PublicAffairs, at 291-294 Sept. 2015.
[156] Andrei Soldatov & Irina Borogan, "Inside the Red Web: Russia's Back Door Onto the Internet—Extract," The Guardian, Sept. 8, 2015.
[157] Ibid.
[158] Jen Tracy, "Who Reads Your E-mail?," Moscow Times, Mar. 16, 1999.

money."[159] According to an investigation by the Associated Press, the Kremlin has also directed state-sponsored hackers to infiltrate the email accounts of political opponents, dozens of journalists, and at least one hundred civil society figures inside Russia—a signal of tactics it would later use against international targets. Its domestic target list includes Mikhail Khodorkovsky, members of Pussy Riot, and Alexey Navalny.[160]

CORRUPTING ECONOMIC ACTIVITY

When news of the so-called "Panama Papers" broke in 2016, shining a light on corruption networks around the globe, a Russian cellist named Sergey Rodulgin found himself center stage. The documents alleged that Rodulgin, an old friend of Putin's, was tied to offshore companies valued at $2 billion that are suspected fronts for stashing pilfered wealth.[161] The documents allegedly showed that Rodulgin directly holds as much as $100 million in assets— a surprising figure for a professional cellist.[162] When pressed to respond to the papers, both Putin and Rodulgin attributed the latter's wealth to his successful philanthropic efforts collecting donations from Russian businessmen for the purchase of fine rare instruments for Russian students' use. "There's nothing to catch me out on here," said Rodulgin. "I am indeed rich; I am rich with the talent of Russia."[163] In fact, the estimated $24 billion that Putin's inner circle of friends and family controls is mostly drawn from business with state-controlled companies, particularly in the oil and gas sector.[164] An October 2017 report, jointly compiled by the Organized Crime and Corruption Project (the investigative network which helped to bring the Panama Papers to light) and Russian newspaper *Novaya Gazeta*, details the wealth of several members of Putin's inner circle and notes that, "Though they hold enormous assets, they stay out of the public eye, seem largely unaware of their own companies, and are at pains to explain the origins of their wealth," suggesting these individuals are "proxies" for holding resources that Putin may have amassed.[165]

The wealth that Putin may have accumulated for himself is the tip of a larger iceberg of crony capitalism in Russia that "has turned loyalists into billionaires whose influence over strategic sectors of the economy has in turn helped [Putin] maintain his ironfisted grip on power."[166] This political-economic ecosystem is distinct from the Yeltsin era, when many oligarchs independently built fortunes out of the chaos of the Soviet Union's collapse and thus represented potential political threats to the government. The Russian population, beset by the economic tumult of the 1990s, grew to resent the entrepreneurial oligarchs and their individual

---

[159] Samuel A. Greene, "Book Review: Andrei Soldatov & Irina Borogan's 'The Red Web,'" *Open Democracy*, Sep. 8, 2015.
[160] Raphael Satter et al., "Russia Hackers Pursued Putin Foes, Not Just US Democrats," *Associated Press*, Nov. 2, 2017.
[161] Shaun Walker, "Russian Cellist Says Funds Revealed in Panama Papers Came From Donations," *The Guardian*, Apr. 10, 2016.
[162] *Ibid.*
[163] *Ibid.*
[164] The Organized Crime and Corruption Reporting Project, *Putin and the Proxies*, https://www.occrp.org/en/putinandtheproxies, Oct. 24, 2017.
[165] *Ibid.*
[166] Steven Lee Myers *et al.*, "Private Bank Fuels Fortunes of Putin's Inner Circle," *The New York Times*, Sept. 27, 2014.

gains, often made through unscrupulous means.[167] As Putin took power, he seized on this resentment to assert the importance of the state over the individual. The new class of "bureaucrat-entre-preneurs" that emerged, former Soviet apparatchiks drawn dis-proportionately from the ranks of the security services, were re-warded with "complete power over any individual" and a helping of corrupt profits as long as they served state interests and re-mained loyal to the top of this pyramid scheme—Putin himself.[168] As Putin gained, so too did his loyalists, helping to reinforce the system and deter jealous challengers to his rule.

Many of these insiders trace their relationships with Putin back to a cooperative he joined in the mid-1990s with seven other own-ers of modest vacation homes a few hours outside of St. Petersburg, which they named Ozero ("Lake"). Putin carefully cultivated and relied on these bonds during his rise to power. He helped one such individual, Yury Kovalchuk, to take ownership in the early 1990s of a small firm, Bank Rossiya, whose shareholders included other members of the Ozero cooperative (see Chapter 4 for more on the Ozero cooperative and Bank Rossiya).[169] With Kremlin help to steer lucrative customers its way, obtain state-owned enterprises at bargain-basement prices, and obscure its financial holdings through murky transactions and shell companies, Bank Rossiya grew exponentially, and along the way also amassed significant media holdings that helped the Kremlin influence public percep-tions.[170] Putin has similarly relied on other longstanding friends, such as his former judo sparring partner Arkady Rotenberg, who controls shadow companies that allegedly made huge payments into Putin's business network, including a loan to an offshore com-pany controlled by Bank Rossiya with no apparent repayment schedule.[171]

A number of these insiders have become the targets of inter-national sanctions after the Russian invasion and illegal annex-ation of Crimea in 2014. Powerful Russian government operators have also been the target of U.S. sanctions under the Sergei Magnitsky Rule of Law Accountability Act of 2012, which requires the United States government to sanction Russian officials con-nected to the violent death in detention of lawyer and whistle-blower Sergei Magnitsky, as well as other officials who are gross violators of human rights in Russia.[172] As of the end of 2017, the U.S. government had sanctioned a total of 49 individuals under the Russia-related Magnitsky Act and 569 individuals or entities under existing Ukraine-related sanctions.[173] The Ukraine-related sanc-tions list in particular reads like a who's-who of Putin insiders: Arkady Rotenberg, Putin's childhood friend, along with Rotenberg's

[167] Ostrovsky, *The Invention of Russia*, at 307.
[168] *Ibid.*
[169] Jake Bernstein *et al.*, "All Putin's Men: Secret Records Reveal Money Network Tied to Rus-sian Leader," *The Panama Papers*, Apr. 3, 2016.
[170] Steven Lee Myers *et al.*, "Private Bank Fuels Fortunes of Putin's Inner Circle," *The New York Times*, Sept. 27, 2014.
[171] Jake Bernstein *et al.*, "All Putin's Men: Secret Records Reveal Money Network Tied to Rus-sian Leader," *The Panama Papers*, Apr. 3, 2016.
[172] Sergei Magnitsky Rule of Law Accountability Act, P.L. 112-208, Title IV, Enacted Dec. 14, 2012 (originally introduced by Senator Ben Cardin as S. 1039, May 19, 2011).
[173] U.S. Treasury Department, Office of Foreign Assets Control,"Sanctions List Search," https://sanctionssearch.ofac.treas.gov (search results under Program "MAGNIT" and the four Ukraine-related Executive Orders, as of Dec. 21, 2017).

brother Boris and nephew Roman; Yury Kovalchuk, Vladimir Yakunin, and Andrei Fursenko of the Ozero cooperative and Kovalchuk's nephew Kirill Kovalchuk; Kremlin insiders Vladislav Surkov and Vyacheslav Volodin; Rosneft chairman and head of the Kremlin's "siloviki" faction of security officials-turned-politicians Igor Sechin; billionaire businessman Gennady Timchenko; and even Aleksandr Dugin, whose philosophy of "Eurasianism" pushes for Russia to extend an ultra-nationalist, neo-fascist worldview across the globe.[174] Putin sought to play off the sanctions as a mere annoyance and soften the blow through directing kickbacks to those impacted, for example by shifting valuable state contracts to Bank Rossiya weeks after it was sanctioned.[175] The Duma also passed a law affording tax privileges to sanctioned individuals.[176] But the combination of sanctions and low oil prices have nevertheless been a drag on the Russian economy in recent years. As *The New York Times* noted, this has reduced "the country's most privileged players ... to fighting over slices of a smaller economic pie, seeking an advantage over rivals through the courts and law enforcement officials who are widely seen as vulnerable to corruption."[177]

The increasing exposure of Putin's network has helped to fuel demand for more transparency and questions over the assumed inviolability of Putin's leadership. A 50-minute video released by Navalny's Anti-Corruption Foundation in March 2017 alleging lavish luxury holdings by Prime Minister Dmitry Medvedev has generated millions of views on YouTube and was seen as instrumental in bringing thousands of Russians to the streets in protests during the year.[178] Moreover, the prospect of consequences—whether inside Russia or abroad—for the Putin regime's graft and abuses is helping to chip away at the culture of impunity that has stymied hopes in Russia for a just, secure society governed by the rule of law. In testimony to the U.S. Senate Foreign Relations Committee nearly two years prior to his murder, opposition leader Boris Nemtsov described the Magnitsky Act as "the most pro-Russian law in the history of any foreign parliament" for its capacity to end impunity against "crooks and abusers."[179] Indeed, since the Act's passage in 2012, the U.S. Congress has subsequently passed a global version of the sanctions that was signed into law in 2016, and by the end of 2017 the U.S. government had sanctioned one Russian individual, Artem Chayka, under this law for significant corruption.[180] Meanwhile, parliaments in Estonia, the United Kingdom, and Canada have passed legislation similar to the U.S.

[174] *Ibid.*; James Carli, "Aleksandr Dugin: The Russian Mystic Behind America's Weird Far-Right," *Huffington Post*, Sept. 7, 2017.
[175] Steven Lee Myers et al., "Private Bank Fuels Fortunes of Putin's Inner Circle," *The New York Times*, Sept. 27, 2014.
[176] "Putin Signs Law Granting Sanctions-Hit Russians Tax Breaks," *Radio Free Europe/Radio Liberty*, Apr. 4, 2017.
[177] Andrew E. Kramer, "In Russia, a Bribery Case Lifts the Veil on Kremlin Intrigue," *The New York Times*, Oct. 21, 2017.
[178] David Filipov, "Russia Dismisses Sweeping Corruption Allegations Against Medvedev," *The Washington Post*, Mar. 5, 2017.
[179] Statement of Boris Nemtsov, Co-Chairman, Republican Party of Russia, *A Dangerous Slide Backwards: Russia's Deteriorating Human Rights Situation*, Hearing before the U.S. Senate Committee on Foreign Relations, June 13, 2013.
[180] Matthew Pennington, "U.S. Levies Sanctions Against Myanmar General, Dozen Others," *Associated Press*, Dec. 21, 2017.

34

Magnitsky laws.[181] Vice Chairman of the Open Russia democratic opposition platform Vladimir Kara-Murza has urged more expansive application of U.S. and European targeted individual sanctions, noting that while the task of building a more just Russia lies with the country's own citizens, outsiders should not "enable Mr. Putin and his kleptocrats by providing safe harbor for their illicit gains." [182]

---

[181] The Global Magnitsky Human Rights Accountability Act, P.L. 114-328, Subtitle F, Title XII, Enacted Dec. 23, 2016 (originally introduced by Senator Benjamin L. Cardin as S.284, Jan. 28, 2015); "The US Global Magnitsky Act" *Human Rights Watch*, Sept. 13, 2017; Mike Blanchfield, "Canada Passes Magnitsky Human Rights Law, Sparking Russian Threats," *The Canadian Press*, Oct. 18, 2017.
[182] Vladimir Kara-Murza, "Answering the Kremlin's Challenge," *World Affairs Journal* (2017).

Chapter 3: Old Active Measures and Modern Malign Influence Operations

A BRIEF HISTORY OF SOVIET ACTIVE MEASURES

The FBI and CIA were involved in the assassination of President John F. Kennedy in 1963. The United States and Israel organized an attack on Mecca in 1979. U.S. government scientists created the AIDS virus as a biological weapon in 1983. All of these bogus stories, and many more, were concocted and disseminated by Soviet propagandists during the Cold War.[183] Some are even still repeated today. For example, in a June 2017 interview, Putin referenced the JFK assassination theory to accuse U.S. intelligence agencies of conducting false flag operations and blaming them on the Russian secret services, saying that "[t]here is a theory that Kennedy's assassination was arranged by the United States special services. If this theory is correct, and one cannot rule it out, so what can be easier in today's context, being able to rely on the entire technical capabilities available to special services, than to organize some kind of attacks in the appropriate manner while making a reference to Russia in the process." [184]

While the technological tools have evolved, Russia's use of disinformation is not a new phenomenon—as one Russian military intelligence textbook says, "Psychological warfare has existed as long as man himself." [185] During the Cold War, "active measures," or disinformation and malign influence operations, were "well integrated into Soviet policy and involved virtually every element of the Soviet party and state structure, not only the KGB." [186] Russian specialists in active measures used official newspapers and radio stations, embassies, and foreign communist parties to create and distribute false stories. Each state organ would use their own capabilities in coordinated campaigns: the KGB was responsible for "black propaganda"—creating forgeries and spreading rumors; the International Information Department was responsible for "white propaganda"—broadcasting the stories through official media organizations; and the International Department was responsible for "gray propaganda"—disseminating the stories through inter-

---

[183] Fletcher Schoen & Christopher Lamb, *Deception, Disinformation, and Strategic Communications: How One Interagency Group Made a Major Difference,* Institute for National Strategic Studies, at 4, 20, 34 (June 2012).
[184] Vladimir Putin, Interview with Megyn Kelly, *NBC,* June 5, 2017, http://en.kremlin.ru/events/president/news/54688.
[185] Alexey Kovalev & Matthew Bodner, "The Secrets of Russia's Propaganda War, Revealed," *The Moscow Times,* Mar. 1, 2017.
[186] Thomas Boghardt, "Soviet Bloc Intelligence and Its AIDS Disinformation Campaign," *Studies in Intelligence,* Vol. 53, No. 4, at 1-2 (Dec. 2009).

national front organizations.[187] And they were intently focused on
their target audience: as one Soviet disinformation practitioner put
it, "every disinformation message must at least partially cor-
respond to reality or generally accepted views." [188] Active measures
also sought to take advantage of pre-existing fissures to further po-
larize the West. As Colonel Rolf Wagenbreth, long-time head of active measures operations for the East German Stasi, reportedly
said, "A powerful adversary can only be defeated through .... sophisticated, methodical, careful, and shrewd effort to exploit even
the smallest 'cracks' between our enemies ... and within their
elites." [189]

Opinions on the effectiveness of Soviet active measures varied
among U.S. national security experts. During the Reagan Administration, Under Secretary of State Lawrence Eagleburger and Deputy CIA Director Robert Gates argued that the operations were
"deleterious but generally not decisive," although, according to
Gates, who cited the Dutch decision on deployment of intermediate
range nuclear weapons and Spain's referendum on NATO participation, "in a close election or legislative battle, they can make the
difference." [190]

Soviet bloc disinformation operations were not a rare occurrence:
more than 10,000 were carried out over the course of the Cold
War.[191] In the 1970s, Yuri Andropov, then head of the KGB, created active measures courses for operatives, and the KGB had up
to 15,000 officers working on psychological and disinformation warfare at the height of the Cold War.[192] The CIA estimated that the
Soviet Union spent more than $4 billion a year on active measures
operations in the 1980s (approximately $8.5 billion in 2017 dollars).
And then, as now with the Kremlin, "the highest level of the Soviet
government" approved the themes of active measures operations.[193]

Active measures campaigns in the 1980s focused on influencing
the arms control and disarmament movements, for example, by
promoting the European peace movement in countries that were
scheduled to base U.S. intermediate-range nuclear forces. That
campaign made use of the West German Communist Party, the
Dutch Communist Party, the Belgian National Action Committee
for Peace and Development, the World Peace Council, and the
International Union of Students, among others.[194] In addition to
political parties and peace organizations, the Soviet Union also
used the Russian Orthodox Church and an affiliate of the Soviet-

---

[187] *Ibid.* at 3.

[188] *Ibid.* at 2.

[189] Statement of Thomas Rid, Professor, Department of War Studies, King's College London,
Disinformation: A Primer in Russian Active Measures and Influence Campaigns, Hearing before
the U.S. Senate Select Committee on Intelligence, Mar. 30, 2017, at 2 (citing Günther Bohnsack,
Herbert Brehmer, Auftrag Irrefuhrung, Carlsen, at 16 (1992)).

[190] Schoen & Lamb, Deception, Disinformation, and Strategic Communications, at 104.

[191] Statement of Thomas Rid, *Disinformation: A Primer in Russian Active Measures and Influence Campaigns,* at 2.

[192] "The Fog Of Wars: Adventures Abroad Boost Public Support at Home," *The Economist,* Oct.
22, 2016.

[193] "Soviet Active Measures in the United States, 1986-87; Prepared by the Federal Bureau
of Investigation," reprinted in the Congressional Record, 133 Cong. Rec. H34262 (Dec. 9, 1987)
(statement of Rep. C.W. Bill Young).

[194] Directorate of Intelligence, Central Intelligence Agency, "Soviet Strategy to Derail US INF
Deployment," Feb. 1983.

backed Christian Peace Conference to influence American church-es, religious organizations, and religious leaders.[195]

Soviet active measures also attempted to influence elections in the West during the Cold War, though without much success. Efforts to defeat Chancellor Helmut Kohl in West Germany's 1983 election included "a massive propaganda campaign of interference," according to the German government at the time. That same year, KGB agents in the United States were ordered "to acquire contacts on the staff of all possible presidential candidates and in both party headquarters ... [and] to popularize the slogan 'Reagan Means War!'"[196] The KGB's efforts notwithstanding, Reagan won 49 of 50 states in the 1984 election. Disinformation campaigns also smeared FBI director J. Edgar Hoover and Senator Henry "Scoop" Jackson, both implacable anti-communists, with rumors to the media about their sexual orientation—a tactic that would resurface many decades later during the 2017 French presidential campaign.[197]

MODERN MALIGN INFLUENCE OPERATIONS

Today, the Kremlin's malign influence operations employ state and non-state resources to achieve their ends, including the security services, television stations and pseudo news agencies, social media and internet trolls, public and private companies, organized crime groups, think tanks and special foundations, and social and religious groups.[198] These efforts have "weaponized" four spheres of activity: traditional and social media, ideology and culture, crime and corruption, and energy. Disinformation campaigns are used to discredit politicians and democratic institutions like elections and independent media.

Cultural, religious, and political organizations are used to repeat the Kremlin's narrative of the day and disrupt social cohesion.

Corruption is used to influence politicians and infiltrate decision-making bodies.

And energy resources are used to cajole and coerce vulnerable foreign governments. The Kremlin coordinates these multi-platform efforts from within the Presidential Administration, which controls the FSB and the Foreign Intelligence Service (SVR), among many other agencies, and is described by observers as "perhaps the most important single organ within Russia's highly de-institutionalized state."[199]

While the Russian government supplies many of the resources for these efforts, Kremlin-linked oligarchs are also believed to help fund malign influence operations in Europe.[200]

Furthermore, the Kremlin's efforts attempt to exploit the advantages of democratic societies. As the former president of Estonia

---

[195] "Soviet Active Measures in the United States, 1986–87; Prepared by the Federal Bureau of Investigation," reprinted in the Congressional Record, 133 Cong. Rec. H34262.

[196] Andrew Weiss, "Vladimir Putin's Political Meddling Revives Old KGB Tactics," *The Wall Street Journal*, Feb. 17, 2017.

[197] *Ibid.*

[198] Last year, the European Parliament passed a resolution recognizing the wide range of tools and instruments that Russia uses to disseminate disinformation and propaganda. *See* European Parliament Resolution, "EU Strategic Communication to Counteract Anti-EU Propaganda by Third Parties," 2016/2030(INI), Nov. 23, 2016.

[199] Mark Galeotti, *Controlling Chaos: How Russia Manages its Political War in Europe*, European Council on Foreign Relations, at 1 (Aug. 2017).

[200] Committee Staff Discussion with Russian Human Rights Activists, May 2017.

put it, "[W]hat they do to us we cannot do to them .... Liberal democracies with a free press and free and fair elections are at an asymmetric disadvantage ... the tools of their democratic and free speech can be used against them."[201] The Russian government's work to destabilize European governments often start with attempts to build influence and exploit divisions at the local level. According to the Office of the Director of National Intelligence:

> Russia's influence campaign is built on longstanding practices. Moscow has been opportunistic in its efforts to strengthen Russian influence in Europe and Eurasia by developing affiliations with and deepening financial or political connections to like-minded political parties and Nongovernmental Organizations. Moscow appears to use monetary support in combination with other tools of Russian statecraft, including propaganda in local media, direct lobbying by the Russian Government, economic pressure, and military intimidation.[202]

The U.S. State Department reports that the Kremlin's efforts to influence elections and referendums in Europe include "overt and covert support for far left and right political parties, funding front groups and NGOs, and making small, low-profile investments in key economic sectors to build political influence over time," and that its tactics "focus on exploiting internal discord in an effort to break centrist consensus on the importance of core institutions."[203] An analysis by the German Marshall Fund's Alliance for Securing Democracy found that the Russian government has used cyberattacks, disinformation, and financial influence campaigns to meddle in the internal affairs of at least 27 European and North American countries since 2004.[204] As one Russian expert puts it, the Russian government's methods to pursue its goals abroad are "largely determined by the correlation between the strength of the countries' national institutions and their vulnerability to Russian influence."[205] Whereas in what Russia considers its "near abroad," composed of the former Soviet Union countries, the Kremlin's goal is to exert control over pliant governments or weaken pro-Western leaders, in the rest of Europe it primarily seeks to undermine NATO and the EU, while amplifying existing political and social discord.[206] The Kremlin also acts with more boldness in its near abroad than it does in NATO and EU states. But it still deploys its full range of malign influence tools throughout the rest of Europe and, increasingly, beyond Europe's borders. These operations

[201] Sheera Frenkel, "The New Handbook for Cyberwar Is Being Written By Russia," *BuzzFeed News*, Mar. 19, 2017 (citing former Estonian President Toomas Hendrick Ilves).
[202] Director of National Intelligence, Assessment on Funding of Political Parties and Nongovernmental Organizations by the Russian Federation, pursuant to the Intelligence Authorization Act for FY2016, (P.L. No. 114-113).
[203] U.S. Department of State, Report to Congress on Efforts by the Russian Federation to Undermine Elections in Europe and Eurasia, Pursuant to the Countering America's Adversaries through Sanctions Act of 2017 (P.L. 115-44), Nov. 7, 2017.
[204] Oren Dorell, "Alleged Russian Political Meddling Documented in 27 Countries Since 2004," *USA Today*, Sept. 7, 2017. The countries included Belarus, Bulgaria, Canada, Cyprus, Czech Republic, Denmark, Estonia, Finland, France, Georgia, Germany, Hungary, Italy, Latvia, Lithuania, Macedonia, Moldova, Montenegro, Norway, Poland, Portugal, Spain, Sweden, Turkey, United Kingdom, Ukraine, and the United States.
[205] Mark Galeotti, *Controlling Chaos: How Russia Manages Its Political War in Europe*, European Council on Foreign Relations, Sept. 1, 2017.
[206] Alina Polyakova et al. *The Kremlin's Trojan Horses*, Atlantic Council, at 4 (Nov. 2016).

require relatively small investments, but history has shown that they can have outsized results, if conditions permit.

New technologies, updated policy priorities, and a resurgent brashness in the Kremlin and among its oligarch allies have converged to enable an expanded range of disinformation operations in Europe. According to a resolution adopted by the European Parliament in November 2016, have the goal of "distorting truths, provoking doubt, dividing Member states, engineering a strategic split between the European Union and its North American partners and paralyzing the decision-making process, discrediting the EU institutions and transatlantic partnerships" and "undermining and eroding the European narrative."[207] Whereas the Kremlin's propaganda inside of Russia glorifies the regime, outside of Russia, it aims to exploit discontent and grievances. Notably, the Kremlin's disinformation operations do not necessarily try to convince foreign audiences that the Russian point of view is the correct one. Rather, they seek to confuse and distort events that threaten Russia's image (including historical events), undercut international consensus on Russia's behavior at home and abroad, and present Russia as a responsible and indispensable global power. Challenging others' facts is simpler than the propaganda advanced by the Soviet Union—it is much harder to convince people that the harvest doubled in their local area than it is to plant doubt about what is happening thousands of miles away.

Ben Nimmo of the Center for European Policy Analysis has characterized the Kremlin's propaganda efforts as four simple tactics: dismiss the critic, distort the facts, distract from the main issue, and dismay the audience.[208] At their core, the Kremlin's disinformation operations seek to challenge the concept of objective truth. As the CEO of the U.S. Broadcasting Board of Governors (BBG), John Lansing, put it, Kremlin messaging is "really almost beyond a false narrative. It's more of a strategy to establish that there is no such thing as an empirical fact. Facts are really what is being challenged around the world."[209]

For Putin and the Kremlin, the truth is not objective fact; the truth is whatever will advance the interests of the current regime. Today, that means whatever will delegitimize Western democracies and distract negative attention away from the Russian government. It means subverting the notion of verifiable facts and casting doubt on the veracity of all information, regardless of the source—as Lansing also put it, "If everything is a lie, then the biggest liar wins."[210] Sometimes, it means going so far as using an image from a computer game as evidence of U.S. misdeeds, as Russia's Defense Ministry did in November 2017 when it posted a screenshot from a promotional video of a computer game called "AC-130 Gunship Simulator: Special Ops Squadron" on social media and claimed that it was "irrefutable proof that the US provides cover for ISIS combat

---

[207] "European Parliament Resolution of 23 November 2016 on EU Strategic Communication to Counteract Propaganda against it by Third Parties," 2016/2030(INI), Nov. 23, 2016.
[208] Edward Lucas and Ben Nimmo, *Information Warfare: What Is It and How to Win It?* Center for European Policy Analysis (Nov. 2015).
[209] Rachel Oswald, "Reality Rocked: Info Wars Heat Up Between U.S. and Russia," *CQ*, June 12, 2017.
[210] Testimony of John Lansing, CEO and Director of the Broadcasting Board of Governors, *The Scourge of Russian Disinformation*, Hearing Before the Committee on Security and Cooperation in Europe, Sept. 14, 2017, at 3.

troops, using them for promoting American interests in the Middle East."[211]

The Kremlin's disinformation operations rapidly deliver a high volume of stories, creating, in the words of two RAND Corporation researchers, a "firehose of falsehood."[212] They note that direct and systematic efforts to counter these operations are made difficult by the vast array of mechanisms and platforms that the Kremlin employs.[213] What's more, disproving a false story takes far more time and effort than creating one does, and, as the false story was the first one to be seen by audiences (and possibly repeatedly across multiple platforms), it may have already made a strong impression. In the meantime, while the fact-checkers are busy disproving one story, the Kremlin's propagandists can put out ten more. As the RAND scholars note, "don't expect to counter the firehose of falsehood with the squirt gun of truth."[214]

That being said, there are some methods of countering propaganda that can reduce the effectiveness of false stories, including being warned upon initial exposure that the story may be false, repeated exposure to a refutation, and seeing corrections that provide a complete alternative story, which can fill the gap created by the removal of the false facts. The RAND analysts also recommend not just countering the actual propaganda, but its intended effects. For example, if the Kremlin is trying to undercut support for a strong NATO response to Russian aggression, then the West should promote narratives that strengthen support for NATO and promote solidarity with NATO members facing threats from Russia.[215] Such a response is far more complicated, however, when Russian disinformation is not just intended to promote Putin or Russian policies, but rather to exacerbate existing divides on hot-button social and political issues like race, religion, immigration, and more.

THE KREMLIN'S DISINFORMATION PLATFORMS

The Kremlin employs an array of media platforms and tools to craft and amplify its narratives. The Russian government's main external propaganda outlets are RT, which focuses on television news programming, and Sputnik, a radio and internet news network. RT and Sputnik target a diverse audience: both far-right and far-left elements of Western societies, environmentalists, civil rights activists, and minorities.

While the stated purpose of these state-owned media networks is to provide an alternative, Russian view of the world (in Putin's words, to "break the monopoly of Anglo-Saxon global information streams"), they appear to be more focused on popularizing conspiracy theories and defaming the West, and seek to foster the impression "that everyone is lying and that there are no unequivocal

---

[211] "Computer Game as 'Irrefutable Proof'," *EU* vs. *Disinfo*, Nov. 15, 2017. The image also appeared on a government-sponsored TV station, presented as a news story. The "EU versus Disinformation" campaign is an anti-disinformation effort run by the European External Action Service East StratCom Task Force, created in response to the EU's calls to challenge Russia's ongoing disinformation campaigns. *See* Chapter 7.
[212] Christopher Paul & Miriam Matthews, *The Russian "Firehose of Falsehood" Propaganda Model,* Rand Corporation, at 9 (2016).
[213] *Ibid.*
[214] *Ibid.*
[215] *Ibid.* at 10 (2016).

facts or truths."[216] Part of RT and Sputnik's appeal—and an explanation for their apparent success—is their high production value and sensational content. According to a 2016 study by the RAND Corporation, RT and Sputnik are "more like a blend of infotainment and disinformation than fact-checked journalism, though their formats intentionally take the appearance of proper news programs."[217] Russian media reports have even gone so far as conducting fake interviews with actors that are paid to pretend they are victims of Ukrainian government aggression.[218]

RT was launched in 2005 and currently reports in six languages: Arabic, English, French, German, Russian, and Spanish. The U.S. State Department reports that the Russian government spends an estimated $1.4 billion per year on disseminating its messaging through various media platforms at home and abroad.[219] In 2016, over $300 million went to RT alone.[220] As a Russian human rights activist put it, the Europeans who see RT as an "alternative" are similar to the left-wing audience—both in Europe and the United States—in the 1970s and 1980s who held favorable views of the Soviet Union.[221] Former Secretary of State John Kerry has referred to RT as a "propaganda bullhorn," and RT regularly gives controversial European political figures a platform on its shows and gives disproportionate coverage to the more extreme factions of the European Parliament.[222]

RT claims to reach between 500 million and 700 million viewers in over 100 countries. However, according to data compiled by the BBG, this likely overstates the viewership, as it represents the number of households in which RT is available, and not the number of households that actually watch RT.[223] As of 2017, RT attracted about 22.5 million Facebook followers, and it deftly drives traffic to its platforms with human interest stories, cat videos, and pseudo conspiracy theories (like op-eds about whether the earth is round or flat).[224] A 2015 analysis found that only one percent of videos on RT's YouTube channel were political in nature, while its

[216] Vladimir Putin, Interview with Margarita Simonyan, *RT*, June 12, 2013; Stefan Meister and Jana Pugleirin, *Perception and Exploitation: Russia's Non-Military Influence in Europe*, German Council on Foreign Relations, (Oct. 2015).
[217] Paul and Matthews, *The Russian "Firehose of Falsehood" Propaganda Model*, 3 Rand Corporation, at 5, 2016.
[218] *Ibid.*
[219] U.S. Department of State, Report to Congress on Media Organizations Controlled and Funded by the Government of the Russian Federation (Nov. 7, 2017).
[220] "RT's 2016 Budget Announced, Down from 2015, MSM Too Stumped to Spin?" *RT*, May 4, 2016; "About RT," RT, https://www.rt.com/about-us/, (visited Dec. 6, 2017).
[221] Committee Staff Discussion with Russian Human Rights Activists.
[222] Brett LoGuirato, "John Kerry Just Gave Russia A Final Warning," *Business Insider*, Apr. 24, 2014; Office of the Director of National Intelligence, Assessment on Funding of Political Parties and Nongovernmental Organizations by the Russian Federation, Report to Congress Pursuant to the Intelligence Authorization Act for FY2016 (P.L. No. 114-113). According to a report from the U.S. Office of the Director of National Intelligence, RT's editor-in-chief, Margarita Simonyan, has close ties to several top officials in the Russian government, including the Deputy Chief of Staff of the Presidential Administration, Aleksey Gromov, who is one of RT's founders and now reportedly manages political TV coverage in Russia. Office of the Director of National Intelligence, *Assessing Russian Activities and Intentions in Recent US Elections": The Analytic Process and Cyber Incident Attribution*, at 9 (Jan. 2017) ("DNI Assessment")
[223] BBG Data on Russian International Broadcasting Reach, IBB Office of Policy and Research, Broadcasting Board of Governors, June 2017. For example, BBG data showed that RT and Sputnik combined only have a total weekly reach of 2.8 percent of Moldova's population, 1.3 percent of Belarus's, and 5.3 percent of Serbia's.
[224] "Comparing Russian and American Government 'Propaganda'," *Meduza*, Sept 14, 2017. (*Meduza* is a Russian online newspaper); Sam Gerrans, "YouTube and the Art of Investigation," *RT*, Sept. 27, 2015.

most popular videos were of natural disasters, accidents, and crime.[225]

The Moscow Times found that when RT reporters strayed from its implicit editorial line, they were told "this is not our angle." [226] Former staff report that RT's editorial line comes from the top down, and managers, not editors, choose what will be covered and how. For example, when foreign staff disagreed with the way that RT was covering Ukraine, they were taken off the assignment and Ukraine-related coverage was handled by Russian staff.[227] And those Russian staff are mostly "apathetic or apolitical, with no prior experience in journalism"—their primary qualification is fluency in English, gained from either linguistic training or being the "children of Russian diplomats." [228] All of which reveals that, while RT may have a large budget and growing reach, it also has several fundamental institutional flaws which limit its ability to operate as a professional news organization. In the words of one former employee, "a combination of apathy, a lack of professionalism and a dearth of real talent keep RT from being more effective than it currently is." [229]

Sputnik is a state-owned network of media platforms launched in November 2014 and includes social media, news, and radio content; in June 2017, it began operating an FM radio station in Washington, D.C.[230] With an annual budget of $69 million, the network operates in 31 different languages and attracts about 4.5 million Facebook followers.[231] Like RT, Sputnik consistently promotes anti-West narratives that undermine support for democracy. A study by the Center for European Policy Analysis found that Sputnik "grant[s] disproportionate coverage to protest, anti-establishment and pro-Russian [members of the European Parliament from Central and Eastern Europe]; that it does so systematically; and that even when it quotes mainstream politicians, it chooses comments that fit the wider narrative of a corrupt, decadent and Russophobic West ... making 'wide use of the protest potential' of the legislature to promote the Kremlin's chosen messages of disinformation." [232]

Sputnik is also often used to "ping pong" a suspect story from lesser-known news sites and into more mainstream press outlets.[233] One well-known example was the purported police cover-up of the "Lisa" rape case in Germany. After initially circulating on Facebook, the story was picked up by Channel One, a Russian government-controlled news channel, and then covered by RT and Sputnik, which argued the case was not an isolated incident. The following week, protests broke out, despite the fact the allegations had since been recanted and the police investigation had debunked

[225] Katie Zavadski, "Putin's Propaganda TV Lies About Its Popularity," *The Daily Beast,* Sept. 17, 2015.
[226] Matthew Bodner et al., "Welcome to The Machine: Inside the Secretive World of RT," *The Moscow Times,* June 1, 2017.
[227] *Ibid.*
[228] *Ibid.*
[229] *Ibid.*
[230] Max Greenwood, "Russian Radio Takes Over Local DC station," *The Hill,* June 30, 2017.
[231] "Comparing Russian and American government 'propaganda'," *Meduza,* Sept 14, 2017.
[232] Ben Nimmo, *Propaganda in a New Orbit: Information Warfare Initiative Paper No. 2,* Center for European Policy Analysis, at 6 (Jan. 2016).
[233] "Ping ponging" is a technique to raise the profile of a story through complementary websites, with the goal of getting the mainstream media to pick it up. *See* Appendix H.

them.[234] Sputnik also reportedly orders its foreign journalists to pursue discredited conspiracy theories—it asked one American correspondent to explore possible connections between the death of Democratic National Committee staffer Seth Rich and the leak of internal DNC documents to WikiLeaks, in an attempt to cast doubt on the U.S. Director of National Intelligence (DNI) assessment that Russian-backed hackers were behind the leak.[235] And during the French presidential elections, Sputnik reported on unfounded rumors about the sexual preferences of the pro-EU candidate, Emmanuel Macron.[236]

In light of the DNI assessment that RT serves as the Kremlin's "principal propaganda outlet," and along with Sputnik form Russia's "state-run propaganda machine" that served as platforms for the Kremlin's efforts to influence the 2016 U.S. election, RT and Sputnik encountered significant pushback in the United States in late 2017.[237] In November, RT complied with an order from the U.S. Department of Justice—which found that it was engaged in "political activities" that were "for or in the interests of" a foreign principal—to register under the Foreign Agents Registration Act (FARA).[238] Registration requires RT to disclose more of its financial information to the U.S. government.[239] A month earlier, Twitter announced that it would no longer allow paid advertisements from RT and Sputnik on its platform, citing the DNI findings and the company's ongoing review of how its platform was used in the 2016 election.[240] In November 2017, Eric Schmidt, the Executive Chairman of Google's parent company, reportedly said that the company was working on "deranking" results from RT and Sputnik from its Google News product.[241] However, according to a Google announcement RT and Sputnik's sites would not be specifically targeted, but rather the company "adjusted [their] signals to help surface more authoritative pages and demote low-quality content," giving less weight to relevance and more weight to authoritativeness.[242]

Beyond RT and Sputnik, the Russian government uses a variety of additional tools to amplify and reinforce its disinformation campaigns.[243] Internet "trolls" are one such tool—individuals who try

[234] Jim Rutenberg, "RT, Sputnik and Russia's New Theory of War," *The New York Times,* Sept. 13, 2017.
[235] Andrew Feinberg, "My Life at a Russian Propaganda Network," *Politico,* Aug. 21, 2017.
[236] "Ex-French Economy Minister Macron could be 'US Agent' Lobbying Banks' Interests," *Sputnik,* Feb. 4, 2017.
[237] DNI Assessment at 3.
[238] Devlin Barrett and David Filipov, "RT Files Paperwork With Justice Department To Register As Foreign Agent," *The Washington Post,* Nov. 13, 2017; Josh Gerstein, "DOJ Told RT To Register As Foreign Agent Partly Because Of Alleged 2016 Election Interference," *Politico,* Dec. 21, 2017; Letter from U.S. Department of Justice to RTTV America, Aug. 17, 2017.
[239] See Foreign Agents Registration Act, 22 U.S.C. § 612; Megan Wilson, "Seven Things to Know About RT's Foreign Agent Registration," *The Hill,* Sept. 14, 2017.
[240] Twitter Public Policy Company Announcement: "RT and Sputnik Advertising," Oct. 26, 2017.
[241] Alex Hern, "Google Plans to 'De-Rank' Russia Today and Sputnik to Combat Misinformation," *The Guardian,* Nov. 21, 2017 (citing Schmidt's remarks at the Halifax International Security Forum, Nov. 18, 2017).
[242] "Our Latest Quality Improvements for Search," *Google Official Blog,* Apr. 25, 2017.
[243] The Kremlin wants its propaganda to reach its audiences first, and it wants to reach them repeatedly. Experimental psychology has shown that first impressions are quite resilient, with individuals more likely to accept the first information they receive on a topic (the "illusory truth effect") and favor that information when confronted with conflicting messages. Furthermore, repeated exposure to a statement increases the likelihood that someone will accept that it is

Continued

to derail online debates and amplify the anti-West narratives prop-
agated by RT and Sputnik. These trolls use thousands of fake social media accounts on Facebook, Twitter, and other platforms to
attack articles or individuals that are critical of Putin and Kremlin
policies, spread conspiracy theories and pro-Kremlin messages, attack opponents of Putin's regime, and drown out constructive debate.[244]

According to a *New York Times* investigation, in 2015 hundreds
of young Russians were employed at a "troll farm" in St. Petersburg known as the Internet Research Agency (IRA), where many
worked 12-hour shifts in departments focused on different social
media platforms.[245] The organization was organized in a kind of
vertically-integrated supply chain for internet news. An NBC interview of a former worker at the IRA, Vitaly Bespalov, revealed that
workers were highly compartmentalized and used to amplify each
other's work: the third floor held bloggers writing posts to undermine Ukraine and promote Russia, on the first floor writers composed news articles that referred back to the blog posts created on
the third floor, and then commenters on the third and fourth floors
posted remarks about the stories under fake Ukrainian identities.
Meanwhile, the marketing team worked to package all of the misinformation into viral-ready social media formats.[246]

At the beginning of each shift, workers were reportedly given a
list of opinions to promulgate and themes to address, all related to
current events. Over a two-shift period, a worker would be expected
to publish 5 political posts, 10 nonpolitical posts (to establish credibility), and 150 to 200 comments on other workers' posts.[247] For
their labor, they made between $800 to $1,000 a month, an attractive wage for recent graduates new to the work force.[248] The professional trolls were also provided "politology" classes that taught
them the Russian position on the latest news.[249] Russian media
outlets have reported that the IRA was bankrolled by a close Putin
associate, Evgeny Prigozhin, a wealthy restaurateur known as the
"Kremlin's Chef," whose network of companies have received a
number of lucrative government contracts, and who was sanctioned
by the Obama Administration in December 2016 for contributing to
the conflict in Ukraine.[250]

According to one former employee, IRA staff on the "foreign
desk" were responsible for meddling in other countries' elections.[251]
In the run up to the 2016 U.S. presidential election, for example,

---

true—especially when they are less interested in the topic—and makes them process it less carefully in discriminating weak arguments from strong ones. Christopher Paul & Miriam Matthews, *The Russian "Firehose of Falsehood" Propaganda Model,"* Rand Corporation, at 4 (2016).

[244] Stefan Meister & Jama Puglierin, *Perception and Exploitation: Russia's Non-Military Influence in Europe,* German Council on Foreign Relations, at 4 (Sept.-Oct. 2015).

[245] Adrian Chen, "The Agency," *The New York Times,* June 2, 2015.

[246] Ben Popken & Kelly Cobiella, "Russian Troll Describes Work in the Infamous Misinformation Factory," *NBC News,* Nov. 16, 2017.

[247] Adrian Chen, "The Agency," *The New York Times,* June 2, 2015.

[248] "The Notorious Kremlin-linked 'Troll Farm' and the Russians Trying to Take it Down," *The
Washington Post,* Oct. 8, 2017.

[249] Adrian Chen, "The Agency," *The New York Times,* June 2, 2015.

[250] David Filipov, "The Notorious Kremlin-linked 'Troll Farm' and the Russians Trying to
Take it Down," *The Washington Post,* Oct. 8, 2017; Thomas Grove and Paul Sonne, "U.S. Im-
poses Sanctions on Russian Restaurateur With Ties to Putin," *The Wall Street Journal,* Dec.
20, 2016.

[251] "An Ex St. Petersburg 'Troll' Speaks Out: Russian Independent TV Network Interviews
Former Troll At The Internet Research Agency," *Meduza,* Oct. 15, 2017.

foreign desk staff were reportedly trained on "the nuances of American social polemics on tax issues, LGBT rights, the gun debate, and more ... their job was to incite [Americans] further and try to 'rock the boat.' "[252] The employee noted that "our goal wasn't to turn the Americans toward Russia. Our task was to set Americans against their own government: to provoke unrest and discontent."[253] Based on conversations with Facebook officials, it appears that Kremlin-backed trolls pursued a similar strategy in the lead up to the 2017 French presidential election, and likely before Germany's national election the same year.[254] The IRA also apparently had a separate "Facebook desk" that fought back against the social network's efforts to delete fake accounts that the IRA had developed into sophisticated profiles.[255] In addition, in the United States, Russian-backed social media accounts linked to the IRA paid for advertisements to promote disinformation and encouraged protests and rallies on both sides of socially divisive issues, such as promoting a protest in Baltimore while posing as part of the Black Lives Matter movement.[256] While the IRA has reportedly been inactive since December 2016, a company known as Glavset is a reported successor, and other related companies, including Teka and the Federal News Agency, may be carrying out similar work.[257]

Many of the fake accounts used to amplify misinformation are bots, or automated social media accounts. Bot networks can be created or purchased wholesale fairly cheaply on the dark web, a part of the internet accessed with special software that gives users and operators anonymity, and thus is often used as a marketplace for illicit goods and services.[258] According to one report, they can be purchased for as little as $45 for 1,000 bots with new, unverified accounts, and up to $100 for 500 phone-verified accounts (which have a unique phone number attached to them).[259] Through automation, bots can spread disinformation at high speed and in great numbers, quickly amplifying a false story's reach and profile and making it trend on social media platforms. For example, during the French presidential election, bots were used to spread memes, gifs, and disinformation stories about Emmanuel Macron. Bots have also been used to attack perceived critics of the Kremlin by flooding their accounts with retweets and followers, clogging the target's account and possibly resulting in temporary suspension from the platform for suspicious activity.[260]

Kremlin-aligned hackers, supported by trolls, bot networks, and friendly propaganda outlets, have also used "doxing" to great effect. Doxing occurs when hackers break into a network, steal propri-

252 *Ibid.*
253 *Ibid.*
254 Committee Staff Discussion with Facebook.
255 "An Ex St. Petersburg 'Troll' Speaks Out: Russian Independent TV Network Interviews Former Troll at the Internet Research Agency," *Meduza*, Oct. 15, 2017.
256 Luke Broadwater, "Second Russia-Linked Effort Promoted Protests During Trial of Freddie Gray Officers," *The Baltimore Sun*, Oct. 12, 2016.
257 Diana Pilipenko, "Facebook Must 'Follow The Money' to Uncover Extent Of Russian Meddling," *The Guardian*, Oct. 9, 2017.
258 Andy Greenberg, "Hacker Lexicon: What is the Dark Web?" *Wired*, Nov. 19, 2014.
259 Joseph Cox, "I Bought a Russian Bot Army for Under $100," *The Daily Beast*, Sept. 13, 2017.
260 "The Surprising New Strategy of Pro-Russia Bots," BBC Trending (BBC News Blog), Sept. 12, 2017.

etary, secret, or incriminating information, and then leak it for public consumption.[261] For example, hackers that have been linked to Russian security services attacked the World Anti-Doping Agency (WADA) after it published a report that revealed Russian sports doping, and then released the private medical information of American athletes.[262] During the 2016 U.S. presidential election campaign, both the Democratic National Committee (DNC) and the campaign manager of the Democratic presidential candidate were victims of doxing by the same Kremlin-backed hackers who attacked WADA in 2016, France's TV5Monde in 2015, and Ukraine's election commission in 2014.[263]

A new tactic is planting fake documents among the authentic ones leaked as part of a doxing operation—the Macron campaign alleged that this happened when it was attacked (though in addition to the fake documents planted by the hackers, the campaign had also created several false email accounts and loaded them with fake documents to confuse the hackers and slow them down).[264] Similarly, hackers have previously placed child pornography on the computers of Kremlin critics living abroad, and then alerted the local police. If the hackers are sophisticated enough, it is extremely difficult to discover the source of the intrusion, or even whether an intrusion has taken place. As the head of one cybersecurity company told *The New York Times,* "to use a technical term, you are completely screwed. If something like this is sponsored by the Russian government, or any government or anyone with sufficient skill, you are not going to be successful [in salvaging your reputation]. It is terrible."[265] It is not hard to imagine similar attacks being carried out on Western politicians who have taken a strong position against Putin's regime, and the subsequent consequences for their campaigns, careers, and legacies.

Combining all of these tools together, the Kremlin can ensure that its disinformation operations are seen early, often, and widely. Furthermore, disinformation efforts can now take advantage of increasingly powerful analytics that identify "customer sentiment," allowing them to target the most susceptible and vulnerable audiences. In the case of the United States, Kremlin-backed propagandists and internet trolls sought not just to promote the Kremlin's narratives, but also to advance divisive narratives that further erode social cohesion. In the words of Germany's intelligence chief, the aim is simply to delegitimize the democratic process, "no matter whom they help get ahead."[266] Such efforts are both harder to detect than traditional propaganda and, arguably, more dangerous to the target society.

---

[261] Bruce Schneier, "How Long Until Hackers Start Faking Leaked Documents?" *The Atlantic,* Sept. 13, 2016.
[262] Andy Greenberg, "Russian Hackers Get Bolder in Anti-Doping Agency Attack," *Wired,* Sept. 14, 2016; *see* Appendix C.
[263] FireEye iSight Intelligence, *APT28: At The Center of The Storm, Russia Strategically Evolves Its Cyber Operations,* at 4-5 (Jan 2017).
[264] Adam Nossiter et al., "Hackers Came, but the French Were Prepared," *The New York Times,* May 9, 2017.
[265] Andrew Higgins, "Foes of Russia Say Child Pornography Is Planted to Ruin Them," *The New York Times,* Dec. 9, 2016.
[266] Esther King, "Russian Hackers Targeting Germany: Intelligence Chief," *Politico,* Nov. 29, 2016.

Chapter 4: Weaponization of Civil Society, Ideology, Culture, Crime, and Energy

Pushing fake news stories with Internet trolls and slickly produced infotainment has proved an effective tool for promoting the Russian government's objectives in Europe, and one it can deploy from a distance. But the Kremlin also benefits from having ideological boots on the ground. The Soviets supposedly referred to extreme left activists and politicians in the West as "useful idiots"—people who the former Soviet Union could count on to agitate against its democratic enemies. Today, the Kremlin applies a far less restrictive ideological filter to its useful idiots, and has also embraced and cultivated a menagerie of right wing, nationalist groups in Europe and further abroad.

These agents of influence abroad can be separated into three distinct tiers, according to an April 2016 study by Chatham House, a UK think tank:

1. Major state federal agencies, large state-affiliated grant-making foundations, and private charities linked to Russian oligarchs;

2. Trusted implementing partners and local associates like youth groups, think tanks, associations of compatriots, veterans' groups, and smaller foundations that are funded by the state foundations, presidential grants, or large companies loyal to the Kremlin; and

3. Groups that share the Kremlin's agenda and regional vision but operate outside of official cooperation channels—these groups often promote an "ultra-radical and neo-imperial vocabulary" and run youth paramilitary camps.[267]

THE ROLE OF STATE FOUNDATIONS, GONGOS, NGOS, AND THINK TANKS

The Kremlin funds, directly or indirectly, a number of government-organized non-governmental organizations (GONGOs), non-governmental organizations (NGOs), and think tanks throughout Russia and Europe. These groups carry out a number of functions, from disseminating pro-Kremlin views to seeking to influence elections abroad.

Following a series of "color revolutions" in former Soviet Union republics like Ukraine and Kyrgyzstan, in 2006 the Russian government established the World Coordination Council of Russian Compatriots, which is responsible for coordinating the activities of

---

[267] Orysia Lutsevych, *Agents of the Russian World: Proxy Groups in the Contested Neighbourhood*, Chatham House, at 10 (Apr. 2016).

Russian organizations abroad and their communications with the Kremlin.[268] Some GONGOs that receive and disburse funds from the Kremlin, such as the Russkiy Mir Foundation and Rossotrudnichestvo, established in 2007 and 2008, are headquartered in Russia but have branches throughout the EU, and are led by senior Russian political figures like the foreign minister or the chair of the foreign affairs committee of the upper house of the parliament.[269] Kremlin-linked oligarchs also sit on the boards of many of the GONGOs.[270] Based on conservative estimates from publicly available data, the Kremlin spends about $130 million a year through foundations like Rossotrudnichestvo and the Gorchakov fund, and, in 2015, channeled another $103 million in presidential grants to NGOs; after including support from state enterprises and private companies, however, actual funding levels may be much higher.[271] Most of the Russian government's funding is focused on post-Soviet "swing states" like Ukraine, Moldova, Georgia, and Armenia, but Kremlin-supported groups also operate in the Baltic states and the Balkans, especially Serbia and Bulgaria.[272]

Some Russian government-funded groups are used to gain sympathy for the Kremlin's narrative in academic circles abroad. One example is the Valdai Discussion Club, a Russian government-funded think tank, which is based in Russia but has branches in the EU.[273] Some analysts assert that the Kremlin uses Valdai to co-opt Western experts and academics, who Lilia Shevtsova of the Brookings Institution believes then "pull their punches when writing about Putin. Experts who go want to be close to power and are afraid of losing their access. Some might believe they can use Valdai as a platform for criticism, but in reality their mere presence at the event means they are already helping legitimize the Kremlin."[274]

Other Kremlin-funded think tanks have allegedly attempted to influence elections abroad. The Russian Institute for Strategic Research (RISS) is a Kremlin think tank based in Moscow that has offices throughout the country, including a Baltic Regional Information-Analytical Center in the exclave of Kaliningrad (the Baltic states are a particular focus for the Kremlin's malign influence operations).[275] RISS, which was established by Putin and is mostly staffed with ex-intelligence officers, has been accused by Kremlin opponents of seeking to prevent Montenegro's accession to NATO, dissuade Sweden from enhancing its ties with the alliance, and influence a national election in Bulgaria (see Chapter 5).[276] Accord-

[268] Vladislava Vojtiskova et al., *The Bear in Sheep's Clothing: Russia's Government-Funded Organisations in the EU*, Wilfried Martens Centre for European Studies, at 34 (July 2016).
[269] *Ibid.*
[270] *Ibid.* at 11.
[271] Orysia Lutsevych, *Agents of the Russian World: Proxy Groups in the Contested Neighbourhood*, Chatham House, at 11 (Apr. 2016).
[272] *Ibid.* at 12.
[273] Vladislava Vojtiskova et al., *The Bear in Sheep's Clothing*, at 11.
[274] Peter Pomerantsev & Micahel Weiss, *The Menace of Unreality: How the Kremlin Weaponizes Information, Culture and Money*, Institute of Modern Russia, at 21 (Nov. 2014).
[275] Russian Institute for Strategic Studies, "About," https://en.riss.ru/about (visited Dec. 15, 2017).
[276] Ivan Nechepurenko, "Kremlin Group Employing Ex-Spies Is Viewed Abroad as Propaganda Mill," *The New York Times*, Apr. 20, 2017; Neil MacFarquhar, "A Powerful Russian Weapon: The Spread of False Stories," *The New York Times*, Aug. 28, 2016.

49

ing to current and former U.S. officials, RISS also reportedly developed a plan to "swing the 2016 U.S. presidential election to Donald Trump and undermine voters' faith in the American electoral system." [277] However, more than a few scholars and independent journalists doubt the efficacy of RISS, with one commenting that "these guys (average age: 70) couldn't have possibly game-planned making a sandwich, let alone rigging [the U.S. election]." [278] Such opinions are likely based on some of RISS's other work, such as a study which reportedly claimed that condoms were one of the factors spreading HIV in Russia. [279]

Other think tanks and GONGOs in Europe that promote the Kremlin's narrative have opaque funding structures that hide potential sources of support. A 2017 report published by the Swedish Defense Research Agency noted that "much of the funding that these GONGOs receive from commercial entities would not happen if there were not a clear understanding that these think tanks are closely connected to the political leadership" and "contributing to activities that do enjoy the trust and patronage of the political leadership could give both enterprises and individual businessmen advantages ... . In a political system where economic and political activity are intrinsically linked, the fact that business finances a think tank does not mean that it is therefore more independent of the political leadership." [280] One such example of a privately funded think tank is the Dialogue of Civilizations Research Institute, which opened in Berlin in 2016, and was co-founded and financed by Vladimir Yakunin, a longtime Putin associate and former head of Russian Railways (who the United States sanctioned for his role in Russia's illegal annexation of Crimea). [281] The Institute's goal, according to a report by the Wilfried Martens Centre for European Studies, is to coordinate a worldwide network of Russian think tanks. [282] One German newspaper reportedly described it as an "instrument of Moscow's hybrid warfare" whose primary purpose is to create an "alternative civilization to the American." [283] The Institute denies any connections to the Kremlin, but does not make its funding transparent, and Yakunin is reported to be investing about $28 million in the Institute over five years, in addition to funding from other Russian businessmen. [284] Such opaque funding is a hallmark of many Kremlin-linked NGOs and think tanks. An Atlantic Council report explains why these financial streams are so difficult to trace:

---

[277] Ned Parker et al., "Putin-Linked Think Tank Drew Up Plan to Sway 2016 US Election-Documents," *Reuters,* Apr. 19, 2017.

[278] Ivan Nechepurenko, "Kremlin Group Employing Ex-Spies Is Viewed Abroad as Propaganda Mill," *The New York Times,* Apr. 20, 2017.

[279] "Kremlin Experts Blame Condoms for Russian HIV Epidemic," *The Moscow Times,* May 31, 2016.

[280] Carolina Vendil Pallin & Susanne Oxenstierna, *Russian Think Tanks and Soft Power,* Swedish Defense Research Agency, at 17-18 (Aug. 2017).

[281] Ben Knight, "Putin Associate Opens Russia-Friendly Think Tank in Berlin," *Deutsche Welle,* Jul. 1, 2016; U.S. Department of the Treasury, Office of Foreign Assets Control, "Ukraine-Related Designations," Mar. 20, 2014. The Institute emerged out of the World Public Forum Dialogue of Civilizations, headquartered in Vienna. "History," Dialogue of Civilizations Research Institute, https://doc-research.org/en/about-us/ (visited Dec. 18, 2017). It has a branch in Moscow, and plans expansions in China.

[282] Vladislava Vojtiskova et al., *The Bear in Sheep's Clothing,* at 12, 41, 42.

[283] Ben Knight, "Putin Associate Opens Russia-Friendly Think Tank in Berlin," *Deutsche Welle,* Jul. 1, 2016.

[284] *Ibid.*

The [Kremlin's] web of political networks is hidden and non-transparent by design, making it purposefully difficult to expose. Traceable financial links would inevitably make Moscow's enterprise less effective: when ostensibly independent political figures call for closer relations with Russia, the removal of sanctions, or criticize the EU and NATO, it legitimizes the Kremlin's worldview. It is far less effective, from the Kremlin's point of view, to have such statements come from individuals or organizations known to be on the Kremlin's payroll.[285]

THE KREMLIN'S CULTIVATION OF POLITICAL EXTREMES

The Kremlin has also adopted a new practice in cultivating relationships with some of the more mainstream far-right parties in Europe, by establishing "cooperation agreements" between the dominant United Russia party and parties in Austria (Freedom Party), Hungary (Jobbik), Italy (Northern League), France (National Front), and Germany (AfD). These cooperation agreements include plans for regular meetings and "collaboration where suitable on economic, business and political projects."[286] Kremlin-linked banks, funds, and oligarchs even lent nearly $13 million in 2014 to France's far-right National Front party to finance its election campaign.[287] And the German newspaper Bild reported that the Russian government clandestinely funded the AfD ahead of 2017 parliamentary elections—perhaps without the AfD's knowledge—by using middlemen to sell it gold at below-market prices.[288] In addition to monetary resources, the Kremlin has reportedly also offered organizational, political, and media expertise and assistance to far-right European parties.[289]

Different Kremlin narratives attract different groups from left and right. Scholars Peter Pomerantsev and Michael Weiss describe how "European right-nationalists are seduced by the [Kremlin's] anti-EU message; members of the far-left are brought in by tales of fighting US hegemony; [and] U.S. religious conservatives are convinced by the Kremlin's stance against homosexuality."[290] The Congressional Research Service reports that many of the far-right European parties linked to the Kremlin are "anti-establishment and anti-EU, and they often share some combination of extreme nationalism; a commitment to 'law and order' and traditional family values; and anti-immigrant, anti-Semitic, or anti-Islamic sentiments."[291] Far-right gatherings are also sponsored by Kremlin-linked oligarchs like Vladimir Yakunin and Konstantin Malofeev who, according to the *EUobserver*, a Brussels-based online news-

[285] Alina Polyakova et al., *The Kremlin's Trojan Horses*, Atlantic Council, at 4 (Nov. 2016).
[286] Alison Smale, "Austria's Far Right Signs a Cooperation Pact with Putin's Party," Dec. 19, 2016.
[287] Marine Turchi, "How a Russian Bank Gave France's Far-Right Front National Party 9mln Euros," *Mediapart*, Nov. 24, 2014; Suzanne Daley & Maia de la Baume, "French Far Right Gets Helping Hand With Russian Loan," *The New York Times*, Dec. 1, 2014.
[288] Andrew Rettman, "Illicit Russian Money Poses Threat to EU Democracy," *EUobserver*, Apr. 21, 2017.
[289] Congressional Research Service, "Russian Influence on Politics and Elections in Europe," June 27, 2017.
[290] Peter Pomerantsev & Micahel Weiss, *The Menace of Unreality: How the Kremlin Weaponizes Information, Culture and Money*, Institute of Modern Russia, at 19 (Nov. 2014).
[291] Congressional Research Service, Russia: Background and U.S. Policy, at 29 (Aug. 21, 2017).

paper, have organized conferences that included "delegates from Germany's neo-Nazi NPD party, Bulgaria's far-right Ataka party, the far-left KKK party in Greece, and the pro-Kremlin Latvian Russian Union party."[292]

Another such conference took place in March 2015, when the leaders of some of Europe's most controversial and fringe right-wing political organizations—as well as some from similar groups in the United States—met in St. Petersburg for the first International Russian Conservative Forum. The event was organized by Russia's nationalistic Rodina ("Motherland") party, and its objective was clearly stated: to unite European and Russian conservative forces "in the context of European sanctions against Russia and the United States' pressure on European countries and Russia."[293] Speakers reportedly urged white Christians to reproduce, referred to gays as perverts, and said that murdered Russian opposition activists were resting in hell.[294] They also decried same-sex marriage, globalization, radical Islam, immigration, and New York financiers, while consistently praising Russia's President Vladimir Putin for upholding and protecting conservative and masculine values. A British nationalist speaker showed a picture of a shirtless Putin riding a bear, and declared: "Obama and America, they are like females. They are feminized men. But you have been blessed by a man who is a man, and we envy that."[295] James Taylor, an American who runs a white nationalist website, spoke at the event, where he called the United States "the greatest enemy of tradition everywhere."[296]

In the United States, many extreme right-wing groups, including white nationalists, look up to Putin—a self-proclaimed champion of tradition and conservative values. At a protest in Charlottesville, Virginia, against the removal of a statue of Confederate general Robert E. Lee, white nationalists repeatedly chanted "Russia is our friend."[297] Andrew Anglin, the publisher of the Daily Stormer, the world's biggest neo-Nazi website, apparently spent much of 2015 and 2016 running his website from inside of Russia, from where his content was promoted by a suspected Russian bot network.[298] In addition, the Kremlin has cultivated ties with organizations that promote gun rights and oppose same-sex marriage. For example, Kremlin-linked officials have also cultivated ties with groups in the United States like the National Rifle Association (NRA). Alexander Torshin, a former senator in Putin's United Russia party who allegedly helped launder money through Spain for Russian mobsters, developed a relationship with David Keene when the latter was the

[292] Andrew Rettman, "Illicit Russian Money Poses Threat to EU Democracy," *EUobserver,* Apr. 21, 2017.
[293] Gabrielle Tetrault-Farber, "Russian, European Far-Right Parties Converge in St. Petersburg," *The Moscow Times,* Mar. 22, 2015.
[294] *Ibid.*
[295] Neil MacFarquhar, "Right-Wing Groups Find a Haven, for a Day, in Russia," *The New York Times,* Mar. 22, 2015.
[296] *Ibid.*
[297] Tom Porter, "Charlottesville's Alt-Right Leaders Have a Passion for Vladimir Putin," *Newsweek,* Aug. 16, 2017; Laura Vozzella, "White Nationalist Richard Spencer Leads Torch-Bearing Protesters Defending Lee Statue," *The Washington Post,* May 14, 2017.
[298] *See* Luke O'Brien, "The Making of an American Nazi," *The Atlantic,* Dec. 2017.

52

NRA's President.[299] In 2015, the NRA sent a delegation to Moscow to meet with Dmitry Rogozin, a Putin ally and deputy prime minister who fell under U.S. sanctions in 2014 for his role in the crisis in Ukraine.[300] U.S. evangelicals, including Franklin Graham, have also supported Putin's suppression of LGBT rights in Russia, saying that Putin "has taken a stand to protect his nation's children from the damaging effects of any gay and lesbian agenda."[301] Brian Brown, who runs the World Council of Families (WCF), a group that opposes same-sex marriage and abortion rights, testified to the Duma before it adopted several anti-gay laws.[302] The WCF planned to hold its annual conference in Moscow in 2014, but cancelled it because of the difficulties presented by new U.S. sanctions legislation related to the crisis in Ukraine, which also hit a member of the WCF's planning committee, Vladimir Yakunin.[303]

The Kremlin's illegal annexation of Crimea and military incursion into eastern Ukraine also affected the rhetoric and focus of its disparate ideological boots on the ground. A year-long study by a Hungarian think tank found that since the beginning of the crisis in Ukraine, far right and extremist organizations that had "previously predominantly focused on ethnic, religious, and sexual minorities as their main enemies, redirect[ed] their attention to geopolitical issues. They are not only agitating against NATO and the EU, but also share a particular sympathy towards Vladimir Putin's Russia, which they regard as an ideological and political model."[304] These groups also benefit from their voices being amplified by Kremlin-linked media networks that peddle in fake news and conspiracy theories. Furthermore, the small size and limited influence of fringe parties and paramilitary groups make it easy for the Kremlin to infiltrate, purchase, and control them. The report also noted that in Central and Eastern Europe, the Kremlin has sought to exploit "the bitter memories of past territorial disputes, nationalist-secessionist tendencies, and the haunting spectres of chauvinist ideologies promising to make these nations great again."[305]

Unlike in Soviet times, the Kremlin no longer limits its support to just one end of the ideological spectrum. In addition to right-wing groups, it still maintains strong ties with former and current communist parties—Ukraine's Ministry of Justice in 2014 sought to ban the country's Communist Party, which was believed to be acting on behalf of the Kremlin.[306] Some European left and far-left

---

[299] Estaban Duarte et al., "Mobster or Central Banker? Spanish Cops Allege This Russian Both," *Bloomberg*, Aug. 9, 2016; Rosalind Helderman & Tom Hamburger, "Guns and Religion: How American Conservatives Grew Closer to Putin's Russia," *The Washington Post*, Apr. 30, 2017.

[300] Tim Mak, "Top Trump Ally Met with Putin's Deputy in Moscow," *The Daily Beast*, Mar. 7, 2017; U.S. Department of the Treasury, Office of Foreign Assets Control, "Issuance of a New Ukraine-Related Executive Order; Ukraine-related Designations," Mar. 17, 2014.

[301] Steve Benen, "Franklin Graham Sees Putin with Moral High Ground," *MSNBC*, Mar. 19, 2014.

[302] Southern Poverty Law Center, "Brian Brown Named President of Anti-LGBT World Congress of Families," June 2, 2016; Rosalind Helderman & Tom Hamburger, "Guns and Religion: How American Conservatives Grew Closer to Putin's Russia," *The Washington Post*, Apr. 30, 2017.

[303] Southern Poverty Law Center, "World Congress of Families Suspends Russia Conference," Mar. 25, 2014.

[304] Peter Kreko et al., Political Capital, *From Russia with Hate: The Activity of Pro-Russian Extremist Groups in Central-Eastern Europe*, at 47 (Apr. 2017).

[305] *Ibid.* at 12.

[306] Peter Pomerantsev & Micahel Weiss, *The Menace of Unreality: How the Kremlin Weaponizes Information, Culture and Money*, Institute of Modern Russia, at 19-20 (Nov. 2014).

53

parties have also adopted more friendly views toward Russia, including Spain's Podemos party, Greece's Syriza Party (which has led the government since 2015), Bulgaria's Socialist Party, and Moldova's Socialist Party, with candidates from the latter two winning presidential elections in November 2016.[307] According to NATO officials, Russian intelligence agencies also reportedly provide covert support to European environmental groups to campaign against fracking for natural gas, thereby keeping the EU more dependent on Russian supplies.[309] A study by the Wilfried Martens Centre for European Studies reports that the Russian government has invested $95 million in NGOs that seek to persuade EU governments to end shale gas exploration.[309]

THE USE OF THE RUSSIAN ORTHODOX CHURCH

Just as the Kremlin has strengthened its relationship with the Russian Orthodox Church and used it to bolster its standing at home, the Russian Orthodox Church also serves as its proxy abroad, and the two institutions have several overlapping foreign policy objectives. According to the former editor of the official journal of the Moscow Patriarchate, "the church has become an instrument of the Russian state. It is used to extend and legitimize the interests of the Kremlin."[310] In a letter to Russian foreign minister Sergei Lavrov, the Russian Orthodox Church's Patriarch, Kirill, wrote: "During your service as foreign minister, the cooperation between the Russian foreign policy department and the Moscow Patriarchate has considerably broadened. Through joint efforts we have managed to make a contribution to the gathering and consolidation of the Russian World."[311] Scholar Robert Blitt notes that "the Russian government, in an effort to restore its lost role as a global superpower, has recruited the Church as a primary instrument for rallying together a dubious assortment of states and religious representatives to support a new international order. This new order is premised on the rejection of universal human rights and the revival of relativism, two principles that serve the Church well."[312] Blitt also notes that the Russian government has linked national security with "spiritual security," and that "abroad, the government benefits from the [Russian Orthodox Church]'s efforts as a willing partner in reinforcing Russia's 'spiritual security,' which in turn boosts the channels available to it for the projection of Russian power abroad."[313]

In 2003, the Russian Orthodox Church and Russia's Ministry of Foreign Affairs established a working group that has, in the words of Foreign Minister Lavrov, allowed them to work "together realizing a whole array of foreign policy and international activity

[307] "In the Kremlin's Pocket," *The Economist*, Feb. 12,, 2015; Cynthia Kroet, "The New Putin Coalition," *Politico*, Nov. 21, 2016.
[308] Sam Jones et al., "NATO Claims Moscow Funding Anti-Fracking Groups," *Financial Times*, June 19, 2014.
[309] Vladislava Vojtiskova et al., *The Bear in Sheep's Clothing*, at 31.
[310] Andrew Higgins, "In Expanding Russian Influence, Faith Combines with Firepower," *The New York Times*, Sept. 13, 2016.
[311] Letter from Patriarch Kirill, Patriarch of Moscow and All Russia, Russian Orthodox Church, to Russian Foreign Minister Sergei Lavrov, Mar. 22, 2010.
[312] Robert Blitt, *Russia's Orthodox Foreign Policy: the Growing Influence of the Russian Orthodox Church in Shaping Russia's Policies Abroad*, 33 U. PA. J. INT'L L., at 379 (2011).
[313] *Ibid.*

thrusts."[314] The Ministry of Foreign Affairs has also used Kirill to promote a relativistic view of human rights at the United Nations, arranging for him to give a speech in 2008 (before he was Patriarch) at the UN Human Rights Council, where he bemoaned that "there is a strong influence of feministic views and homosexual attitudes in the formulation of rules, recommendations and programs in human rights advocacy."[315] According to a report by Chatham House, in Ukraine, Georgia, and Armenia, Orthodox parent committees, modelled on similar Russian Orthodox committees, have launched attacks on LGBT and feminist groups.[316] These committees "claim that gender equality is a Western construct intended to spread homosexuality in Eastern Europe, blaming the United States and the EU for the decay of 'moral health' in the respective societies."[317] The Russian Orthodox Church also enjoys strong financial backing from Kremlin-linked oligarchs Konstantin Malofeev and Vladimir Yakunin, who are both under U.S. sanctions.[318] In Bulgaria and Romania, the Kremlin even allegedly co-opted Orthodox priests to lead anti-fracking protests.[319] In Moldova, senior priests have worked to halt the country's integration with Europe (leading anti-homosexual protests and even claiming that new biometric passports for the EU were "satanic" because they had a 13-digit number), and priests in Montenegro led efforts to block the country from joining NATO.[320]

THE NATIONALIZATION OF ORGANIZED CRIME

During his time in St. Petersburg in the 1990s, Putin allegedly collaborated with two major organized crime groups to assert control over the city's gambling operations, helped launder money and facilitated travel for known mafia figures, had a company run by a crime syndicate provide security for his Ozero ("Lake") house cooperative, and helped that criminal organization gain a monopoly over St. Petersburg's fuel deliveries.[321] According to a report by scholar Ilya Zaslavskiy, the latter operation would teach Putin useful skills that he could later use at the national level, including "monopolization of the downstream energy market, management of the city's oil and gas assets through nominal front men and offshore accounts, and the use of ex-Stasi and other Warsaw Pact operatives in energy schemes across Europe."[322]

[314] *Ibid.* at 381.
[315] Metropolitan Kirill, Chairman of the Moscow Patriarchate DECR, Address on the Panel Discussion on Human Rights and Intercultural Dialogue at the 7th Session of the UN Human Rights Council, Mar. 22, 2008.
[316] Orysia Lutsevych, *Agents of the Russian World: Proxy Groups in the Contested Neighbourhood*, Chatham House, at 26 (Apr. 2016).
[317] *Ibid.* at 26.
[318] *Ibid.* at 25-26; Gabriela Baczynska & Tom Heneghan, "How the Russian Orthodox Church Answers Putin's Prayers in Ukraine," *Reuters*, Oct. 6, 2014; U.S. Department of the Treasury, Office of Foreign Assets Control, "Ukraine-related Designations," Mar. 20, 2014; U.S. Department of the Treasury, Office of Foreign Assets Control, "Issuance of a New Ukraine-related Executive Order and General License; Ukraine-related Designations," Dec. 19, 2014.
[319] Sam Jones et al., "NATO Claims Moscow Funding Anti-Fracking Groups," *Financial Times*, June 19, 2014.
[320] Andrew Higgins, "In Expanding Russian Influence, Faith Combines with Firepower," *The New York Times*, Sept. 13, 2016.
[321] Brian Whitmore, "Putinfellas," *Radio Free Europe/Radio Liberty*, May 3, 2016 (citing Karen Dawisha, *Putin's Kleptocracy: Who Owns Russia?* Simon & Schuster, Sept. 2015).
[322] Ilya Zaslavskiy, *Corruption Pipeline: the Threat of Nord Stream 2 to EU Security and Democracy*, Free Russia, at 4 (2017).

From the Kremlin, Putin has allegedly continued to use Russian-based organized crime groups to pursue his interests both at home and abroad, including to smuggle arms, assassinate political opponents, earn "black cash" for off-the-books operations, conduct cyberattacks, and support separatist movements in Moldova, Georgia, and Ukraine.[323] Euan Grant, an expert in transnational crime, told *The Moscow Times* that Russians linked to organized crime groups have formed a large quasi-intelligence agency for the Kremlin, acting as "political Trojan horses" that use their money to "undermine morale, compromise officials and weaken Western resolve."[324]

In 2016, a judge investigating Russian mafia operations in Spain issued international arrest warrants for several current and former Russian government officials with alleged connections to a money laundering operation run by a Russia-based crime group in Spain. Spanish prosecutors also alleged that a senior member of the Duma, Vladislav Reznik, helped the head of the Russian crime syndicate in Spain, Gennady Petrov, get his allies into senior positions in the Russian government in exchange for assets in Spain.[325] Spanish investigators tapping Petrov's phones heard him speak with a deputy prime minister and five other cabinet ministers, as well as various legislators, including Reznik, a founder and vice president of Putin's United Russia party and head of the Duma's finance committee.[326] Reznik and Petrov regularly socialized and did business together, sharing a private jet and the same secretary, lawyer, and financial adviser in Spain.[327] Reznik was also a member of the board of directors of Bank Rossiya, which fell under U.S. sanctions in 2014 for its role in Ukraine and was described by the U.S. Treasury Department as "the personal bank for senior officials of the Russian Federation."[328] And from 1998-99, Petrov was reportedly a co-owner of Bank Rossiya, along with several men belonging to Putin's Ozero cooperative of dacha owners (the Panama Papers also revealed that Bank Rossiya transferred at least $1 billion to Putin's friend, the musician Sergei Roldugin).[329]

There are also multiple historical links between Putin and Petrov's gang in St. Petersburg. The gang was then led by Vladimir Barsukov and started out in St. Petersburg in the early 1990s, the same time that Putin served as the city's deputy mayor. In addition to illicit activities, the gang was allegedly involved in real estate, banking, and energy, including the Petersburg Fuel Company (PTK), which, thanks to a decision involving Putin, won a contract

[323] Mark Galeotti, *Crimintern: How the Kremlin Uses Russia's Criminal Networks in Europe,* European Council on Foreign Relations, at 1 (Apr. 2017); Brian Whitmore, "Putinfellas," *Radio Free Europe/Radio Liberty,* May 3, 2016.
[324] Peter Hobson, "How Europe Became a Russian Gangster Playground," *The Moscow Times,* May 12, 2016.
[325] *Ibid.* The arrest warrants were later thrown out, reportedly because some of the named individuals were cooperating with the investigation.
[326] *Ibid.*
[327] *Ibid.*
[328] *Ibid.*; U.S. Department of the Treasury, "Treasury Sanctions Russian Officials, Members of the Russian Leadership's Inner Circle, and an Entity for Involvement in the Situation in Ukraine," Mar. 20, 2014.
[329] Alec Luhn & Luke Harding, "Spain Issues Arrest Warrants for Russian Officials Close to Putin," *The Guardian,* May 4, 2016.

in 1995 to be the sole supplier of gasoline in St. Petersburg.[330] It is worth noting that, according to an investigation by *Newsweek,* the then-owner of PTK was Vladimir Smirnov (also a member of the Ozero cooperative), who partnered with Barsukov for the gasoline business. Smirnov also once led the Russian operations of the St. Petersburg Real Estate Holding Company (SPAG), of which Putin was an advisory board member until his inauguration as president.[331] In 1999, U.S. and European intelligence agencies began to suspect that SPAG was involved in a money laundering scheme in Lichtenstein for Russian organized crime gangs and Colombian drug traffickers, including the Cali cocaine cartel (though SPAG denies wrongdoing and no charges were ever filed).[332] Furthermore, Barsukov was also reportedly a board member of a SPAG subsidiary.[333] Alexander Litvinenko, the former spy who Putin allegedly ordered the assassination of (see Appendix B for more information), and another former KGB agent, Yuri Shvets, had compiled a report on Barsukov and the Tambov gang in 2006, and found that, as deputy mayor, Putin had provided political protection for criminal activity related to Barsukov's gang in St. Petersburg.[334]

Russian security expert Mark Galeotti of the European Council on Foreign Relations, estimates that Russian-based organized crime is now responsible for one-third of Europe's heroin supply, a large portion of the trafficking of non-European people, and most illegal weapons imports.[335] Galeotti reports that Russian-based crime groups in Europe largely operate with (and behind) indigenous European gangs.[336] They are not fighting for territory anymore, but working as "brokers and facilitators" for regional and international criminal activities and supply chains. One supposedly retired Russian criminal told Galeotti in 2016 that "we have the best of both worlds: from Russia we have strength and safety, and in Europe we have wealth and comfort."[337] And, according to a Western counter-intelligence officer, the strength and safety that these groups enjoy in Russia are what give the Kremlin power over them.[338] Galeotti asserts that, under Putin's rule, connections between Russia-based organized crime groups and Russian intelligence services, including the FSB, have grown substantially. Their interconnectedness now goes well beyond the institutionalization of corruption and the growing grey area between legal and illegal activity. In effect, during Putin's rule the state has nationalized organized crime: the underworld now serves the "upperworld."[339]

---

[330] Sebastian Rotella, "A Gangster Place in the Sun: How Spain's Fight Against the Mob revealed Russian Power Networks," *ProPublica,* Nov. 10, 2017.
[331] Mark Hosenball, "A Stain on Mr. Clean," *Newsweek,* Sept. 2, 2001.
[332] *Ibid.*
[333] *Ibid.*; United Kingdom House of Commons, *The Litvinenko Inquiry: Report into the Death of Alexander Litvinenko,* at 112 (Mar. 2015).
[334] Damien Sharkov, "'Putin Involved in Drug Smuggling Ring,' Says Ex-KGB Officer," *Newsweek,* Mar. 13, 2015.
[335] Mark Galeotti, *Crimintern: How the Kremlin Uses Russia's Criminal Networks in Europe,* European Council on Foreign Relations, at 1 (Apr. 2017).
[336] *Ibid.*
[337] *Ibid.* at 1-2.
[338] *Ibid.* at 3.
[339] *Ibid.* at 2.

THE EXPORT OF CORRUPTION

The Kremlin has also exported economic corruption to its periphery and throughout Europe. Anton Shekhovtsov, a scholar who studies the Kremlin's links with far-right and extremist groups, believes that the Kremlin even prefers using corruption over cultivating such groups, saying that "Russia would rather destroy the EU through corruption ... than through the support of anti-EU forces."[340]

In the report "Stage Hands: How Western Enablers Facilitate Kleptocracy," journalist and author Oliver Bullough describes how Western countries are used by corrupt officials to protect their ill-gotten gains:

> In Stage One, the kleptocrat secures his newly acquired assets by getting his money and company ownership off-shore. This successfully insulates him against unexpected political changes at home. In Stage Two, the kleptocrat secures himself and his children by physically moving his family offshore. This insulates those closest to him against the consequences of the misgovernment that made him rich, while providing both them and him with a more amenable environment in which to spend his wealth. In Stage Three, the kleptocrat secures his reputation by building a network among influential people in Western countries. In simple terms, the goal of Stage Three is to make sure that a Google search returns more news stories about good deeds than about allegations of corruption and loutishness.[341]

The scale of how much illicit money has moved out of Russia is staggering. A report by Global Financial Integrity that tracked illicit financial flows from developing countries found that, between 2004 and 2013, over $1 trillion left Russia, averaging over $100 billion a year.[342] Several recent investigations have uncovered how that illicit money flows out of Russia. An exhaustive investigation by the Organized Crime and Corruption Reporting Project (OCCRP) tracked over $20 billion in illicit money that travelled from 19 Russian banks to 5,140 companies with accounts at 732 banks in 96 countries, including nearly every country in the EU.[343] The International Committee of Investigative Journalists' (ICIJ) Panama Papers probes have traced $2 billion in illicit funds linked to Vladimir Putin that were moved abroad using a Cypriot bank and a Swiss law firm.[344] Investigations of Deutsche Bank have found that it assisted Russian clients covertly transfer $10 billion to other jurisdictions.[345] In 2015, Deutsche Bank reported that $1.5

[340] Andrew Rettman, "Illicit Russian Money Poses Threat to EU Democracy," *EUobserver,* Apr. 21, 2017.
[341] Oliver Bullough, *Stage Hands: How Western Enablers Facilitate Kleptocracy,* Hudson Institute, at 2 (May 2016).
[342] Dev Kar and Joseph Spanjers, "Illicit Financial Flows from Developing Countries: 2004-2013," Global Financial Integrity, at 8 (Dec. 2015).
[343] Organized Crime and Corruption Reporting Project, *The Russian Laundromat Exposed,* Mar. 20, 2017.
[344] Jake Bernstein, et al., International Committee of Investigative Journalists, "All Putin's Men: Secret Records Reveal Money Network Tied to Russian Leader," Apr. 3, 2016.
[345] Ed Caesar, "Deutsche Bank's $10-Billion Scandal," *The New Yorker,* Aug. 29, 2016.

billion entered the UK each month without being recorded in official statistics, and that half of that money comes from Russia.[346] Hermitage Capital's investigation of the Klyuev organized crime group found that it used EU banks to launder portions of the $230 million the group stole through fraudulent tax refunds.[347] Of that amount, some $39 million ended up in Germany, $33 million in France, and $30 million in Britain, where it was reportedly spent on yachts, private jets, designer dresses, and boarding school fees.[348] All of this illicit money is reportedly a boon for real estate agents, lawyers, and luxury service providers in the West.[349]

Recent years have seen some progress in cracking down on Russian organized crime in Europe, especially Spain, and uncovering illicit money flowing out of Russia. But the size of the problem still far outweighs the response, particularly in prime destinations for illicit funds like Britain and the United States, where corrupt Russian government officials and criminals can easily hide and protect the assets they have stolen from the Russian people. In the United States, current law allows the true owners of shell corporations to remain anonymous and hidden from public sight. In addition, opaque bank accounts held by law firms are used to launder illicit funds into the country to purchase real estate and other assets, making the United States an attractive conduit and destination for the ill-gotten gains of corrupt Russian officials and other bad actors around the world.[350]

THE LEVERAGING OF ENERGY SUPPLIES FOR INFLUENCE

Russia's use of energy to influence politics in Europe is part of the Kremlin's "energy superpower" strategy, coined by Igor Shuvalov when he was Putin's chief economic aide. As Putin's sherpa to the 2005 G8 summit, Shuvalov developed a new energy policy approach for Russia and proposed that the Kremlin make the European countries an offer at the upcoming G8 summit:

> Moscow would take care of ensuring a flow of fuel sufficient to supply every house in Europe, and in return Europe would show friendship, understanding, and loyalty, as Silvio Berlusconi had. The concept appealed very much to Putin. It allowed him to demonstrate a new, more pragmatic approach to relations with Europe. He did not want to talk to European leaders about human rights, freedom of speech, or Chechnya. He was tired of hearing only criticism. The only way to silence the liberals was to steer the conversation toward business matters. Putin appointed Shuvalov as his chief economic negotiator, whereupon the latter began to represent Russia in the G8, in the WTO,

---

[346] Peter Hobson, "How Europe Became a Russian Gangster Playground," *The Moscow Times*, May 12, 2016.

[347] Neil Buckley & Richard Milne, "French Probe Danske Bank Link to Alleged Russian Fraud," *Financial Times*, Oct. 12, 2017; Russian Untouchables, "Attack On Hermitage, $230 Million Tax Theft," June 23, 2012.

[348] Neil Buckley, "Magnitsky Fraud Cash Laundered Through Britain, MPs Hear," *Financial Times*, May 3, 2016; Neil Buckley & Richard Milne, "French Probe Danske Bank Link to Alleged Russian Fraud," *Financial Times*, Oct. 12, 2017.

[349] Peter Hobson, "How Europe Became a Russian Gangster Playground," *The Moscow Times*, May 12, 2016.

[350] Rachel Louise Ensign & Serena Ng, "Law Firms' Accounts Pose Money-Laundering Risk," *The Wall Street Journal*, Dec. 26, 2016.

at Davos, and in talks with the European Union. His strategic aim was essentially to convert Russian oil and gas into political influence and make Putin the energy emperor of Europe.[351]

The past decade-plus has seen Putin and the Kremlin pursue this "energy superpower" strategy with extreme vigor, not only using energy supplies as leverage, but also accumulating large stakes in energy infrastructure throughout Europe. Control of supplies and infrastructure has also allowed the Kremlin to extend influence over local businessmen and politicians, and exercise undue political influence over the countries of Europe, especially those on its periphery.

Central and Eastern European countries are dependent on Russia for approximately 75 percent of their gas imports and, by some estimates, pay 10 to 30 percent more for their gas imports than countries in Western Europe.[352] According to Heather Conley, a senior vice president at the Center for Strategic and International Studies (CSIS), a U.S. think tank, this "provides additional graft to deepen a country's energy dependency on Russia and make it vulnerable to political manipulation."[353] Serbia provides a telling example of how such a situation might play out. The country is reliant on Russia for its natural gas imports, and its state-owned gas company, Srbijagas, has in recent years accumulated debts of over $1 billion, leading Russia to pressure Serbia in 2014 by reducing gas deliveries by 30 percent. Dusan Bajatovic, the director of Srbijagas, is also the deputy chairman of the pro-Russian Socialist Party of Serbia, and serves in parliament, where he is on the Committee on Finance, State Budget, and Control of Public Spending. Russia is reported to have relied on Bajatovic as "a guarantor of the matters agreed [to] in [the] South Stream project"—a now-defunct pipeline project on which Serbia has already lost some $30 million. Despite Serbia's debts and dependency on the Kremlin's gas supplies, Bajatovic insists that his country still "benefits from contracts with Russia."[354]

The Kremlin also has a long track record of using energy resources and investments to funnel state resources into the pockets of Putin's friends and allies ("privatizing profit and nationalizing losses"), while at the same time maintaining or increasing its leverage and influence over the countries of Europe, which are largely dependent on Russia for natural gas supplies. While 90 percent of Europe's oil imports arrive by sea, most of its natural gas imports come via pipeline, limiting the flexibility of European countries to change suppliers or supply routes.[355] Furthermore, European countries' ambitious carbon dioxide reduction targets mean that they are likely to become increasingly reliant on natural gas. While nat-

[351] Zygar, *All the Kremlin's Men,* at 118-19 (emphasis added).
[352] Statement of Heather Conley, Senior Vice President for Europe, Eurasia and the Arctic, Center for Strategic and International Studies, *The Modus Operandi and Toolbox of Russia and Other Autocracies for Undermining Democracies Throughout the World,* Hearing before the U.S. Senate Committee on the Judiciary, Subcommittee on Crime and Terrorism, at 3, Mar. 15, 2017.
[353] *Ibid.*
[354] Heather Conley et al., *The Kremlin Playbook: Understanding Russian Influence in Central and Eastern Europe,* Center for Strategic and International Studies, at 7 (Oct. 2016).
[355] Michael Ratner et al., *Europe's Energy Security: Options and Challenges to Natural Gas Supply Diversification,* Congressional Research Service, at 5 (Nov. 2015).

ural gas accounted for about 23 percent of the EU's energy consumption in 2015, that figure is expected to grow to 30 percent by 2030, and 70 percent of the natural gas consumed in the EU is imported.[356] In 2014, the EU imported 40 percent of its natural gas and 30 percent of its oil from Russia (Norway accounted for 35 percent of the EU's natural gas imports and 12 percent of oil imports).[357] Several of the EU's member states rely on Russia for all of their natural gas imports: Bulgaria, Estonia, Finland, Latvia, Slovakia, and Slovenia (and Latvia uses natural gas for approximately 40 percent of its primary energy needs). Germany and Italy get nearly 40 percent of their gas imports from Russia, and Germany's decision to phase out nuclear power plants by 2020, as well as some EU members' potential prohibitions on shale gas development, could result in a greater need for natural gas imports in the EU.[358]

In addition to their roles as energy suppliers, Russian energy companies have large ownership stakes in European energy infrastructure such as pipelines, distribution, and storage facilities. A 2014 study commissioned by members of the European parliament found that Gazprom, Russia's state-owned natural gas company, controls large amounts of shares—sometimes even majority stakes—in energy trading, distribution, pipeline, and storage facilities in several Central and Eastern European countries. Gazprom also owns large stakes in storage facilities in Western Europe, including in Germany, Austria, and the UK.[359]

The placement of and control over energy pipelines provides the Russian government with a key source of leverage. Pipeline routes are chosen to exert maximum influence over the countries they are going through, as well as the countries that they circumvent. According to a *Berlin Policy Journal* article by Ilya Zaslavskiy, "these projects serve a purpose beyond mere economic gain: they are primarily driven by the Kremlin for political expediency, with Russian leadership sacrificing efficiency and commercial viability for the sake of international political partnerships and the economic security of President Vladimir Putin's inner circle. This approach gives the Russian regime a political and economic tool which is powerful and unavailable to its Western counterparts."[360]

For example, the proposed Turkish Stream pipeline is not economically expedient, as the Blue Stream and Trans-Balkan pipelines already give Russia excess export capacity to Turkey. However, in addition to providing lavish contracts to Putin's inner circle and further cementing ties with Turkey's President Recep Erdogan, the new pipeline will give the Kremlin more leverage over Ukraine by further reducing its role in transiting Gazprom's gas to Europe and Turkey.[361] Gazprom also uses long-term contracts (LTCs) that prohibit buyers from selling its gas to third parties, allowing it to implement "take-or-pay" clauses that require the buyer to purchase a set amount or pay a penalty, instead of more flexible contracts

---

[356] *Ibid.*
[357] *Ibid.*
[358] *Ibid.*
[359] Deutsches Institut fur Wirtschaftsforschung, *European Natural Gas Infrastructure: The Role of Gazprom in European Natural Gas Supplies*, at VI (Spring 2014).
[360] Ilya Zaslavskiy, "Putin's Art of the Deal," *Berlin Policy Journal*, May 18, 2017.
[361] *Ibid.*

that would be based on fluctuating pricing and demand.[362] According-
ing to an Atlantic Council report, "many countries that were heavily depending on Gazprom's gas were thus given a de facto choice:
compromise with Russia on sensitive political and economic issues
and receive favorable LTCs, or defy the Kremlin and pay high gas
prices for years to come."[363] Such practices led the European Commission to open an antitrust investigation of Gazprom in 2012,
looking at its activities in eight EU countries.[364] In 2015, the European Commission formally charged Gazprom for illegally parti-
tioning EU gas markets, denying access to gas pipelines by third
parties, and unlawful pricing, all of which could strengthen the
Kremlin's political and economic stranglehold over Central and
Eastern European countries.[365]

The Nord Stream pipelines provide another example of Russia
forgoing economic logic in the name of political expediency. Nord
Stream 1 (NS1), which went into service in 2011, is a 760-mile sub-
sea natural gas pipeline that connects Germany to Russia via the
Baltic Sea.[366] According to some analysts, NS1 has been an economic disaster for Russia: transit costs are equal to or greater than
the cost of transporting gas across Ukraine, and capacity increases
have been minimal as gas transited through NS1 is just diverted
from pipelines that cross Ukraine (before NS1 opened, as much as
80 percent of Europe's gas imports from Russia were transported
through Ukraine).[367] As a result, Ukraine's transit revenue has declined from approximately $4 billion in 2013, to some $3 billion in
2014, and an expected $2 billion in 2015.[368] Gazprom has treated
the pipeline as "a stranded investment which never makes the
promised return on capital," in the words of one analyst. But NS1
has given the Kremlin increased leverage over Ukraine and entan-
gled Germany as a principal hub for Russian gas in Europe. NS1
has also advanced the Russian government's goal to "divide and
conquer" the EU with its energy supplies.[369]

Even though NS1 only runs at about 50 percent capacity, the
Kremlin has assiduously pursued the construction of Nord Stream
2 (NS2), which it aims to put into service by 2019 and would dou-
ble the capacity of NS1 by laying two new pipelines parallel to the
original pair.[370] The $11 billion project would also give Gazprom a
stronger "strategic foothold" in Germany, which would become the
main hub for transit and storage of Russian gas exports to Eu-

[362] Ilya Zaslavskiy, *The Kremlin's Gas Games in Europe: Implications for Policy Makers*, Atlantic Council, at 2 (May 2017).
[363] *Ibid.*
[364] European Commission, "Commission Opens Proceedings against Gazprom," (Antitrust Case
No. 39816), Sept. 4, 2012.
[365] European Commission, "Commission Sends Statement of Objections to Gazprom for Alleged Abuse of Dominance on Central and Eastern European Gas Supply Markets," (Antitrust
Case No. 39816), Apr. 22, 2015; Nicholas Hirst, "Commission Charges Gazprom," *Politico Europe*, Apr. 22, 2015. In March 2017, the Commission provisionally accepted concessions by
Gazprom, which the Commission said will address competition its concerns and better integrate
European markets. European Commission, "Commission Invites Comments on Gazprom Commitments Concerning Central and Eastern European Gas Markets," Mar. 13, 2017.
[366] Nord Stream, "The Pipeline," https://www.nord-stream.com/the-project/pipeline (visited
Dec. 19, 2017).
[367] Ilya Zaslavskiy, "Putin's Art of the Deal," *Berlin Policy Journal*, May 18, 2017; Jon Henley,
"Is Europe's Gas Supply Threatened by the Ukraine Crisis?" *The Guardian*, March 3, 2014.
[368] Vladimir Socor, "Nordstream Two in Ukrainian Perspective," Jamestown Foundation Eurasia Daily Monitor, Sep. 21, 2015.
[369] Ilya Zaslavskiy, "Putin's Art of the Deal," *Berlin Policy Journal*, May 18, 2017.
[370] Zaslavskiy, *The Kremlin's Gas Games in Europe*, at 6-7.

rope.[371] The geopolitical rationale for the Kremlin is clear: if both the Turkish Stream and NS2 pipelines are built, the Russian government would have the transport capacity to fully divert all Russian gas supplies that currently transit Ukraine, thereby depriving the government of Ukraine of billions of dollars in transit fees that are essential to its budget.[372] An analysis published by the Atlantic Council in May 2017 concluded that NS2 "is a politically motivated project that presents a major challenge to European law and EU principles, and jeopardizes the security interests of the United States and its EU allies."[373] The U.S. State Department's former special envoy for international energy affairs said in 2016 that NS2 would put an "economic boot" on the necks of governments in the Balkans and Eastern Europe.[374]

Under the project's current structure, Gazprom will be the sole shareholder of the NS2 project company, though five European energy firms—Engie (France), OMV (Austria), Shell (Britain and the Netherlands), and Uniper and Wintershall (Germany)—have committed to providing long-term financing for 50 percent of the project's total costs.[375] As of November 2017, the European Commission was proposing to extend to offshore pipelines rules that govern internal energy markets, which would lead to more stringent regulation of the project.[376] Proposals to enhance the EU's regulatory oversight of NS2 led Russian Prime Minister Medvedev to complain that the EU was attempting to complicate the project's implementation or force Russia to abandon it.[377]

Given the threat this project poses to governments in Ukraine and the Balkans, as well as the Kremlin's history of leveraging energy supplies for political purposes, several U.S. government officials have come out in clear opposition to NS2. In February 2017, the Director of the State Department's Bureau of Energy Resources office for Europe, the Western Hemisphere, and Africa told a conference in Croatia that NS2 was "a national security threat."[378] The State Department's Assistant Secretary for European and Eurasian Affairs, A. Wess Mitchell, has stated that Moscow's construction of NS2 and the Turkish Stream pipeline, if completed, would "bypass Ukraine as a transit country, heighten the vulnerability of Poland and the Balkans, and deepen European dependence on the Russian gas monopoly."[379] And Deputy Assistant Secretary of State John McCarrick, from the Department's Bureau of Energy Resources, has noted that construction of NS2 "would concentrate 75 to 80 percent of Russian gas imports to the EU through a single route, thereby creating a potential choke point that would signifi-

[371] *Ibid.* at 2.
[372] *Ibid.* at 6-7.
[373] *Ibid.* at 1.
[374] Anca Gurzu & Joseph Schatz, "Great Northern Gas War: Gazprom Project Worries the US and Divides Europe," *Politico,* Feb. 17, 2016.
[375] "New EU Amendment on Gas Pipelines Regulations Could Affect Nord Stream 2," *Radio Free Europe/Radio Liberty,* Nov. 8, 2017.
[376] "EU Plans Rule Change to Snag Russian Pipeline," *Reuters,* Nov. 4, 2017.
[377] "Medvedev Says EU Trying to Force Russia to Abort Nord Stream 2 Pipeline Project," *Radio Free Europe/Radio Liberty,* Nov. 14, 2017.
[378] Dariusz Kalan, "Nord Stream 2 'a Security Threat'—US Official," *Interfax Global Energy,* Feb. 17, 2017.
[379] Statement of A. Wess Mitchell, Assistant Secretary of State, Bureau of European and Eurasian Affairs, *European Energy Security: U.S. Interests and Coercive Russian Diplomacy,* Hearing before the U.S. Senate Committee on Foreign Relations, Subcommittee on Europe and Regional Security Cooperation, Dec. 12, 2017, at 2.

cantly increase Europe's vulnerability to supply disruption, whether intentional or accidental." [380]

Energy supply disruption is a tactic that the Kremlin has repeatedly used to pursue its political objectives in Europe. A report by the Swedish Defense Research Agency showed that between 1992 and 2006, Russia imposed 55 energy cutoffs. [381] Though Russian officials claimed the cutoffs were for technical reasons, analysts note that they "almost always coincided with political interests, such as influencing elections or energy deals in Central and Eastern Europe." [382] In addition, the Russian government has been suspected of sponsoring cyberattacks on energy infrastructure throughout Europe, especially in Ukraine and the Baltic states. [383] Cybersecurity experts have linked Russian-backed hackers to multiple attacks in Ukraine, including one that crippled much of the country's power grid in December 2016. [384] Some experts have said that Russia has used Ukraine as a training ground for cyberattacks on energy infrastructure. [385] Such attacks on the United States are also possible, as a hacking group known as Dragonfly, which is reportedly linked to the Russian government, has reportedly hacked into dozens of companies that supply power to the U.S. electricity grid. [386] These efforts are in line with a Russian military doctrine known as Strategic Operations to Destroy Critical Infrastructure Targets (SODCIT). General Martin Dempsey, former Chairman of the Joint Chiefs of Staff, has said that the doctrine "calls for escalating to deescalate. That's a very dangerous doctrine. And they are developing capabilities that could allow them to do that." [387] Given the tremendous potential damage of such attacks on energy grids in both Europe and the United States, stronger cyber defense efforts in the United States and more robust cooperation between U.S. and European governments is of the utmost necessity.

---

[380] Statement of John McCarrick, Deputy Assistant Secretary of State, Bureau of Energy Resources, *European Energy Security: U.S. Interests and Coercive Russian Diplomacy,* Hearing before the U.S. Senate Committee on Foreign Relations, Subcommittee on Europe and Regional Security Cooperation, Dec. 12, 2017, at 4.

[381] Robert L. Larsson, *Nord Stream, Sweden and Baltic Sea Security,* Swedish Defense Research Agency, at 80, (Mar. 2007). At least 20 occurred during Putin's tenure. *Ibid.*

[382] Peter Pomerantsev & Micahel Weiss, *The Menace of Unreality: How the Kremlin Weaponizes Information, Culture and Money,* Institute of Modern Russia, at 22 (Nov. 2014).

[383] "Dragonfly: Western Energy Sector Targeted By Sophisticated Attack Group," *Symantec,* Oct. 20, 2017; Suspected Russia-Backed Hackers Target Baltic Energy Networks, *Reuters,* May 11, 2017.

[384] Andy Greenberg, "How an Entire Nation Became Russia's Test Lab for Cyberwar," *Wired,* June 20, 2017.

[385] *Ibid.*

[386] "Dragonfly: Western Energy Sector Targeted By Sophisticated Attack Group," Symantec, Oct. 20, 2017; Kevin Collier, "Electricity Providers Targeted In Massive Hack," *BuzzFeed News,* Sept. 6, 2017.

[387] Martin Dempsey, Interview with Peter Feaver, Duke University, Apr. 11, 2016.

Chapter 5: Kremlin Interference in Semi-Consolidated Democracies and Transitional Governments[388]

The former states of the Soviet Union, as well as the former Communist countries of Central and Eastern Europe, remain perhaps the most vulnerable to Russian aggression. Geographically, the countries in Russia's "backyard" have populations that are most receptive to Kremlin propaganda, and, in some cases, have their own Russian-speaking populations. They are also the most vulnerable to interference due to weak governing institutions, justice systems that allow for higher levels of corruption, and underdeveloped or beleaguered independent media and civil society.

The Russian tactics of interference follow two main trends in this region. First, Russia aggressively targets countries that have taken tangible steps to integrate with western institutions like the EU or NATO in order to impede integration processes. Georgia, Ukraine, and Montenegro are the most recent cases in a long history of Russian aggression along the periphery that stretches back generations—and as they have drawn closer to NATO and the EU, they have been the focus of arguably the most brazen Kremlin efforts to keep them from sliding across the finish line. Montenegro's accession to NATO in 2017 is an anomaly within this group, where, despite an onslaught of Russian pressure to deter it, the country was able to become a full member of the alliance.

Second, Russian interference in places like Serbia is less visibly aggressive and focuses more on cultivating sympathetic elements of society to deter government efforts to integrate with the West. In addition to disinformation and the co-opting of political forces, Russia employs energy resources as a weapon to gain leverage in these countries. The Kremlin also targets NATO and EU members where corruption or vulnerabilities in the rule of law provide openings to erode their bonds to European values and institutions. This includes undermining their support for EU sanctions on Russia or NATO exercises on the continent. These tactics are most acute in

---

[388] The countries in this chapter are defined as "semi-consolidated democracies" or "transitional or hybrid regimes" by the Freedom House Nations in Transit study, which ranks and measures the progress toward or backsliding from democracy of 29 countries from Central Europe to Central Asia. The ranking is determined by an assessment of a country's national democratic governance, electoral process, civil society, independent media, local democratic governance, judicial framework and independence, and corruption. Countries classified as semi-consolidated democracies are defined as "electoral democracies that meet relatively high standards for the selection of national leaders but exhibit weaknesses in their defense of political rights and civil liberties," while transitional or hybrid regimes are "typically electoral democracies where democratic institutions are fragile, and substantial challenges to the protection of political rights and civil liberties exist." Freedom House, *Nations in Transit 2017: The False Promise of Populism, at 22 (2017).*

Bulgaria and Hungary. Hungary represents a case where the government has enabled space for Kremlin interference to shore up its own political strength, which is largely based on anti-migrant and anti-European integration policies.

Finally, the country examples in the following two chapters are not an exhaustive compilation of Russian government interference throughout Europe, but an illustrative list of examples from recent years. The examples provide important lessons about tried and true Kremlin interference tools, as well as best practices to neutralize them. President Putin and the Russian government are not master strategists, nor are they always successful in their assaults on democracies. But a few notable qualities make the Russian Federation a considerable opponent: scale, persistence, and adaptability. The United States and our allies, then, must also develop a more nimble, adaptable toolkit to deter and defend against continued meddling by the Kremlin.

UKRAINE

Perhaps more than any other country, Ukraine has borne the brunt of Russian hybrid aggression in all of its forms—a lethal blend of conventional military assaults, assassinations, disinformation campaigns, cyberattacks, and the weaponization of energy and corruption. Russian government action on all of these fronts spiked after the Euromaidan protests of 2014 brought President Petro Poroshenko to power, and they have continued at an intense tempo in the years since. Ukraine has also been the target and testing ground for Russian cyberattacks that have crossed into direct strikes on physical infrastructure, such as its electricity grid.[389] As with Georgia, the goal of Russia's interference appears to be to weaken Ukraine to the point that it becomes a failed state, rendering it incapable of joining Western institutions in the future and presenting the Russian people with another example of the "consequences" of democratization.

The Russian military assault on Ukraine has been well documented since the illegal occupation of Crimea and support for separatists in Donbas began in 2014.[390] This chapter will focus on those other elements of the Russian government's asymmetric arsenal at play in Ukraine, namely its use of cyberattacks, disinformation, and corruption.

Putin's interference in Ukraine's internal affairs was on full display in the 2004 presidential election between pro-Russian candidate Viktor Yanukovych and a pro-Western candidate, Viktor Yuschenko. Yanukovych's campaign was supported by a large cadre of Russian political strategists, and just three days before the election, Putin attended a parade in Kiev where he stood alongside Yanukovych.[391] Putin's interference created an unprecedented situation where "Yuschenko's main rival in the elections was not Yanukovych, in fact, but Putin, who carried on as if it were his own personal campaign."[392] And Russia's secret services allegedly performed darker acts to assist Yanukovych. Most disturbingly, FSB agents were reportedly involved in the poisoning of Yuschenko in September 2004 with TCDD, the most toxic form of dioxin, which nearly killed him and left his face permanently disfigured.[393] And according to Ukraine expert Taras Kuzio, alleged FSB-hired operatives also planted a car bomb—large enough to destroy every building within a 500-meter radius—near Yuschenko's campaign offices.[394] But in spite of Putin's best efforts, the Ukrainian people came to the streets to protect the ballot box, culminating in the Orange Revolution and the elevation of Yuschenko to the presidency.

Yanukovych would later assume power in February 2010, and in 2014, as Ukraine sought to finalize an Association Agreement with the European Union, a key step in the EU accession process,

---

[389] Kim Zetter, "Inside the Cunning Unprecedented Hack of Ukraine's Power Grid," *Wired*, Mar. 3, 2016.

[390] The congressionally supported provision of lethal assistance to the Ukrainian military is long overdue and will hopefully increase the battlefield cost for Russian forces active in the country.

[391] Zygar, *All the Kremlin's Men*, at 89-90.

[392] *Ibid.* at 91.

[393] Taras Kuzio, *Russian Policy Toward Ukraine During Elections*, 13 Demokratizatsiya: The Journal of Post-Soviet Democratization 491, at 497-499, 512-513 (Sept. 2005).

[394] *Ibid.* at 498.

Yanukovych backtracked on the deal in response to pressure from Moscow.[395] The Ukrainian people rose up in a "Revolution of Dignity" in Kiev, which ousted Yanukovych, but also emboldened Russian forces to invade Crimea and eastern Ukraine under the pretext that Russian-speaking compatriots faced threats from Ukrainian nationalists. Using techniques honed during the invasion of Georgia, Russia expertly combined all the elements of hybrid warfare in its assault on Ukraine—conventional and unconventional forces, cyberattacks, and propaganda.

Today, Russia continues to illegally occupy Crimea and maintains an active military presence in eastern Ukraine in support of separatists there. In that context, Ukraine seems to have emerged as Russia's favorite laboratory for all forms of hybrid war.

Cyberattacks have been a primary tool of Russia's hybrid warfare operations in Ukraine. Virtually every sector of its society and economy—media, finance, transportation, military, politics, and energy—has been the repeated target of pro-Kremlin hackers over the past three years.[396] According to Kenneth Geers, an ambassador to the NATO Cooperative Cyber Defense Center of Excellence: "The gloves are off. This is a place where you can do your worst without retaliation or prosecution ... Ukraine is not France or Germany. A lot of Americans can't find it on a map, so you can practice there."[397]

And the Kremlin has not wasted any opportunity to test and refine its cyber warfare skills. CyberBerkut, a pro-Russian group with ties to the hackers that breached the Clinton campaign and DNC in 2016, attacked Ukraine's Central Election Commission website in 2014 to falsely show that ultra-right presidential candidate Dmytro Yarosh was the winner.[398] The extent of attacks on Ukrainian institutions quickly widened to include the ministries of infrastructure, defense, and finance as well as the country's pension fund, treasury, and seaport authority.[399]

Russian cyberattacks in Ukraine have graduated from simply exfiltrating data and taking down websites to attacks on physical infrastructure. On at least two occasions, in December 2015 and December 2016, hackers have attacked Ukraine's electricity distribution system, putting thousands of citizens in the dark for extended periods of time.[400] Cyber experts say that the sophistication of the attacks show a marked evolution. According to Marina Krotofil, an industrial control systems security researcher for Honeywell: "In 2015 they were like a group of brutal street fighters. In 2016, they were ninjas."[401]

The United States has sought to provide support to Ukrainian cyber defense efforts, but challenges remain. In the aftermath of the attacks on Ukraine's energy grid, U.S. officials from the De-

---

[395] Will Englund & Kathy Lally, "Ukraine, Under Pressure from Russia, Puts Brakes on E.U. Deal," *The Washington Post*, Nov. 21, 2013; James Marson, et al. "Ukraine President Viktor Yanukovych Driven From Power," *The Wall Street Journal*, Feb. 23, 2014.
[396] Andy Greenberg, "How an Entire Nation Became Russia's Test Lab for Cyberwar," *Wired*, June 20, 2017.
[397] *Ibid.*
[398] *Ibid.*
[399] *Ibid.*
[400] *Ibid.* Kim Zetter, "Inside the Cunning Unprecedented Hack of Ukraine's Power Grid," *Wired*, Mar. 3, 2016.
[401] Andy Greenberg, "How an Entire Nation Became Russia's Test Lab for Cyberwar," *Wired*, June 20, 2017.

69

partment of Energy, Department of Homeland Security, FBI, and the North American Electric Reliability Corporation deployed to assist Ukrainian authorities in assessing the attack.[402] In 2017, USAID started a project in Ukraine to help the country build its cyber defenses, but given the scale and consistency of the Kremlin-directed barrage of cyberattacks, these assistance efforts pale in comparison to the threat.[403]

As the Kremlin has made Ukraine the front line in its battle against Western institutions, Ukrainian civil society organizations have developed cutting-edge innovations to counter Russian disinformation. In March 2014, the Kyiv Mohyla School of Journalism helped establish StopFake.org—a fact-checking website that works to refute Russian disinformation and promote media literacy, which has expanded to produce a weekly TV show and podcasts. StopFake's show has debunked Russian propaganda that said the Islamic State terrorist group had opened a training camp in Ukraine and that Ukrainian nationalists had crucified Russian-speaking children.[404] StopFake has become one of the most internationally recognized organizations for successfully countering Russian disinformation.[405] Another program conducted by a U.S.-based organization helped train more than 15,000 Ukrainians on how to critically read and share information.[406] Over the course of the program, the number of trainees who cross-checked the news they consumed rose by 22 percent.[407]

The Ukrainian government has also sought to push back against disinformation, though with uneven results. In May 2017, President Poroshenko ordered Ukrainian service providers to block access to Russian websites including the social networking site VK (formerly VKontakte), Odnoklassniki, search engine Yandex, and the email service Mail.ru, prompting freedom of speech concerns from groups like Human Rights Watch.[408]

Ukraine's most significant vulnerability to the Kremlin's influence operations is corruption (Ukraine ranks 131 out of 167 countries on Transparency International's 2016 Corruption Perceptions Index).[409] Since Ukraine's independence, the Russian government has used corruption as a tool to weaken the development of the country's fragile democratic institutions. While many political figures in Ukraine have been mired in corruption scandals, the scale that apparently took place during the Yanukovych regime was striking—in order to maintain power, Ukrainian watchdogs asserted that he paid $2 billion in bribes, which amounted to $1.4 million for every day that he was in office. Election commissioners

---

[402] Ibid.
[403] U.S. Department of State, Congressional Notification of Programs to Counter Russian Influence, Jan.19, 2017.
[404] Andrew E. Kramer, "To Battle Fake News, Ukrainian Show Features Nothing But Lies," *The New York Times*, Feb, 26, 2017.
[405] *See, e.g.,* "2017 Democracy Dinner Explores the Global Threat of Disinformation," National Democratic Institute for International Affairs, Nov. 2, 2017.
[406] Tara Susman-Pena & Katya Vogt, "Ukrainians' Self-defense against Disinformation: What We Learned from Learn to Discern," *IREX*, June 12, 2017.
[407] Ibid.
[408] "Ukraine's Poroshenko to Block Russian Social Networks," *BBC News*, May 16, 2017; Human Rights Watch, "Ukraine: Revoke Ban on Dozens of Russian Web Companies," May 16, 2017.
[409] Transparency International, *Corruption Perceptions Index 2016*, Jan. 25, 2017.

who guaranteed his party's good fortunes at the polls were especially well compensated.[410]

Corruption is now seen in many circles as a threat to Ukraine's national security, and the country's civil society and the current government have developed several important anti-corruption measures, building the resilience of their institutions to defend against malign Russian government influence. Ukrainian civil society has established the Anti-Corruption Action Center (AntAC), which has courageously uncovered cases of high-level corruption despite mounting pressure by the authorities.[411] And under substantial pressure from donors, the Ukrainian government has also taken important reform steps: it removed a controversial Prosecutor General who was accused of protecting corrupt actors in the country; it introduced transparency measures like an e-declaration system for public officials to report their assets, and it established investigatory bodies like the National Anti-Corruption Bureau (NABU). But few high-level prosecutions have taken place, calling into question the government's political will to pursue genuine reform.[412] Moreover, institutions like NABU have come under increased pressure. In December 2017, the General Prosecutor's office was accused of unmasking a NABU investigation and some NABU officials were arrested. In response, the U.S. State Department said, "These actions ... undermine public trust and risk eroding international support for Ukraine."[413] Until Ukrainian institutions, especially the judiciary, prove capable of prosecuting senior level officials from the former and current regime, the country will remain severely exposed and vulnerable to the Kremlin's interference in their country's affairs.

The military conflict in Ukraine grinds on and the Russian government's asymmetric arsenal seeks to damage Ukraine in other ways. But despite the overwhelming pressure from its more powerful neighbor, Ukraine has proven remarkably resilient with help from friends in the international community. Ukraine is ground zero for Russian government aggression and deserves continued support. This support, however, is a two-way street. Oksana Syroyid, a deputy speaker of Ukraine's Parliament Ukraine said in 2017 that Ukraine had become a testing ground "for a lot of Russia's evil strategies," and that "unfortunately, we have to put up with this. Ukraine's experience can be used by Europe and America to understand the real Russian threat."[414] The deputy speaker is right—despite the significant challenges remaining in Ukraine, the country has many valuable lessons learned since 2014.

While Ukraine is the main laboratory for Russian aggression abroad, it is also generating some of the most effective responses, through collaborations between the Ukrainian government and civil society, along with partners in the international community. The United States should proactively work with Ukraine to docu-

---

[410] Maxim Tucker, "Ukraine's Fallen Leader Victor Yanukovych 'Paid Bribes of $2 billion' or $1.4 Million for Every Day He was President," *The Guardian*, May 31, 2016.

[411] Josh Cohen, "Something is Very Wrong in Kyiv," The Atlantic Council Blog, May 18, 2017.

[412] Hrant Kostanyan, "Ukraine's Unimplemented Anti-Corruption Reform," Center for European Policy Studies, Feb.10, 2017.

[413] Matthias Williams & Natalia Zinets, "Ukraine Tries to Fend Off Critics as West Cranks Up Pressure on Corruption," *Reuters*, Dec. 6, 2017.

[414] Andrew E. Kramer, "To Battle Fake News, Ukrainian Show Features Nothing But Lies," *The New York Times*, Feb. 26, 2017.

ment and disseminate these lessons to other democracies facing the asymmetric arsenal.

Lessons Learned

- *Cybersecurity Cooperation Can Reap Benefits for the United States:* The Russian cyber assault on Ukraine has been relentless and multi-faceted since 2014. Ukraine is where the Russian government experiments and sees what can work. The United States and others in the international community have taken steps to help Ukraine build its defenses, but this cooperation can also offer insight into how the Russian government conducts these operations and thus provide a forecast for the types of attacks we will see in the future. Cooperation with Ukraine to counter these threats is a critically important element of building the United States' defenses.

- *Countering Disinformation Begins with Awareness:* Civil society organizations like StopFake have led the way in developing innovative techniques to dispel lies in the media, which has in turn helped to build resilience and skepticism within the Ukrainian population. This critical thinking ability is the first step towards blunting the effect of lies from Moscow. NGOs in vulnerable countries should look to StopFake as a model, not only for the effectiveness of its techniques, but the courage of its staff.

- *Civil Society Matters:* Since the 2014 Euromaidan demonstrations, civil society organizations in Ukraine have played a key watchdog role in holding the government accountable and calling for reform. This pressure from the Ukrainian people, channeled through these groups has led to concrete reforms, particularly in building anti-corruption institutions. International efforts to support civil society in Ukraine are critical; even though they have grown in strength and effectiveness, these groups still face pressure from anti-reform elements in the country.

- *Corruption is Russia's Best Weapon in Ukraine:* The best defense against the Russian government's asymmetric arsenal in Ukraine, and indeed across Europe, is the existence of durable democratic institutions that are less susceptible to corruption. While the Ukrainian government has established credible anti-corruption institutions, resistance to genuine reform remains very strong and Ukraine has yet to embark on significant efforts to prosecute some of the country's most egregious corrupt actors. Until Ukraine shows the political will to confront corruption, the country will remain dangerously vulnerable to Russian aggression.

- *High Level U.S. Engagement is Key:* The Obama Administration, primarily through former Vice President Joe Biden's personal engagement, was instrumental in pressuring the Ukrainian government to reform despite the attendant political difficulties in making such decisions. This approach garnered results, but sustainable progress can only come with consistent engagement and pressure from the United States.

72

- *Sanctions Pressure Has Been Insufficient:* U.S. and EU sanctions have not resulted in the implementation of the Minsk Agreements nor the return of Crimea to Ukrainian control.[415] The Russian government appears to have been able to resist this pressure because the cost imposed by sanctions has been manageable. In order to achieve the desired outcomes of the Minsk Agreements and return Crimea to Ukrainian control, the U.S. government should significantly increase pressure and use the mandates and authorities outlined in the Countering America's Adversaries Through Sanctions Act (CAATSA) to ramp up sanctions on pro-Kremlin entities, in concert with the European Union.[416]

---

[415] The Minsk Agreements were negotiated by Germany, France, Russia, and Ukraine in talks in Minsk, Belarus in February 2015, under auspices of the Organization for Security and Co-operation in Europe (OSCE). They are comprised of a 13-point plan for resolving the conflict in eastern Ukraine, including a ceasefire and the withdrawal of heavy weapons from the front lines, to be monitored by the OSCE. The Agreements were concluded after the collapse of a ceasefire previously negotiated in Minsk ("the Minsk Protocol") in September 2014; the terms have yet to be fulfilled.

[416] Countering America's Adversaries Through Sanctions Act, P.L. 115-44, Enacted Aug. 2, 2017 (originally introduced by Senator Ben Cardin as the Counteracting Russian Hostilities Act of 2017, S. 94, January 11, 2017).

GEORGIA

The 2008 invasion of Georgia is a stark example of how Russia exerts power—by taking territory inside another country. After years of rising tensions, Russian troops supported separatists in the South Ossetia and Abkhazia regions in August 2008, resulting in the Russian government's recognition of their independence. The conflict also represents the first time that cyberattacks were used alongside a military invasion—an innovation that the Russian government was to hone with the invasion of Ukrainian territory six years later. Since 2008, Russian government propaganda and Russian support for political parties and civil society groups remains a significant problem in Georgia as pro-democratic forces in the country seek to deepen integration with the west.

Leading up to August 2008, tensions had been growing in South Ossetia and Abkhazia, regions that had been contested since Georgia's independence in 1991. South Ossetian separatists shelled Georgian villages in early August, which led to the deployment of the Georgian military to the area.[417] The Russian military responded by pushing the Georgian troops out of South Ossetia with a heavy assault of tanks.[418] It soon became clear that the Russian attack was not limited to just conventional military means, but was much more comprehensive in scope.

Despite the seemingly sudden escalation into a hot war, the Georgian government accused the Russian government of preparing the hybrid battlefield a month before the invasion. As early as July 20, the Georgian government experienced distributed denial of service (DDoS) attacks and President Mikhail Saakashvili's website was forced to shut down for 24 hours.[419] As Russian troops entered Georgian territory on August 8, the websites of the Georgian president, the parliament, the ministries of defense and foreign affairs, the national bank, and several news outlets were hit with cyberattacks.[420] The Georgian government accused the Russian government of conducting these attacks, which the Kremlin denied.[421]

Michael Sulmeyer, a senior Pentagon official in charge of cyber policy during the Obama Administration, said that Russia's invasion was "one of the first times you've seen conventional ground operations married with cyber activity. It showed not just an understanding that these techniques could be useful in combined ops but that the Russians were willing to do them. These guys implemented."[422]

---

[417] Jim Nichol, "Russia-Georgia Conflict in August 2008: Context and Implications for U.S. Interests," *Congressional Research Service,* at 5, Mar. 3, 2009.

[418] Anne Barnard et al., "Russians Push Past Separatist Area to Assault Central Georgia," *The New York Times,* Aug. 10, 2008.

[419] Swedish Defense Research Agency, Emerging Cyber Threats and Russian Views on Information Warfare and Information Operations, at 44 (Mar. 2010); John Markoff, "Before the Gunfire, Cyberattacks," *The New York Times,* Aug. 13, 2008.

[420] Swedish Defense Research Agency, Emerging Cyber Threats and Russian Views on Information Warfare and Information Operations, at 44; "Georgia: Russia 'Conducting Cyber War,'" *The Telegraph,* Aug. 11, 2008.

[421] Joseph Menn, "Expert: Cyber-Attacks On Georgia Websites Tied to Mob, Russian Government, *LA Times,* Aug. 13, 2008; "Georgia: Russia 'Conducting Cyber War,'" *The Telegraph,* Aug. 11, 2008.

[422] Evan Osnos et al., "Trump, Putin, and the New Cold War: What Lay Behind Russia's Interference in the 2016 Election—And What Lies Ahead?," *The New Yorker,* Mar. 6, 2017.

The governments of Estonia and Poland quickly mobilized to assist the Georgian government to get back online, with the Estonians sharing experience from the attack on their cyber infrastructure the year before (see Chapter 6).[423]

Saakashvili came to power in the wake of the Rose Revolution in 2003 and he quickly sought to establish stronger ties with Western institutions, drawing Putin's ire. At an April 2008 summit in Bucharest, NATO pledged to review the possibility of offering a Membership Action Plan to Georgia.[424] Putin responded to the statement by saying that expansion of NATO to Russia's borders "would be taken in Russia as a direct threat to the security of our country."[425] While not the only factor in Russia's 2008 invasion, Georgia's active steps to deepen ties with NATO appears to have been a critical element of Russia's decision to invade.

The short war would presage future Russian hybrid warfare in Europe, meant to resist NATO and EU enlargement and the consolidation of democracy on the continent. Today, Russia recognizes the "independence" of South Ossetia and Abkhazia, and, with the support of separatist forces, continues to station troops in the two breakaway regions.[426] Moscow has also entered into treaties of partnership and strategic alliance with the two regions, further solidifying the frozen conflict.

The timing of the war in Georgia coincided with a political transition in the United States from the Bush to Obama Administrations. The outgoing Bush Administration seemed reluctant to impose sanctions on Russia for its aggression in the waning days of its term. The incoming Obama Administration sought a reset with Russia, which also precluded significant coercive measures to respond to the Kremlin's aggression. Despite the lack of a more aggressive response to Russian actions, both administrations did invest significantly in building governing institutions in Georgia and its integration into NATO structures.[427]

Beyond its military assaults on Georgian territory, the Russian government also supports a variety of pro-Kremlin political parties, NGOs, and propaganda efforts in the country. For example, Obiektivi TV, a media outlet, reportedly relied on Russian funding in its support of the ultra-nationalistic Alliance of Patriots political party.[428] Obiektivi's xenophobic, homophobic, and anti-western narrative helped the Alliance of Patriots clear the threshold to enter parliament during the October 2016 election.[429] Russian propaganda in Georgia borders on the bizarre. For example, Russian propaganda asserts that the United States uses the "Richard Lugar Public Health Research Center" to carry out biological tests on the

[423] Swedish Defense Research Agency, Emerging Cyber Threats and Russian Views on Information Warfare and Information Operations, at 44-45 (March 2010).
[424] North Atlantic Treaty Organization, "Bucharest Summit Declaration," Apr. 3, 2008.
[425] Michael Evans, "Vladimir Putin Tells Summit He Wants Security and Friendship," The Times, July 24, 2008.
[426] "Russia Recognizes Abkhazia, South Ossetia," Radio Free Europe/Radio Liberty, Aug. 26, 2008; Damien Sharkov, "Russian Troops Launch 3,000-Strong Drill In 'Occupied' Georgian Region," Newsweek, June 13, 2017.
[427] U.S. Department of State, "U.S. Relations with Georgia Fact Sheet," Nov. 28, 2016.
[428] IREX, Media Sustainability Index 2017: The Development of Sustainable Independent Media in Europe and Eurasia, at 154 (2017).
[429] Ibid.

Georgian population.[430] According to the Georgian government, several pro-Russian groups are active in the country, including the Russian Institute for Strategic Studies and Russkiy Mir Foundation, two well-known institutions that the Kremlin uses to exert its influence abroad (see Chapter 4).[431]

Despite these ongoing pressures, Georgia completed an Association Agreement and a Deep and Comprehensive Free Trade Area with the EU in June 2014, both important steps in the integration process.[432] In addition, the country was granted visa-free travel by the EU in December 2015.[433] And at NATO's 2014 summit in Wales, the Alliance approved a Substantial NATO-Georgia Package (SNGP), which includes "defense capacity building, training, exercises, strengthened liaison, and opportunities to develop interoperability with Allied forces."[434].

Cooperation in this area was given a significant boost at the 2014 NATO Summit in Wales, where Allied leaders endorsed a Substantial NATO-Georgia Package (SNGP), including defense capacity building, training, exercises, strengthened liaison, and opportunities to develop interoperability with Allied forces. These measures aim to strengthen Georgia's ability to defend itself as well as to advance its preparations towards NATO membership.

The United States has also provided substantial assistance to Georgia since the Russian invasion in 2008, though the Trump Administration has requested sharp cuts in funding. Georgia received $47.5 million through the Assistance to Europe, Eurasia, and Central Asia Account in FY16; for FY18, the Administration requested only $28 million.[435]

Lessons Learned

- *Hybrid War is Here to Stay:* The Georgia war was the first instance in which cyberattacks occurred alongside a military strike. These tools would be replicated and refined six years later in Ukraine. The Georgia case has and should continue to be very instructive for other states, like the Baltics, that are vulnerable to similar attacks by the Russian government.

- *The Asymmetric Arsenal is Flexible:* After using military aggression in Georgia, the Russian government maintained pressure and influence by using disinformation, support for NGOs, and interference in political affairs. While difficult to measure, the Russian government is able to exert considerable influence in Georgia using these different avenues.

- *Western Commitment is Key:* The United States and the EU have provided significant assistance and political support to

---

[430] Embassy of Georgia, Information Provided in Response to Questions from U.S. Senator Ben Cardin, Aug. 29, 2017.
[431] *Ibid.*
[432] European Commission, "Trade Policy, Countries and Regions: Georgia," http://ec.europa.eu/trade/policy/countries-and-regions/countries/georgia (visited Dec. 31, 2017); European Commission, "EU-Georgia Association Agreement Fully Enters Into Force," July 1, 2016.
[433] European Commission, "Commission Progress Report: Georgia Meets Criteria for Visa Liberalisation," Dec. 18, 2015.
[434] North Atlantic Treaty Organization, "Relations with Georgia," Aug. 23, 2017.
[435] The Senate Appropriations Committee has approved $63 million for Georgia in this account for FY2018. Department of State, Foreign Operations, and Related Programs Appropriations Bill, 2018, S. 1780, S. Rept. 115-153, at 51. The legislation awaits consideration by the full Senate.

Georgia in the years since the 2008 war in order to bolster democratic institutions and protect against Russian government aggression. This support has been essential in helping to prevent renewed Russian military aggression, but has not been sufficient in helping Georgia to confront the full range of Russian interference techniques.

MONTENEGRO

Russian malign influence in Montenegro has long been present and intensified in 2016 in an effort to derail the country's NATO bid. This renewed focus included propaganda, support for NGOs and political parties, and culminated in an alleged Russian effort to overthrow the government following the 2016 parliamentary election. While Russia was strongly opposed to Montenegro's desire to join NATO, it did not resort to the conventional military tactics used in Ukraine and Georgia, but instead relied on a hybrid mix of disinformation and threat of force to send the same message that integration with the West was unacceptable.

That threat of force came in the form of an alleged coup plot, which was hatched sometime in mid-2016 when former Russian intelligence officers Eduard Shishmakov (who also used the alias Shirakov) and Vladimir Popov went to Serbia and met with anti-western Serbian nationalist Aleksandar Sindjelic, where they reportedly discussed a plan to overthrow the Montenegrin government following parliamentary elections that October.[436] According to Senate testimony by Damon Wilson of the Atlantic Council, Sindjelic was the leader of a Serbian paramilitary group called the "Serbian Wolves," which sent fighters to support separatists in Eastern Ukraine—where Sindjelic reportedly first met Shishmakov and Popov.[437] The plot was simple, and, if successful, would have been devastating. First, Montenegro's pro-Russian Democratic Front (DF) political party would stage a rally in front of the Montenegrin parliament on Election Day. Then a broader group of coup plotters, dressed as policemen but with blue ribbons on their shoulders to differentiate them from actual officers, would open fire on the crowd, storm the parliament, and capture or kill Montenegrin Prime Minister Milo Djukanovic.[438] Following the meeting, Sindjelic reportedly paid €130,000 to Mirko Velimirovic, a Montenegrin, to organize logistics and buy 50 rifles and three boxes of ammunition.[439]

But the plot would not come to pass. Days before the election, Velimirovic turned himself in to police and exposed the conspiracy. Montenegrin security forces swept up the plotters, but reports have suggested that Shishmakov and Popov escaped and were among a group of individuals detained by the Serbian authorities shortly after the October election.[440] But after a visit to Serbia by the head of Russia's Security Council (and former FSB director), Nikolai Patrushev, Shishmakov and Popov were reportedly released and al-

[436] "Kremlin Rejects Claims Russia Had Role in Montenegro Coup Plot," *The Guardian,* Feb. 20, 2017; Ben Farmer, "Reconstruction: The Full Incredible Story Behind Russia's Deadly Plot to Stop Montenegro Embracing the West," *The Telegraph,* Feb. 18, 2017.

[437] Testimony by Damon Wilson, Vice President of the Atlantic Council, *Attempted Coup in Montenegro and Malign Russian Influence in Europe,* Hearing before the U.S. Senate Committee on Armed Services, July 13, 2017, at 1.

[438] Ben Farmer, "Reconstruction: The Full Incredible Story behind Russia's Deadly Plot to Stop Montenegro Embracing the West," *The Telegraph,* Feb. 18, 2017.

[439] *Ibid.*

[440] Julian Borger et al., "Serbia Deports Russians Suspected of Plotting Montenegro Coup," *The Guardian,* Nov. 11, 2016.

lowed to return to Russia.[441] The Russian government denies any role in the attempted coup plot.[442]

The purpose of the coup plot was to create such discord in Montenegro that its NATO bid, or any prospects for integration with Europe, would be disrupted. Russia sought to destabilize Montenegro in the same way that it had Georgia and Ukraine, seeking to render it incapable of integration with Western democracies. This coup attempt, however, was not a one-off event, but the culmination of a sustained propaganda and interference campaign to persuade the Montenegrin people to oppose NATO membership.

Following Montenegro's announcement of its intention to join NATO, the Russian government spoke out forcefully against the bid in the hopes of swaying public opinion. The Russian Ministry of Foreign Affairs declared that "to launch NATO accession talks with Montenegro [is] an openly confrontationist move which is fraught with additional destabilizing consequences for the system of Euro-Atlantic security," and said the move "directly affects the interests of the Russian Federation and forces us to respond accordingly."[443]

That response would come in short order. Soon after Montenegro announced its intention to join NATO, Russia unleashed a propaganda campaign that included support for pro-Russian political parties and the cultivation of anti-NATO civil society groups.[444] The Democratic Front (DF) political party, believed to have received millions of dollars in Russian support, has grown from being a marginal force into Montenegro's main opposition party.[445] Sergei Zheleznyak, a former Deputy Speaker of the Russian Duma, reportedly traveled to Montenegro to work with members of the Democratic Front.[446] On one such visit, he allegedly sought to advance the idea of neutrality for Montenegro, calling it the "Balkans Switzerland" and encouraged DF activists to use it as a messaging tool to push back against NATO membership.[447] The DF was very active throughout the debate on NATO, which sometimes resulted in violence. For example, activists from the DF were behind a demonstration in October 2015 which led to clashes with police.[448]

Propaganda also flowed freely through Sputnik and the pro-Russia web portals inf4.net, and Russia reportedly directed resources to the non-governmental organizations "NO to War, NO to NATO" and the "Montenegrin Movement for Neutrality" to push back publicly against NATO accession.[449]

[441] Ibid.

[442] "Russia Says It Won't Extradite Suspect In Montenegro Alleged Coup Attempt," Radio Free Europe/Radio Liberty, Nov. 1, 2017.

[443] The Ministry of Foreign Affairs of the Russian Federation, "Comment by the Information and Press Department on Invitation for Montenegro to Start Talks on Joining NATO," Dec. 2, 2015.

[444] Statement of Vesko Garcevic, Professor of the Practice of International Relations, The Frederick Pardee School of Global Studies, Boston University, Russian Interference in European Elections, Hearing before the U.S. Senate Select Committee on Intelligence, June 28, 2017, at 5.

[445] Ben Farmer, "Reconstruction: The Full Incredible Story Behind Russia's Deadly Plot to Stop Montenegro Embracing the West," The Telegraph, Feb. 18, 2017.

[446] Garcevic, Russian Interference in European Elections, at 5.

[447] Ibid.

[448] Janusz Bugajski & Margarita Assenova, "Eurasian Disunion: Russia's Vulnerable Flanks," The Jamestown Foundation, June 2016.

[449] Garcevc, Russian Interference in European Elections, at 4.

The Montenegrin government called for elections in October 2016 in order to bolster its case that the public supported Montenegro's membership in NATO. As Mr. Wilson of the Atlantic Council testified, "in the run up to this election it was pretty remarkable to see street signs, billboards all across the country, [all part of an] anti-NATO campaign. So the plan was to defeat the pro-NATO forces in this election through using the Orthodox Church, the Serbian Orthodox Church, the telecommunications company and the media empire, this small country of 600,000 was flooded with resources to tip the balance."

Prime Minister Milo Djukanovic, who was the main backer of NATO, emerged victorious with 41 percent of the vote, which he heralded as an indication of public support for NATO membership.[450] It was not until days after the election that the foiling of the coup plot was made public.

In May 2017, Montenegro's chief prosecutor formally indicted 14 individuals for allegedly plotting to overthrow the government. They include the two alleged Russian "masterminds" of the coup, Shishmakov and Popov, who are being tried in absentia.[451] During the trial, witnesses have also testified that Chechen Republic President Ramzan Kadyrov had a role in the alleged conspiracy. Mr. Sindjelic testified that Shishmakov told him Kadyrov received a large amount of money to bribe a mufti in Montenegro to form a parliamentary coalition with the DF.[452]

U.S. officials have also weighed in on the Kremlin's complicity in the coup attempt. In a June 2017 Senate Foreign Relations Committee hearing, Deputy Assistant Secretary of State Hoyt Yee said that there were:

> Russian or Russian-supported actors who tried to undermine the elections and probably undermine the government, if not actually overthrow the government or even assassinate the prime minister. This is, I think, consistent with where we've seen Russia trying to interfere in elections around the world, around Europe, including our own country. It's consistent with Russia's attempts to prevent countries of the Western Balkans from joining NATO, from integrating further with Euro-Atlantic institutions.[453]

And in testimony before the Senate Armed Serviced Committee in July 2017, Montenegro's Ambassador said that the "Special Chief Prosecutor, in charge of the case, has publicly stated that the evidence in this case is (I quote) 'undisputable' and 'iron clad.'"[454]

Despite the enormous pressure from Russia described in this chapter, Montenegro formally joined NATO on June 5, 2017.

---

[450] *Congressional Research Service,* "Russian Influence on Politics and Elections in Europe," June 27, 2017.
[451] *Ibid.*; Ben Farmer, "Reconstruction: The Full Incredible Story behind Russia's Deadly Plot to Stop Montenegro Embracing the West," *The Telegraph,* Feb. 18, 2017.
[452] Alec Luhn & Ben Farmer, "Chechnya Leader Accused of Involvement in Montenegro Coup," *The Telegraph,* Nov. 29, 2017.
[453] Testimony of Hoyt Brian Yee, Deputy Assistant Secretary of State, Bureau of European and Eurasian Affairs, *Southeast Europe: Strengthening Democracy and Countering Malign Foreign Influence,* Hearing before the U.S. Senate Committee on Foreign Relations, June 14, 2017.
[454] Statement of Nebojsa Kaluderovic, Ambassador of Montenegro to the United States, *Attempted Coup in Montenegro and Malign Russian Influence in Europe,* Hearing before the U.S. Senate Committee on Armed Services, July 13, 2017, at 1. At the time of this writing, the trial of the alleged coup plotters was ongoing.

Montenegro's NATO membership at this time has outsized importance, as it shows other NATO aspirants that it is possible to stand
up to Russian government pressure and propaganda efforts and integrate with the West. This case should be kept in mind as the
international community looks to engage another tier of vulnerable
countries with aspirations to integrate further with the West. Russia should never get a veto over the decisions of NATO, and the
Alliance should be willing to accept any country which meets the
membership requirements and has support from its citizenry.

Lessons Learned

* *NATO Membership Matters:* Montenegro pursued NATO membership at great risk and after having to implement far reaching reforms. Its determination to join the alliance is a testa-
ment to NATO's seminal importance in the world today. The
leading countries in NATO, including the United States,
should recognize the commitment made by our most vulnerable
allies to the alliance and continuously reciprocate by reit-
erating the United States' commitment to the importance of
NATO, particularly Article 5.

* *Russia's Asymmetric Arsenal Now Includes the Alleged Use of
Violence Outside of the Former Soviet Space:* Montenegrin authorities were fortunate to uncover the coup plot before it occurred, but evidence presented at the trial shows that the plotters were very close to succeeding. The Montenegro case shows
how far the Russian government was willing to go in order to
stop a country's membership in the Alliance—it should serve
as a wake-up call for other NATO and EU aspirants, especially
in the Balkans.

* *The NATO Reform Process Can Itself Build Resilience:* In a
July 2017 statement before the Senate Armed Services Committee regarding the coup attempt, Montenegrin Ambassador
to the United States Nebojsa Kaludjerovic said, "it was thanks
to those [NATO] reforms aimed at strengthening the capacity
and independence of institutions to uphold the rule of law that
helped those very institutions to tackle such a challenge we are
talking about today that would have put to test much more established democracies than ours."[455] NATO should take heed
and require a series of reforms by aspirant countries directly
focused on building resiliency against threats from the Russian
government's asymmetric arsenal.

* *Montenegro Must Remain Vigilant:* Now that Montenegro has
joined NATO, heavy-handed and overtly violent tactics by Russia are less likely, but Moscow could continue to exert pressure
and influence in ways similar to those seen in countries like
Bulgaria. The international community should not rest on its
laurels now that Montenegro is a NATO member, but should
actively help the government to bolster its defenses against
other soft power tools in Russia's asymmetric arsenal.

---

[455] *Ibid.*

SERBIA

Russian malign influence in the Republic of Serbia manifests itself through cultural ties, propaganda, energy, and an expanding defense relationship. Moscow also highlights deep roots between the countries through the Orthodox Church and a shared Slavic culture. This narrative has been carefully cultivated over the years such that Russian government disinformation campaigns find very fertile ground among the population of Serbia.[456] Despite its close relationship with Moscow, the government of Serbia has made clear that its top priority is joining the European Union. Serbia's desire to maintain good relations with both the EU and Russia is reflective of public opinion, but may not be sustainable, as deeper integration may mean adopting EU decisions that run counter to Russian interests.[457] Therefore, closer ties between Serbia and the EU could result in a significant surge in Russian malign influence in the country. The government of Serbia has done little to prepare for this eventuality and has taken few discernable actions to defend against Russian malign influence.

Serbian government officials' differing opinions on EU integration reflect a tension within the broader society itself. In remarks at the Serbian Economic Summit in Belgrade in October 2017, U.S. Deputy Assistant Secretary of State Hoyt Brian Yee said that those countries who wished to join the European Union "must very clearly demonstrate this desire." Referring to Serbia's long-standing relationship with Moscow, he said, "You cannot sit on two chairs at the same time, especially if they are that far away."[458] The mixed reaction from the Serbian government to Yee's remarks reflected the point that Yee was trying to make. Tanja Miscevic, the Ministry of Foreign Affairs negotiator on Serbia's EU Accession bid, said that Yee's statement was taken out of context and that he understood that Serbia's "clear foreign political strategic orientation" was towards the EU.[459] Serbia's Defense Minister Aleksandar Vulin, on the other hand, lashed out and said, "This is not a statement made by a friend or a man respecting Serbia, our policy, and our right to make our own decisions." He also said that Serbia will choose its course regardless of what the "great powers" want.[460]

Serbia has made significant progress in talks with the EU, having opened 12 out of the 35 "chapters" required for EU membership.[461] It also has the closest ties to Russia of any of the prospective candidates. And as it continues to make progress towards integration with Europe, there are signs that Moscow plans to increase pressure on the Balkan country to prevent this outcome. As Serbia's EU bid becomes more serious, Belgrade would be well served

---

[456] Forty-two percent of Serbian citizens see Russia as Serbia's most supportive partner, compared to 14 percent for the EU and 12 percent for China. Public Opinion Survey of 1,050 Serbian Adults, Sept. 2017 (unpublished).

[457] While 49 percent of Serbian citizens supported joining the EU in September 2017, that number drops to only 28 percemt if joining the EU meant "spoiling Serbia's relationship with Russia." Public Opinion Survey of 1,050 Serbian Adults, Sept. 2017 (unpublished).

[458] "Serbian Defense Minister Denounces U.S. Official's 'Unfriendly' Remarks," *Radio Free Europe/Radio Free Liberty*, Oct. 24, 2017.

[459] *Ibid.*

[460] *Ibid.*

[461] "EU Opens New Negotiation Chapters With Montenegro, Serbia," *Radio Free Europe/Radio Free Liberty*, Dec. 11, 2017.

to examine the tools used by Russia laid out throughout this report and work closely with the EU to build its defenses.

The government of the Republic of Serbia has dedicated substantial resources and political capital towards joining the EU.[462] But unfortunately, it has taken little action to defend itself from anti-EU Russian government propaganda that circulates throughout the country with little resistance. According to the U.S. State Department, the "number of media outlets and NGOs taking pro-Russian stands has grown from a dozen to over a hundred in recent years, and the free content offered by Russian state outlets such as Sputnik make them the most quoted foreign sources in the Serbian press."[463] For example, Sputnik articles in recent years have falsely claimed that Kosovar Albanians planned pogroms against Kosovar Serbs with the blessing of the West and that the West is fomenting instability in the Balkans to create a pretext for invasion.[464] This propaganda appears to have had an impact. Since Sputnik was launched in Serbia in January 2015, Russia's favorability numbers among Serbians have increased from 47.8 percent to 60 percent in June 2017.[465]

Most EU aspirants adopt the foreign policy directives of the European Union as a way to show commitment to solidarity even before they join. For example, Montenegro has adopted a top foreign policy priority of the EU—the sanctions regime on Russia—even though it is not a member. Once in the EU, countries are expected to adopt the foreign policies of the block on agreed-upon issues. Serbia has not signed onto the EU's Russia sanctions, and, given its relationship with Russia, it is difficult to see Belgrade agreeing to such measures in the foreseeable future. This tension with the EU on a central foreign policy priority for Brussels makes a challenging situation for Serbia even more difficult.

A similar dynamic is playing out next door in Bosnia and Herzegovina, where parts of the government have expressed a desire to join NATO.[466] In order to move forward, however, all three constituent ethnicities represented in the Bosnian presidency—the Croats, Bosniaks, and Serbs—would have to agree on Bosnia's NATO bid and make the commensurate reforms. Bosnia's Republika Srpska (RS), or Serbian Republic, is one of two largely autonomous constitutional entities in Bosnia. It is majority Serb and maintains close relations with Moscow. An RS objection to joining NATO would collapse any deal. Although the central government in Sarajevo has expressed support for Bosnia's implementation of a NATO Membership Action Plan (MAP), the parliament in RS passed a non-binding resolution in October 2017 opposing Bosnia's potential membership in the military alliance.[467] In recent years, Russia has intensified its relationship with RS Prime Min-

[462] See, e.g., Republic of Serbia, Ministry of Foreign Affairs, EU Integration Process of the Republic of Serbia, http://www.mfa.gov.rs/en/themes/public-consultation-on-the-eu-strategy-for-the-adriatic-and-ionian-region (visited Dec. 19, 2017).

[463] U.S. Department of State, Background Information on Serbia provided to Committee Staff, June 30, 2017.

[464] Andrew Rettman, "Western Balkans: EU Blindspot on Russian Propaganda," EUobserver, December 10, 2015.

[465] Public Opinion Survey of 1,050 Serbian Adults, Sept. 2017 (unpublished).

[466] "Bosnia Making Military Progress in NATO Bid—Alliance General," Reuters, Nov. 14, 2017.

[467] "Bosnian Serbs Pass Non-Binding Resolution against NATO Membership," Associated Press, Oct. 18, 2017.

ister Milorad Dodik, which could prove useful in hampering Bosnia's NATO bid. Though Dodik is not the head of Bosnia's government, Vladimir Putin has met with him on multiple occasions, despite not meeting the central government in Sarajevo—a breach of diplomatic protocol that makes clear that he is Russia's preferred interlocutor.[468] The Russian government has also publicly expressed its support for a 2017 independence referendum in RS, which the Constitutional Court found violated the rights of non-Serbs in the country.[469] If Bosnia were to make significant progress towards NATO, Russia could exert influence in RS to hamper forward progress. The media space is already prepared for that possibility, as RS media outlets rely on anti-NATO and anti-EU content from Sputnik's Belgrade outlet.[470] Russian influence in Banja Luka, the de facto capital of RS, is pervasive—downtown kiosks are filled with t-shirts, coffee mugs, and other memorabilia praising the Russian Federation and Vladimir Putin.[471]

As Serbia continues to work through chapters in its EU accession talks, Russia has employed several of the interference tools seen in this report, especially propaganda and disinformation. For example, according to Stratfor Worldview, the Russian state newspaper Rossiyskaya Gazeta prints Nedeljnik, a widely read weekly magazine, in Moscow before delivering it to Serbia.[472] According to the *Financial Times,* Sputnik provides online stories and news bulletins to 20 radio stations across Serbia free of charge.[473] More than 100 media outlets and NGOs in Serbia can be considered pro-Russian, a number that has spiked considerably in recent years.[474] The response from the West has been sparse, but there are signs of competition in the information space. The BBC has announced plans to reengage in Serbia in 2018, seven years after it closed its Serbian language service. The service will be funded at around £600,000 annually and will employ 20 local staff.[475]

Press freedom has also declined sharply in recent years in Serbia. Freedom House reported in 2017 that "press freedom has eroded under the SNS-led administration of Prime Minister [now President] Vucic. Independent and investigative journalists face frequent harassment, including by government officials and in progovernment media. Physical attacks against journalists take place each year, and death threats and other intimidation targeting media workers are a serious concern."[476] If Serbia's journalists are not able to conduct investigations without threat of censorship, vio-

---

[468] Danijel Kovacevic, "Putin-Dodik Comradeship Causes Uncertainty for Bosnia," *BIRN/Balkan Insight,* June 8, 2017.
[469] Milivoje Pantovic et al., "Russia Lends Full Backing to Bosnian Serb Referendum," *Balkan Insight,* Sept. 20, 2016.
[470] John Cappello, "Russian Information Operations in the Western Balkans," *Real Clear Defense,* Feb. 1, 2017.
[471] Observed during Committee Staff Visit to Banja Luka, July 2017.
[472] "Russia Stirs up the Hornet's Nest," *Stratfor Worldview,* Mar. 28, 2017.
[473] Andrew Byrne, "Kremlin Backed Media Adds to Western Fears in Balkans" *Financial Times,* March 19, 2017. In conversations with U.S. officials and civil society groups during a visit to Belgrade in 2017, Committee staff were told Serbian outlets pick up content from Sputnik and other Russian outlets because it is free; however, *Radio Free Europe/Radio Liberty* also provides free content that is objective and does not contain the same Russian propaganda messages.
[474] U.S. Department of State, Background Information on Belgrade provided to Committee Staff, June 30, 2017.
[475] *Ibid.*
[476] Freedom House, *Freedom of the Press 2017: Serbia* (2017).

lence, or intimidation, the ability of the country to significantly counter Russian propaganda may not be possible. The government of Serbia has an important role to play in fostering an environment where press freedom can thrive.

Russia also exerts considerable influence through Serbia's energy sector. In 2014, Russia provided 40 percent of the natural gas consumed in Serbia, and, in December 2017, Serbia's state-owned natural gas company, Srbijagas, announced that it would increase imports from Gazprom by 33 percent in 2018.[477] Russia's energy dominance also extends to Serbia's domestic oil, where Gazprom has majority ownership of the national oil company.[478] While the cancellation of the South Stream project (see Chapter 4) caught Serbia and other countries in the region by surprise, there are indications that Serbia could be invited to participate in its replacement, Turkish Stream, Russia's proposed pipeline deal with Turkey.[479] While the EU and United States are working with Belgrade to diversify its energy resources through projects like the Bulgaria-Serbia Interconnector, Serbia's viable short-term diversification options remain limited.[480]

Russia is able to engage with the citizens of Serbia through cultural institutions, including the Orthodox Church, civil society associations, and under the guise of humanitarian assistance. Leonid Reshetnikov, a retired lieutenant general in the Russian intelligence service SVR and then director of the Russian Institute for Strategic Studies, spoke at a 2015 conference in Serbia entitled "Balkan Dialogue—Russia's Soft Power in Serbia." Reshetnikov has been described by former senior government officials in the Balkans as "a propaganda fist" and "the right hand of Mr. Putin" in their countries.[481] He commented on the roots of the orthodox bond between Serbia and Russia:

> [W]e have forgotten that we are a civilization that is an alternative to the Anglo-Saxon civilization. Our mission is to carry our civilization into the world and to propose our view. Our soft power is to be loyal to the principles of the Orthodox civilization. That is the idea we should have in mind when we talk about the influence of Russia. Why do Serbs and Russians so easily find a common language? Because we have the same root, we easily find a common language with the Serbs.[482]

---

[477] Janusz Bugajski and Margarita Assenova, "Eurasian Disunion: Russia's Vulnerable Flanks," *The Jamestown Foundation*, June 2016, at 242; "Gazprom to Increase by 33% Natgas Exports to Serbia in 2018," *SeeNews*, Dec. 20, 2017.

[478] U.S. Department of State, Background Information on Belgrade provided to Committee Staff, June 30, 2017.

[479] Andrew Roth, "In Diplomatic Defeat, Putin Diverts Pipeline to Turkey," *The New York Times*, Dec. 1, 2014; Vincent L. Morelli, "Serbia: Background and U.S. Relations," *Congressional Research Service*, Oct. 16, 2017.

[480] In January 2017, Serbia and Bulgaria signed a memorandum of understanding to establish a natural gas line between the cities of Sofia and Nis, contributing to regional efforts to diversify energy supplies away from Moscow. "Bulgaria, Serbia Agree to Work on Pipeline to Cut Reliance on Russian Gas," *Reuters*, Jan. 19, 2017.

[481] Joe Parkinson & Georgi Kantchev, "Document: Russia Uses Rigged Polls, Fake News to Sway Foreign Elections," *The Wall Street Journal*, Mar. 23, 2017. In addition, Reshetnikov was sanctioned by the United States in December 2016 for his role in a bank that financed the government of Syria's Bashar al-Assad. *Ibid.*

[482] The Center for Euro-Atlantic Studies, *Eyes Wide Shut: Strengthening of Russian Soft Power in Serbia: Goals, Instruments, and Effects*, May 2016 (citing *"Soft Power" of Russia in Serbia—Possibilities and Perspectives*, NSPM [Nova Srpska Politicka Misao], Dec. 15, 2014 (in Serbian)).

A core element of the Russian government narrative on its relationship with Serbia rests on its common heritage in the Orthodox Church. Church leadership in Russia and Serbia amplify traditional conservative messages that frequently carry anti-EU or anti-western tones, often focused on gay rights. These ties between the churches are cultivated by senior political leaders—Russian officials emphasize these ties on visits to Serbia, often making time to meet with Serbian Orthodox Church leaders.[483]

The Center for Euro-Atlantic Studies (CEAS) has documented 51 pro-Kremlin associations and student organizations active in Serbia.[484] Among the most influential, according to CEAS, is SNP Nashi, a group modeled on the Russian pro-Kremlin youth organization Nashi (see Chapter 2).[485] SNP Nashi was created in 2006 and sought to build closer ties with Moscow, while opposing Serbia's membership in the EU. The group's leadership has led efforts against pro-western voices in Serbia and has been sued for creating a list of "the 30 biggest Serb haters."[486] Similar organizations include the Patriotic Front, which has reportedly facilitated paramilitary training for Serbian children in Siberia, and the Serbian Patriotic Movement Zavetnici, which includes many student members and has advocated against Kosovo independence as well as Serbia's proposed EU membership.[487] In the southern city of Nis, the Russian government established a Russian-Serbian Humanitarian Center (RSHC) in 2012, ostensibly to help Serbia improve its emergency response capabilities and respond to natural disasters.[488] U.S. officials, however, have questioned the center's true purpose. The former Commander of U.S. Army forces in Europe, Lieutenant General Ben Hodges noted his skepticism about Russian intentions in Nis, which is close to U.S. military personnel stationed across the border in Kosovo, saying, "I don't believe it's a humanitarian center. That's the facade, but that's not what it's for."[489] In June 2017, testifying before the U.S. Senate Foreign Relations Committee, Deputy Assistant Secretary Yee stressed that if Serbia "allows Russia to create some kind of a special center for espionage or other nefarious activities, it will lose control over part of its territory."[490] The Russian government has requested diplomatic status for their staff at the facility, a request that Serbia has not yet honored.

Security cooperation presents Russia with another powerful inroad into Serbia's government and society. The narrative that Russia is Serbia's protector on the world stage has a particular resonance with Serbia's population. A 2017 public opinion survey by the Belgrade-based Demostat research center found that 41 percent

[483] See Ibid. at 71-73.
[484] Ibid. at 82-99.
[485] Ibid. at 84. For more on Nashi, see Chapter 2.
[486] Ibid.
[487] Ibid. at 88-89.
[488] Russian-Serbian Humanitarian Center, "About," http://en.ihc.rs/about (visited Dec. 19, 2017).
[489] "US General: Russian Center in Serbia is Not Humanitarian," In Serbia Today, Nov. 16, 2017. Lt. Gen. Hodges retired in December 2017.
[490] Statement of Hoyt Brian Yee, Deputy Assistant Secretary, Bureau of European and Eurasian Affairs, U.S. Department of State, Southeast Europe: Strengthening Democracy and Countering Malign Foreign Influence, Hearing before the U.S. Senate Committee on Foreign Relations, June 14, 2017.

perceive Russia as Serbia's greatest friend.[491] The Russian government takes a hard line against recognition of Kosovo's statehood and blocking resolutions at the UN on the 1995 Srebrenica massacre. Serbian President Aleksandar Vucic frequently meets with President Putin, and as recently as December 2017 called upon Russia to play a more active role in negotiations on Serbia's relationship with Kosovo.[492]

This theme also plays out in the defense relationship between Russia and Serbia. In the last year, Serbia signed a major arms deal with Russia and sent a member of its Defense Attaché team in Moscow to observe a Russian military exercise in Crimea.[493] In October 2017, Russia provided six MiG-29 jets, and reportedly agreed to provide 30 T-72 tanks and 30 BRDM-2 patrol combat vehicles to Serbia, all at no charge. President Vucic reportedly said that Serbia is also negotiating the purchase of the S-300 air defense system from Russia, a deal which could trigger recently adopted U.S. law which mandates sanctions on any significant transaction with the Russian military or intelligence sectors.[494]

Despite close military ties with Russia, Serbia also seeks to maintain security cooperation with NATO and the United States. According to the Congressional Research Service, Serbia participates in NATO's Partnership for Peace (PfP) program, including through joint exercises and training opportunities.[495] According to John Cappello, a former Acting Defense Attaché at the U.S. Embassy, Serbia held around 125 military-to-military exchanges with the United States in 2016, compared to only four with Russia.[496]

The Russian government's asymmetric arsenal in Serbia is multifaceted and very effective at maintaining public support for a strong relationship with Moscow. This has been achieved with little counter-messaging efforts on the part of the European Union and the United States. Given Serbia's central role and influence in the Balkans, any strategy to counter malign influence should start with Belgrade. Since the Russian government could significantly ramp up its malign influence efforts beyond current levels in the event that Serbia made clear strides towards joining the European Union, the international community should prepare for this eventuality by incorporating some of the best lessons learned from other countries across Europe.

Lessons Learned

- *More Domestic Leadership is Needed to Defend Against Kremlin Interference:* Serbia is an important country in the region, given its geographical centrality and complicated recent history during the breakup of Yugoslavia. As its leaders navigate a

---

[491] Filip Rudic, "Serbians Support Military Neutrality, Research Says," *Balkan Insight,* Sept. 5, 2017.

[492] Filip Rudic, "Serbia Seeks Russia Role in Kosovo Talks," *Balkan Insight,* Dec. 20, 2017.

[493] U.S. Department of State, Background Information on Serbia provided to Committee Staff, June 30, 2017.

[494] "Serbia Takes Delivery of First of Six MiG-29 Fighters from Russia," *Radio Free Europe/Radio Liberty,* Oct. 2, 2017; Countering America's Adversaries Through Sanctions Act, P.L. No. 115-44, § 231 (Enacted Aug. 2, 2017).

[495] Vincent L. Morelli, "Serbia: Background and U.S. Relations," *Congressional Research Service,* Oct. 16, 2017.

[496] Kaitlin Lavinder, "Russia Ramps Up Media and Military Influence in the Balkans," *The Cipher Brief,* Oct. 13, 2017.

challenging political environment, there is no doubt that Serbia faces pressure in trying to "sit on two chairs." But leadership matters, and if Serbia wants to join the EU, it needs to take steps to counter the Russian asymmetric arsenal. Without any significant defense, Russian propaganda will continue to have an impact on public opinion in Serbia.

- *The United States Must Reengage with Resources:* U.S. assistance to Serbia has been on a downward trajectory in recent years. According to the Congressional Research Service, the United States provided $22.9 million in FY2014, $14.2 million in FY2015, and $16.8 million in FY2016. For FY2017, the Obama Administration requested approximately $23 million. The FY2018 budget from the Trump Administration requested $12.1 million.[497] In light of substantial assistance increases authorized in the 2017 Countering America's Adversaries Through Sanctions Act, USAID missions across the region must reorient towards a more robust effort to counter Russian malign influence.[498] For years, these missions have been on a glide path to wind down operations with insufficient focus on the threat posed by Russian malign influence. The challenge faced by the United States and its allies across the Balkans and throughout Europe requires a reorientation of assistance. In approaching this reality, the United States must reverse years of thinking about shrinking its footprint, and instead work towards an expansive and entrepreneurial approach that makes long-term investments in building resiliency and strengthening democratic institutions, including their ability to counter disinformation. The United States should also continue to support Serbia's efforts to become more energy independent, and work with the EU on comprehensive efforts across the region.

- *U.S. Officials Need to Show Up:* In addition to aid, countries like Serbia also need senior level and consistent U.S. diplomatic engagement. The United States must send a clear message that it is willing to spend the time and effort necessary to support those who want a democratic future in Europe. High-level attention by the United States has been noticeably diminished in the region since the fall of Slobodan Milosevic, more than 17 years ago. Russian engagement with Serbia's leadership stands in stark contrast to that of the United States. President Vucic has met with President Putin at least twelve times since 2012.[499] The last U.S. President to visit Belgrade was Jimmy Carter in 1980.[500] To fill this void, senior U.S. officials, including members of Congress, should regularly travel to the region and host high profile visitors to Washington. The United States needs to send a clear message that

[497] Morelli, "Serbia: Background and U.S. Relations," U.S. Department of State, Congressional Budget Justification, Department of State, Foreign Operations, and Related Programs, Fiscal Year 2018 (May 23, 2017).
[498] Countering America's Adversaries Through Sanctions Act, P.L. No. 115-44, § 254 (Enacted Aug. 2, 2017).
[499] U.S. Department of State, Background Information on Belgrade provided to Committee Staff, June 30, 2017.
[500] U.S. Department of State Office of the Historian, *Presidential and Secretaries Travel Abroad: Jimmy Carter* (1980).

it is back and ready to work seriously in cooperation with host countries and allies across Europe to defend against malign influence and help countries complete the integration process.

89

Russia exerts influence in Bulgaria through its dominant role in the economy, primarily in the energy sector, as well as propaganda, relationships with political parties, cultural ties, and a relationship with a Bulgarian military that continues to rely on Soviet-era equipment. Bulgaria's longstanding historical relationship with Russia makes it unique among the other EU and NATO countries, requiring continued vigilance on the nature and effect of Russian influence on the country.

From a bird's eye view of downtown Sofia, Bulgaria's capital city, one can see the second biggest Orthodox Church in the Balkan Peninsula, the St. Alexander Nevsky Cathedral. Named after a Russian prince, the cathedral is meant to honor the memory of Russian soldiers killed during the Russo-Turkish War of 1877-1878. Yards away stands a monument honoring Russian Tsar Alexander II, who led the effort to liberate Bulgaria from the Ottoman Empire. Alexander is sitting on a horse, facing the Bulgarian parliament building, an imposing reminder to the country's legislators of how the country gained its independence.

These iconic buildings on Sofia's skyline are a telling perspective on Bulgaria's history and current position. Among the group of countries profiled in this report, Bulgaria has perhaps the most longstanding historical ties to Russia. During the Cold War, Bulgarian leaders like Todor Zhivkov sought to make Bulgaria the 16th Soviet Republic.[501] Today, the Bulgarian Socialist Party maintains good relations with Moscow and its leader, Kornelia Ninova, has called for EU sanctions on Russia (which Bulgaria is required to implement as an EU member) to be lifted.[502] The pro-Kremlin Ataka party has called for a closer relationship with Russia and has stridently opposed the European Union through a xenophobic, far-right agenda. Ataka's leader, Volen Siderov, opened his party's 2014 election campaign at an event in Moscow, where he criticized the "sodomite NATO."[503] While public support for the party has diminished in recent years, its messaging continues to resonate with elements of the electorate. At the same time, the government of Prime Minister Boyko Borisov has taken measures to push back against Russian influence, such as in September 2015, when he denied overflight rights to Russian aircraft in support of its mission in Syria.[504] The apparent disconnect between Bulgarian society and government—a broad affinity for Russia among the population combined with a strong EU and NATO partner in the Bulgarian government—argues for deeper U.S. engagement across all sectors of Bulgarian society.

While the history of Bulgaria's relationship with Russia is rooted in its military liberation from Ottoman rule, the modern manifestation of Moscow's influence is more focused on soft power, energy economics, and political and cultural influence.

---

[501] Heather A. Conley et al., Center for Strategic & International Studies, *The Kremlin Playbook: Understanding Russian Influence in Central and Eastern Europe*, at 43 (Oct. 2016).
[502] *Ibid.*
[503] John R. Haines, "The Suffocating Symbiosis: Russia Seeks Trojan Horses Inside Fractious Bulgaria's Political Corral," *Foreign Policy Research Institute*, Aug. 5, 2016.
[504] "Russia Says Bulgaria's Refusal of Flyovers to Syria Is a U.S. Plot," *Los Angeles Times*, Sept. 8, 2015.

Bulgarian public opinion polls clearly reflect an affinity for Russia. In its recent Trends 2017 Survey, the think tank GLOBSEC found that 70 percent of Bulgarians had a favorable opinion of Vladimir Putin, the highest of any EU country.[505] Bulgaria joined NATO in 2004, but public support for the Alliance is tepid. When asked about Article 5 of the NATO charter—which considers an attack on one member as an attack on all—less than half of Bulgarian respondents said that they would support coming to the aid of a NATO ally under attack.[506]

A report by the Center for Strategic and International Studies (CSIS), a U.S. think tank, has characterized Russia's outsized role in the Bulgarian economy as "bordering on state capture" and asserts that "the Kremlin uses a complex and opaque network of colluding officials within the governing apparatus and business community" to advance its interests.[507] Nowhere is Russian government dominance more apparent than in the energy sector. Bulgaria is almost completely dependent on Russia for oil and natural gas—90 percent of Bulgaria's natural gas is imported from Russia and the country completely depends on Moscow to supply nuclear fuel for its two reactors, which generate 35 percent of the country's electricity.[508] The CSIS report also argues that Moscow's ability to influence the policy making process in Bulgaria is considerable. During debate on the South Stream pipeline in the Bulgarian parliament, MPs introduced amendments which would have circumvented EU energy law. Gazprom also reportedly sent an official letter to the Bulgarian Energy Holding company, which provided advice on changes to the Bulgarian energy law in Gazprom's interests.[509]

Russia canceled the Gazprom-led South Stream project in 2014 after it attracted significant pushback from other countries, which in turn enabled Bulgaria to support the EU-backed Southern Gas Corridor.[510]

Societal challenges also create openings for Russian influence. Bulgaria is one of the poorest countries in Europe—it has experienced slow economic growth and many of its young people are leaving for Western Europe.[511] The population is aging and likely more inclined towards nostalgia for Bulgaria's warm relations with Moscow during the Cold War. The migrant crisis also provides an opening for anti-Europe propaganda, one that political parties like Ataka have been eager to exploit. In 2014, its leader warned that, "Bulgaria was melting away without a war" as "abortion, emigration, homosexuality, and permanent economic crisis destroyed the population."[512] The Russian government, through the Russkiy Mir

[505] GLOBSEC Policy Institute, *GLOBSEC Trends 2017: Mixed Messages and Signs of Hope from Central and Eastern Europe,* at 20 (Jan. 8, 2017).
[506] *Ibid.* at 17.
[507] *Ibid.*
[508] U.S. Department of State, Background Information on Bulgaria provided to Committee Staff, Feb. 9, 2017.
[509] *The Kremlin Playbook,* at 46.
[510] Stanley Reed & James Kanter, "Putin's Surprise Call to Scrap South Stream Gas Pipeline Leaves Europe Reeling," *The New York Times,* Dec. 2, 2014; Radislov Dikov, Bulgaria Becomes Part of Southern Gas Infrastructure, *Radio Bulgaria,* Mar. 21, 2015.
[511] Ivan Krastev, "Britain's Gain is Eastern Europe's Brain Drain," *The Guardian,* Mar. 24, 2015.
[512] John R. Haines, "The Suffocating Symbiosis: Russia Seeks Trojan Horses Inside Fractious Bulgaria's Political Corral," *Foreign Policy Research Institute,* Aug. 5, 2016.

Foundation, supports organizations outside Russia "in partnership with the Russian Orthodox Church ... to promote Russian language and Russian culture."[513] Russkiy Mir operates six "Russia Centers" in Bulgaria focused on cultural and educational programs in addition to Russian-language instruction.[514]

Russia reportedly sought to exploit Bulgarian politics during the 2016 presidential election using techniques seen elsewhere across Europe.[515] Prior to the 2016 presidential election, Leonid Reshetnikov, then director of the Russian Institute for Strategic Studies (RISS), visited Bulgaria, where he reportedly provided the Socialist Party with "a secret strategy document proposing a road to victory at the ballot box" with recommendations to "plant fake news and promote exaggerated polling data."[516] The document also urged the Socialist Party to adopt a platform that aligned with Kremlin interests: end sanctions on Russia, criticize NATO, and encourage Brexit.[517] Reshetnikov told the Bulgarian and Russian media that he met with the head of the Socialist party, but he denies providing the dossier.[518] Later that year, Rumen Radev, the Bulgarian Socialist Party candidate, would go on to win the presidency with 59 percent of the vote, though how much of its success was due to following the reported RISS plan is impossible to determine.[519] And despite the alleged Russian support and initial concerns about Radev's candidacy, since becoming President, his expressions of strong support for NATO and the EU indicate an intention to maintain the status quo with these institutions.[520]

The Kremlin has also reportedly interfered in more recent Bulgarian national elections. Prior to the 2017 parliamentary elections, Bulgarian analysts asserted that upwards of 300 Bulgarian websites were dedicated to advancing pro-Russian propaganda.[521] A 2017 report by the Human and Social Studies Foundation, a Bulgarian think tank, asserts that domestically-generated pro-Russian propaganda is used as a tool to advance domestic political goals.[522] For example, Bulgarian national Stefan Proynov runs a small troll farm in the village of Pliska.[523] According to the Russian investigative website Coda:

> Proynov's mission runs on vengeance—specifically, against the generally pro-European, center-right, GERB party of Prime Minister Boyko Borisov, who won re-election last

[513] *Ibid.* The Foundation is a joint project of the Ministry of Foreign Affairs and the Ministry of Education and Science, and has a stated purpose of "promoting the Russian language, as Russia's national heritage and a significant aspect of Russian and world culture, and supporting Russian language teaching programs abroad." Russkiy Mir Foundation, "About Russkiy Mir Foundation," https://russkiymir.ru/en/fund/index.php (visited Dec. 31, 2017).

[514] *See* Russkiy Mir Foundation, "Russian Centers of the Russkiy Mir Foundation," https://russkiymir.ru/en/rucenter (visited Dec. 31, 2017).

[515] Parkinson & Katchev, "Document: Russia Uses Rigged Polls, Fake News to Sway Foreign Elections," *The Wall Street Journal*, Mar. 23, 2017.

[516] Joe Parkinson & Georgi Kantchev, "Document: Russia Uses Rigged Polls, Fake News to Sway Foreign Elections," *The Wall Street Journal*, Mar. 23, 2017.

[517] *Ibid.*

[518] *Ibid.*

[519] Tsvetelia Tsolova & Angel Krasimirov, "Russia-Friendly Political Novice Wins Bulgaria Presidential Election: Exit Polls," *Reuters*, Nov. 12, 2016.

[520] North Atlantic Treaty Organization, "Joint Press Point with NATO Secretary General Jens Stoltenberg and the President of the Republic of Bulgaria, Rumen Radev," Jan. 31, 2017.

[521] Committee Staff Interview of Project Members Examining Russian Disinformation, Sofia University, Sofia, Bulgaria, Feb. 23, 2017.

[522] "Anti-Democratic Propaganda in Bulgaria," *Human and Social Studies Foundation*, 2017.

[523] Michael Colborne, "Made in Bulgaria: Pro-Russian Propaganda," *Coda*, May 9, 2017

month. Proynov claims that in 2011, GERB, then Bulgaria's ruling party, and the police cooked up criminal charges against him (for the illegal possession of antiquities, weapons and narcotics) to silence his criticism of their policies.[524]

This mutually beneficial propaganda loop is in some respects more powerful and more difficult to counter than Moscow-generated propaganda on its own.

Despite the lukewarm support for NATO within the general population, Bulgaria should be lauded for its active role in the Alliance. It deployed troops and suffered casualties in the NATO-led missions in Iraq and Afghanistan.[525] According to the U.S. State Department, the U.S. Department of Defense is funding increased exercises and training at four joint U.S.-Bulgarian military facilities.[526] In September 2016, the United States and Bulgaria conducted a NATO Joint Enhanced Air Policing (EAP) Mission, the first of its kind in the country.[527] And in 2017, Bulgaria co-hosted the Saber Guardian exercise, the largest U.S. and NATO exercise in Europe of the year.[528] Bulgaria's active role in NATO, however, remains somewhat hampered by the country's continued reliance on Russian-made military equipment, a legacy of the Warsaw Pact. In particular, Bulgarian government officials have expressed concern about the country's Soviet-era air defense systems as well as ongoing maintenance of equipment across the armed forces.[529] In light of the Counteracting America's Adversaries Through Sanctions Act (CAATSA) that mandates sanctions on those who conduct significant transactions with the Russian defense and intelligence sectors, the Bulgarian government should be working with urgency to diminish its reliance on Russian arms.

Lessons Learned

- *Despite Pressure, Bulgaria Remains Resilient:* In November 2006, former Russian Ambassador to the EU, Vladimir Chizhov, said that "Bulgaria is in a good position to become our special partner, a sort of a Trojan horse in the EU."[530] More than 10 years later, this prediction has not come to pass, as Bulgarian citizens continue to support membership in the EU and the country is an active participant in NATO.[531] Bulgaria has chosen a pro-Western path and while it has had to manage pressure from Moscow, especially in the energy sector, it has proven resilient on important issues like security co-

---

[524] *Ibid.*
[525] U.S. Department of State, Background Information on Bulgaria for Committee Staff, Feb. 9, 2017.
[526] *Ibid.*
[527] *Ibid.*
[528] Eric Schmitt, "U.S. Troops Train in Eastern Europe to Echoes of the Cold War," *The New York Times,* Aug. 6, 2017.
[529] Nick Thorpe, "Bulgaria's Military Warned of Soviet-Era 'Catastrophe,'" *BBC News,* Oct. 14, 2014.
[530] John R. Haines, *The Suffocating Symbiosis: Russia Seeks Trojan Horses Inside Fractious Bulgaria's Political Corral,* Foreign Policy Research Institute, Aug. 5, 2016 (citing a November 2006 interview with Kapital, a Bulgarian language weekly business newspaper).
[531] In a public opinion poll conducted by the European Commission in 2016, 49 percent of Bulgarian citizens expressed trust in the EU, a rate higher than several other countries across Western Europe. European Commission, Directorate-General for Communication, Standard Eurobarometer 86: Public opinion in the European Union, Nov. 2016, at 93.

operation with the West and support for EU sanctions on Russia. As described above however, significant vulnerabilities to the Russian asymmetric arsenal do persist and would benefit from additional assistance and engagement from Bulgaria's democratic allies.

- *Diminished U.S. Assistance has Consequences:* The United States provided more than $600 million in assistance for political and economic reforms in Bulgaria from 1990 to 2007, but this assistance was largely discontinued when the country joined the EU.[532] These aid programs gave the United States the ability to engage with broad swaths of Bulgarian society on the merits of democratic values and the rule of law. Without this programming, the United States' ability to engage on these issues has been significantly hampered while Russian propaganda and malign influence has thrived. While the U.S. Embassy has sought to continue to engage with limited resources, the diplomatic challenge in countering Russian malign influence remains considerable. With the dedication of more diplomatic attention and resources—particularly on energy diversification, addressing corruption, and building up the democratic rule of law—the United States will be in a position to help leaders within the Bulgarian government and civil society counter Russia's asymmetric arsenal.

---

[532] Congressional Research Service, "Background on Bulgaria for the Nomination of Eric S. Rubin to be United States Ambassador to the Republic of Bulgaria," Oct. 2, 2015.

94

In Hungary, the Russian government's asymmetric arsenal includes support for extreme political parties and organizations within the country, propaganda, and the use of corruption. The Russian government also enjoys a warm relationship with the country's Prime Minister, Viktor Orbán. Despite Hungary's proud history of resistance to Moscow during the Cold War and its membership in the European Union and NATO, Orban has increasingly sought to deepen ties with Russia in recent years, calling into question the government's commitment to the principles which underlie these international institutions.

Within the EU and NATO, Prime Minister Orbán is perhaps the most supportive leader of Vladimir Putin, his style of leadership, and his worldview. The platform of his party, Fidesz, includes an "Eastern Opening" foreign approach focused on an accommodating relationship with Moscow.[533] Orbán has reportedly said on several occasions that Hungary has shot itself in the foot by supporting sanctions against Russia, and that Moscow should be praised for opposing "Western attempts of isolation, regime change."[534] So while many citizens may remember with great pride the Hungarian Uprising of 1956 against the Soviets, today's government in Budapest is closer now to Moscow than at any time since the fall of the Berlin Wall.

Given Orbán's positive orientation towards Moscow, his government has taken no discernable steps to stop or even discourage Russian malign influence, and appears to applaud the anti-EU, anti-U.S., and anti-migrant Russian propaganda because it aligns with the themes that Orbán promotes. Instead of defending Hungary against Russian malign interference, Orbáln appears to have welcomed it. Russia has exploited this relatively unimpeded access by flooding Hungary with pro-Kremlin and anti-western propaganda and reportedly providing support to far-right political parties and fringe militant groups.

For example, in December 2017 Hungarian prosecutors charged Hungarian businessman and Jobbik party politician Bela Kovacs with spying on EU institutions on behalf of Russia.[535] Kovacs joined the Jobbik party, which has espoused anti-Semitic and racist views, in 2005 and helped turn around its financial prospects.[536] In 2010, he was elected to the European Parliament. Kovacs has denied the charges and no date has been set for his trial.

Russian intelligence also appears to be cultivating relationships with far-right groups in Hungary. In October 2016, the police raided the house of Istvan Gyorkos, the leader of a fringe neo-Nazi group called the Hungarian National Front, to search for illegal

[533] Lorant Gyori & Peter Kreko, "Russian Disinformation and Extremism in Hungary," *The Warsaw Institute Review*, Oct. 16, 2017.
[534] Lorant Gyori et al., Political Capital (Hungarian Think Tank), *Does Russia Interfere in Czech, Austrian and Hungarian Elections?*, at 12 (2017) (translated from Hungarian, citing Orbán's comments in August 2014, available at http://mandiner.hu/cikk/20140815—orban—az—oroszorszag—elleni—szankciokkal—labon—lottuk—magunkat, and his speech at the Lamfalussy Lectures Conference, Jan. 23, 2017, available at http://www.miniszterelnok.hu/orban-viktor-beszede-lamfalussy-lectures-szakmai-konferencian/).
[535] Marton Dunai & Gergely Szakacs, "Hungary Charges Jobbik MEP with Spying on EU for Russia," *Reuters*, Dec. 6, 2017.
[536] Andrew Higgins, "Intent on Unsettling E.U., Russia Taps Foot Soldiers from the Fringe," *The New York Times*, Dec. 24, 2016.

weapons. A shootout ensued, and a police officer was killed.[537] The New York Times reported that in the investigation that followed, Hungarian intelligence officials told a parliamentary committee that Gyorkos gathered regularly with Russian intelligence officers to conduct mock combat exercises in the area around his house.[538] The Hungarian online news portal Index also reported that Gyorkos had been meeting with Russian intelligence officers for years.[539] Hungarian security officials believe that the Russian intelligence sector's main goal in cultivating Gyorkos was to gain control of Hidfo (the Bridgehead), a website that was controlled by his Hungarian National Front and had a significant following among extremists in the country.[540] Following its efforts to cultivate a relationship with Gyorkos, Russian intelligence was reportedly successful in commandeering the site and moving its server to Russia where it has been used as a platform to broadcast propaganda targeting the West and the United States.[541] For example, the website circulated a fake U.S. Department of Homeland Security assessment that the 2016 U.S. election was not a victim of cyberattacks.[542] It also issued false reports that Austria sought to lift sanctions against Russia and that NATO Secretary General Jens Stoltenberg had sought to make European nations vassals of Washington.[543]

Russian government propaganda also finds fertile ground in Hungary's domestic media landscape. Content by Sputnik and RT is widely referenced by pro-government news sources in Hungary.[544] The pro-government daily newspaper Magyar Idok (*The Hungarian Times*) has published pieces by the Strategic Culture website, a well-known Russian propaganda outlet.[545] The Russian propaganda site New Eastern Outlook has also been reportedly referenced by pro-Fidesz websites like 888.hu and Magyar Hirlap (*Hungarian Gazette*).[546] There does not appear to be discernable effort by the government to counter this disinformation.

A lack of transparency in the political process has also allowed for increased corruption, another opening that Russia can exploit. In 2016, Jozsef Peter Martin, the executive director of Transparency International in Hungary, said that "a centralised form of corruption has been developed and systematically pursued in Hungary."[547] He also directly criticized the government and asserted that "turning public funds into private wealth using legal instruments is an important element of corruption in Hungary."[548] In 2014, Russia directly benefitted from this lack of transparency with

[537] *Ibid.*
[538] *Ibid.*
[539] Lili Bayer, "Moscow Spooks Return to Hungary, Raising NATO Hackles," *Politico*, July 19, 2017.
[540] Andrew Higgins, "Intent on Unsettling E.U., Russia Taps Foot Soldiers from the Fringe," *The New York Times*, Dec. 24, 2016.
[541] *Ibid.*
[542] *Ibid.*; Lili Bayer, "Moscow Spooks Return to Hungary, Raising NATO Hackles," *Politico*, July 19, 2017.
[543] Andrew Higgins, "Intent on Unsettling E.U., Russia Taps Foot Soldiers from the Fringe," *The New York Times*, Dec. 24, 2016.
[544] Lili Bayer, "Fidesz-Friendly Media Peddling Russian Propaganda," *The Budapest Beacon*, Nov. 17, 2016.
[545] *Ibid.*
[546] *Ibid.*
[547] Transparency International: Hungary, "Corruption Perceptions Index: 2015."
[548] *Ibid.*

the Paks nuclear deal, in which the Russian nuclear operator Rosatom was awarded a sole source contract to construct two plants, and the Hungarian parliament subsequently passed legislation which would keep details related to the deal classified for 30 years.[549]

Since returning to power in 2010, Orbán has embraced the concept of "illiberal democracy" modeled on the "sovereign democracy" advanced by Vladislav Surkov in Russia.[550] As Orbán deepens relations with Russia abroad, he has steadily eroded the democratic process at home, where Hungary's political opposition has been marginalized and civil society watchdogs have a diminished voice.[551] Without the critical scrutiny provided by political opposition or civil society, Russian malign influence is able to spread with little resistance.

The Hungarian public does not seem to share Orbán's affinity for Russia or his antagonism toward western institutions. According to a survey by the think tank GLOBSEC, 79 percent of Hungarians want to stay in the EU and 61 percent think the union is a good thing.[552] A resounding 81 percent of Hungarians believe that NATO is important for their safety and 71 percent believe that liberal democracy is the best political system for Hungary, as opposed to an autocracy.[553] However, 45 percent of Hungarians hold a favorable view of Orban, a number nearly matched by Vladimir Putin, who was seen sympathetically by 44 percent of Hungarians.[554]

The international community, working through existing watchdog efforts like the EU East StratCom Task Force, should aggressively uncover and publicize the scope and scale of Russian influence in Hungary.[555] Orbán appears to have cast his lot with Moscow, but the Hungarian people chose a western path after the fall of communism and continue to embrace those values. With parliamentary elections due in the spring of 2018, the international community should proactively seek to build resilience within the Hungarian population so that they are made fully aware of the level of Russian interference in the affairs of the country.

Lessons Learned

- *Opposing the Asymmetric Arsenal without a Government Partner is Difficult, But not Impossible:* As the United States and its allies look to build resilience to Russian interference in Europe, they will unfortunately not find a partner in the Hungarian government. Regardless, the international community should increase support for transparency and anti-corruption efforts in the country—the denial of U.S. visas for six Hun-

[549] Budapest Times, "Paks Data to Be Classified for 30 Years," *The Budapest Times,* Mar. 6, 2015.

[550] Zoltan Simon, "Orbán Says He Seeks to End Liberal Democracy in Hungary," *Bloomberg,* July 28, 2014.

[551] Daniel Hegedus, "Nations in Transit 2017 Hungary Chapter," *Freedom House,* 2017.

[552] GLOBSEC Policy Institute, *GLOBSEC Trends 2017: Mixed Messages and Signs of Hope from Central and Eastern Europe,* at 13 (Jan. 8, 2017).

[553] *Ibid.* at 20.

[554] *Ibid.* at 23.

[555] *See* European Union External Action Service, "Questions and Answers about the East StratCom Task Force," https://eeas.europa.eu/headquarters/headquarters-homepage/2116/-questions-and-answers-about-the-east-stratcom-task-force—en (visited Dec. 14, 2017); see also Chapter 7.

garian officials suspected of corruption in 2014, for example, was an effective step that should be replicated when possible.[556]

---

[556] Rick Lyman, "U.S. Denial of Visas for 6 in Hungary Strains Ties," *The New York Times,* Oct. 20, 2014.

Chapter 6: Kremlin Interference in Consolidated Democracies [557]

Countries with long-standing membership in the European Union or NATO are increasingly aware of the nature and scope of Russian government threats to their populations and democratic processes, and have developed a series of strong responses to deter and defend against Kremlin interference. Geographically, these countries are further away from the eastern flanks of NATO and the EU, and are generally less susceptible to Russian cultural, political, or linguistic influences, yet many remain vulnerable to Russian government threats to their energy security. While these countries benefit from healthy democratic political systems and vibrant independent media and civil societies, the bonds within these systems have come under increasing strain as societal frustrations have grown over economic inequalities and the pressures of migration. These societal tensions have been a focus for exploitation by the Russian government.

The Russian tactics of interference follow two main trends in this region. First, Russia seeks to exacerbate divisions within countries that have membership in Western institutions like NATO and the EU, but where corruption or vulnerabilities in the rule of law provide openings to erode their bonds to European values and institutions. This includes undermining their support for EU sanctions on Russia or NATO exercises on the continent. A primary goal is to sow discord and confusion—since more frontal attacks by the Kremlin against these states are likely to invite unacceptable blowback for the Russian government.

Second, Russia seeks to exacerbate divisions in consolidated democracies who are seen as the flagbearers for European values and institutions, and thus staunchly opposed to the Russian government's agenda to undermine those values and institutions. And in its attempts to weaken the democratic systems of these nations, the Kremlin amplifies their perceived weaknesses and problems to countries on Russia's periphery, in an attempt to show that consolidated democracy is not a goal worth pursuing.

---

[557] The countries in this chapter are defined as "consolidated democracies," a term drawn from the Freedom House Nations in Transit study, which ranks and measures the progress toward or backsliding from democracy of 29 countries from Central Europe to Central Asia. The ranking is determined by an assessment of a country's national democratic governance, electoral process, civil society, independent media, local democratic governance, judicial framework and independence, and corruption. Countries receiving the consolidated democracy classification are defined as ones that "embody the best policies and practices of liberal democracy, but may face challenges—often associated with corruption—that contribute to a slightly lower score." Freedom House, *Nations in Transit 2017: The False Promise of Populism*, at 22 (2017).

BALTIC STATES: LATVIA, LITHUANIA, AND ESTONIA

The Russian government has sought to influence the Baltic countries through military intimidation, energy dependence, trade relations, business links, cultural ties, corruption, disinformation, and cyberattacks. As in Ukraine, the Kremlin has used the Baltics as a laboratory for its malign influence activities, especially in deploying hackers to engage in cyberwarfare.

Because of their relatively small size, large Russian-speaking populations in Latvia and Estonia, and geographic proximity to Russia, the Baltic countries are subject to more intensive pressure from the Kremlin than other EU countries. Lithuania's Ambassador to the United States testified to the U.S. Senate that, in addition to aggressive intelligence operations and cyberattacks on members of parliament, the Kremlin has also "used supply of energy resources, investment in strategically important sectors of economy and trade relations as a tool to influence domestic and foreign policy of Lithuania." [558] Latvia's head intelligence agency has said that Russia is responsible for "the most significant security threats in the Baltic sea region," [559] and Lithuania's government has called Russia "a major source of threats posed to the national security of the Republic of Lithuania." [560] In addition, all three presidents of the Baltic states have also taken strong and public positions against the Kremlin's disinformation campaigns and supported building resiliency against them. [561]

The Kremlin has long used the Baltic states as a testing ground for its asymmetric arsenal. One infamous incident occurred on a morning in late April 2007, when the government of Estonia decided to move a six-and-a-half-foot statue of a Soviet soldier out of the center of its capital, Tallinn, to another part of town. Removing the statue, placed there during Soviet occupation in 1947, was a controversial act—protests by ethnic Russians and violence the night before had damaged property, injured dozens, and left one person dead. Russia's Foreign Minister, Sergey Lavrov, called the move "blasphemous." Other Russian officials declared that removing the statue was glorifying Nazism, and both the Duma and the Federation Council called on Putin to sanction Estonia or cut off bilateral relations. [562]

What happened next was described by Estonia's then-president, Toomas Hendrik Ilves, as "the first time a nation-state had been targeted using digital means for political objectives." [563] The Inter-

---

[558] Statement of Rolandas Krisciunas, Ambassador of the Republic of Lithuania, *Russian Policies & Intentions Toward Specific European Countries,* Hearing before the U.S. Senate Committee on Appropriations Subcommittee on State, Foreign Operations, and Related Programs, Mar. 7, 2017, at 8.

[559] The Constitution Protection Bureau of the Republic of Latvia, *Annual Public Report 2016,* at 1 (Mar. 2017). The Constitution Protection Bureau (SAB) is one of three state security institutions of the Republic of Latvia, and is responsible for foreign intelligence and counter-intelligence. *Ibid.*

[560] State Security Department and Ministry of National Defense of Lithuania, *National Security Threat Assessment 2017,* at 2.

[561] Eriks Selga & Benjamin Rasmussen. "Defending the West from Russian Disinformation: The Role of Leadership" Foreign Policy Research Institute, Nov. 13, 2017

[562] Steven Lee Myers, "Russia Rebukes Estonia for Moving Soviet Statue," *The New York Times,* Apr. 27, 2007.

[563] Statement of Toomas Hendrik Ilves, Former President of Estonia, *The Modus Operandi and Toolbox of Russia and Other Autocracies for Undermining Democracies Throughout the World,* Hearing before the U.S. Senate Judiciary Subcommittee on Crime and Terrorism, Mar. 15, 2017, at 3.

net servers of the country's government, security, banking, and media institutions were hit by distributed denial of service (DDoS) attacks for two straight weeks, causing many of their websites to go down.[564] Ilves believes the attack was coordinated by the Kremlin and executed by organized criminal groups, "a public-private partnership" with "a state actor that paid mafiosos."[565] As a senior former Pentagon official told *The New Yorker*, the attack showed that "Russia was going to react in a new but aggressive way to perceived political slights."[566]

The Kremlin's disinformation operations in the Baltics, especially in Latvia and Estonia, are mostly aimed at the countries' Russian-speaking populations (which constitute nearly 27 percent of the population in Latvia and 25 percent in Estonia, compared to just under 6 percent in Lithuania).[567] After the fall of the Soviet Union, the Russian government's disinformation campaigns in the 1990s were largely directed at post-communist states like Poland and the Baltics. While serving as Estonia's ambassador to the United States in the first half of the 1990s, Ilves recalled having to respond to Western diplomats who showed him false news stories about his country. At the time, he said, Russian government disinformation was "primarily an exercise in providing new democracies extra work to debunk invented news."[568] While a factor, these measures did not have much of an impact in societies accustomed to questioning the veracity of Soviet propaganda efforts, and their half-hearted nature reflects the sclerotic state of the Russian security services at the time. But over the past decade, the Kremlin has supercharged its disinformation operations in the Baltics. Those efforts, which also include the use of internet trolls and NGOs, seek to portray the countries "as failures—blighted by emigration and poverty—and run by a sinister elite of Western puppets with ill-disguised fascist sympathies."[569]

In the Baltic states, the Kremlin's influence operations in the region appear to seek several objectives:

- Divide the populations along ethnic lines to establish and maintain control over the local Russian diaspora, which can be used as a tool of influence.
- Create mistrust among the general population toward their own governments by portraying them as ethnocratic regimes that are overseeing the rebirth of fascism.
- Undermine Western values and democracy and promote populism and radicalism, especially by emphasizing the West's degradation while playing up Russia's growing prosperity.
- Weaken or paralyze the alliances Baltic states belong to, like NATO and the EU, especially by portraying their governments

---

[564] Evan Osnos et al., "Trump, Putin, and the New Cold War," *The New Yorker*, Mar. 6, 2016.
[565] *Ibid.*
[566] *Ibid.*
[567] Tomas Cizik, "Russia Tailors Its Information Warfare to Specific Countries," *European Security Journal*, Nov. 6, 2017.
[568] Statement of Toomas Hendrik Ilves, Former President of Estonia, *The Modus Operandi and Toolbox of Russia and Other Autocracies for Undermining Democracies Throughout the World*, Hearing before the Senate Judiciary Subcommittee on Crime and Terrorism, Mar. 15, 2017, at 5.
[569] Edward Lucas, *The Coming Storm: Baltic Sea Security Report*, Center for European Policy Analysis, at 11 (June 2015).

as puppets of those supranational organizations that are being used to provoke Russia into military conflict.

- Ridicule or marginalize the culture, history, traditions, and achievements of the Baltic states, to weaken the will of local populations to defend their countries in the event of a military conflict with Russia.

Multiple studies have found that Russian-speaking populations in the Baltics have absorbed the narratives that the Kremlin's propaganda machines have concocted. For example, during the war between Russia and Georgia in 2008, the majority of ethnic Russians in Estonia were more likely to believe reports from Russian media than Estonian and foreign media. A similar result occurred during the conflict between Russia and Ukraine, with ethnic Russians in Latvia and Estonia believing the narrative put forth by Russian media and subsequently holding Kiev, not Moscow, responsible for the conflict.[570]

Pro-Russian narratives are also promoted by Kremlin-linked groups throughout the Baltic states. A 2014 report commissioned by the Swedish Defense Research Agency found that a large number of organizations that are directly or indirectly governed by the Russian federal government are helping to implement a strategy that aims to undermine "the self-confidence of the Baltic states as independent political entities" and interfere in their domestic political affairs.[571] The study also concluded that these efforts were all "reinforced by systematic Russian attempts—through political, media and cultural outlets—to portray the Baltic states as 'fascist', not least in terms of their treatment of their Russian minorities .... As a whole, the Russian strategy can be considered as aiming at destabilizing the Baltic states."[572]

The head of the Latvian security service also reported that there is a clear link between organizations that promote the Kremlin's narrative and Russian-funded NGOs.[573] According to the Baltic Centre for Investigative Journalism, also known as *re:Baltica,* more than 40 NGOs in the Baltics have received grants from large Russian GONGOs (government-controlled NGOs) over the past several years, though the figure could be much higher as NGOs are not required to publish financial reports in every Baltic country.[574] Furthermore, nearly 70 percent of those grant recipients are linked to pro-Kremlin political parties in the Baltics.[575] Disbursing grants to NGOs is an important element of Russia's "compatriots policy," which the Kremlin has stated involves "always defend[ing] [the interests of Russians and Russian-speakers abroad] using political, diplomatic, and legal means."[576] The director of Estonia's domestic intelligence service has noted that "the Russian population or the Russian-speaking minority is a target for the so-called compatriots

---

[570] Vladislava Vojtiskova et al., *The Bear in Sheep's Clothing: Russia's Government-Funded Organisations in the EU,* Wilfried Martens Centre for European Studies, at 63 (July 2016).
[571] Mike Winnerstig *Tools of Destablization: Russian Soft Power and Non-military Influence in the Baltic States,* Swedish Defense Research Agency, at 4 (Dec. 2014).
[572] *Ibid.*
[573] *Ibid.* at 61
[574] Sanita Jemberga et al., "Money From Russia: Kremlin's Millions," *re:Balitca,* Aug. 27, 2015. For more on Russia's use of GONGOs, see Chapter 2.
[575] *Ibid.*
[576] Heather A. Conley et al., *The Kremlin Playbook: Understanding Russian Influence in Central and Eastern Europe,* Center for Strategic & International Studies, at 51 (Oct. 2016).

103

policy, the goal of which has been the establishment of organized groups linked to Russia capable of influencing another country's sovereign decisions."[577]

The Kremlin allegedly uses its embassies in the Baltics to disburse funding to NGOs that promote its narrative. According to the Lithuanian ambassador to the United States, the "Russian Embassy in Lithuania directly controls, coordinates, and finances [the] activities [of a] variety of pro-Russian organizations, clubs and groups ranging from political protests to cultural events."[578] Yet sometimes the culture of corruption among the Russian government bureaucracy can hamper the Kremlin's disinformation efforts, with embassy officials reportedly taking kickbacks from organizations that receive grants. For example, in 2016, the Russian embassy in Estonia disbursed $30,000 in grant money for the publication of the *Baltiysky Mir* journal. However, no issue was published in 2016, and Estonia's lead security agency notes that "the best way to receive grants [from the Russian embassy] is to share them with Russian officials and diplomats."[579]

Estonia's government also reports that "[t]he Kremlin constantly supports and funds people who promote anti-Estonian propaganda narratives at events held by international organizations" such as the Organization for Security and Co-operation in Europe, where Estonian "activists," whose travel was paid for by the Russian government, complained about government suppression of the ethnic Russian minority in Estonia.[580] And in one example from 2015, a skinhead from St. Petersburg "was sent to Estonia to be captured on film as a 'local Nazi activist'" at a WWII battle memorial, and "Kremlin-controlled media was eager to pick this up as an example of events in Estonia."[581]

Kremlin disinformation operations have also targeted NATO exercises, especially after NATO established four multinational battlegroups led by the United Kingdom, Canada, Germany, and the United States, known as the Enhanced Forward Presence (EFP), to deter Russian military aggression in the Baltics and Poland. Pro-Kremlin media outlets falsely reported that German troops raped a 13-year-old Lithuanian girl just two days after the soldiers arrived to participate in NATO's EFP exercise.[582] Because of its similarity to a fake story pushed in German media, it became known as the "Lithuania Lisa" case.[583] Ambassador Sorin Ducaru, NATO's Assistant Secretary General for Emerging Security Challenges, noted that it was "a clear example of information manipulation with a sense of weaponization, because it really was supposed

[577] Michael Weiss, "The Estonian Spymasters: Tallin's Revolutionary Approach to Stopping Russian Spies," *Foreign Affairs,* June 3, 2014.
[578] Statement of Rolandas Krisciunas, Ambassador of the Republic of Lithuania, *Russian Policies & Intentions Toward Specific European Countries,* Hearing before the U.S. Senate Committee on Appropriations Subcommittee on State, Foreign Operations, and Related Programs, Mar. 7, 2017, at 10.
[579] Estonian Internal Security Service, *Estonian Internal Security Service Annual Review 2016,* at 8 (Apr. 17, 2017).
[580] *Ibid.* at 7.
[581] *Ibid.* at 8.
[582] 582 Statement of Toomas Hendrik Ilves, Former President of Estonia, *The Modus Operandi and Toolbox of Russia and Other Autocracies for Undermining Democracies Throughout the World,* Hearing before the Senate Judiciary Subcommittee on Crime and Terrorism, Mar. 15, 2017, at 6.
[583] *See* Damien McGuinness, "Russia Steps into Berlin 'Rape' Storm Claiming German Cover-Up," *BBC News,* Jan. 27, 2016; infra, section on Germany.

to affect the perception about the presence of German troops as the [EFP] framework nation in Lithuania. It was supposed to affect morale; it was supposed to affect everything—the operational functioning."[584]

Before another NATO exercise, hackers infiltrated the Lithuanian military's website and replaced the statement announcing the exercise with a fake one proclaiming that it was part of a plan for Lithuania to annex Kaliningrad, a small Russian exclave to the west. The head of Lithuania's National Cyber Security Center noted that the announcement was obviously fake and quickly taken down, but still spread through online networks and colored discussions about NATO. He summarized the effectiveness of such disinformation operations when he told a reporter that "I don't believe in aliens, but if you see enough articles about aliens visiting Earth, you start to think 'Who knows, maybe the government is hiding something.'"[585]

As elsewhere in Europe and beyond, an extensive network of social media bots spread Kremlin disinformation narratives. According to a report by the NATO Strategic Communications Centre of Excellence, bot-generated messages are targeted at different audiences: those aimed at the West emphasize how much smaller Russian exercises are than NATO ones, while those targeting domestic audiences rarely mention Russian military exercises.[586] In addition, approximately 70 percent of all Russian messages about NATO in the Baltics and Poland are created by Russian-language bots. NATO's report also found that Twitter was less effective at removing Russian-language material generated by bots than messages in English, but did note improvement in the platform's policing of content and urged continued pressure to ensure further improvements.[587] NATO's analysts also noted that "increased interest by Twitter and other social media companies in tackling state-sponsored trolls and bots may offer an explanation for the low levels of activity in the current observation window."[588] That conclusion underscores the point that social media companies have not only great responsibility, but also strong potential to successfully counter Kremlin disinformation operations (and fake news in general).

The Baltic states have all taken concerted actions against Russian state-sponsored propaganda outlets, with methods ranging from outright censorship to public disregard. Since 2014, Latvia and Lithuania have placed restrictions on several Russian television channels, including three-to six-month bans on one station owned by a Russian state broadcaster, because of what government authorities deemed to be dangerous and unbalanced reporting on the situation in Ukraine, incitement of discord and unrest, and warmongering.[589] In March 2016, Latvia's local domain registry

[584] Teri Schultz, "Why the 'Fake Rape' Story Against German NATO Forces Fell Flat in Lithuania," *Deutsche Welle*, Feb. 23, 2017.
[585] Andrew Higgins, "Foes of Russia Say Child Pornography Is Planted to Ruin Them," *The New York Times*, Dec. 9, 2016.
[586] NATO Strategic Communications Centre of Excellence, *Robotrolling 2017*, Issue 2, at 2, 4 (Nov. 8, 2017).
[587] *Ibid.* at 2.
[588] *Ibid.* at 6.
[589] Congressional Research Service, "European Efforts to Counter Russian Influence Operations," July 24, 2017.

suspended Sputnik's domestic website (Sputniknews.lv) a few weeks after it was established, with a Foreign Ministry spokesman declaring that "we don't regard Sputnik as a credible media source but as something else: a propaganda tool."[590] Sputnik responded by placing its content under a .com domain and accusing Latvia of attacking media freedom.[591]

The Estonian government, while not censoring the activities of Kremlin-sponsored media outlets, has publicly stated that it does not recognize Sputnik as an independent media outlet and therefore its officials will not grant the organization any interviews. Estonia also established three Russian-language TV channels to provide alternate sources of news to its large Russian-speaking population; a poll from 2016 showed that the stations had captured about 20 percent of that audience.[592] The Baltic states also have educational awareness programs that aim to counter the influence of Kremlin disinformation, such as a national information influence identification and analysis ecosystem project in Lithuania, which quickly noticed the fake story about the alleged rape of a teenage girl by a German soldier during a NATO exercise and worked to immediately debunk it.[593] Latvia's ministries of defense and education have also paired up to improve their country's school curriculum to emphasize critical thinking skills and media literacy.[594] Furthermore, the Baltic Centre for Media Excellence (BCME), based in Latvia, serves as a hub for professional Russian-language journalism in the Baltics as well as the countries of the Eastern Partnership. The BCME also supports media literacy programs and research to better understand audiences that are most susceptible to propaganda.[595]

In addition to counter-disinformation efforts by the state and the media, a network of hundreds of concerned citizens has sprung up in the Baltics (starting in Lithuania but later spreading to Latvia and Estonia, and even Finland) to fight against Kremlin-linked internet trolls. Styling themselves "elves," they push back against false comments on Facebook and on Lithuanian news websites, working not to promote their own propaganda but only to, in the words of their founder, "expose the bullshit." The elves have even taken their activities onto the street, counter-demonstrating at pro-Kremlin events, draped in EU and U.S. flags and wearing large smiles—thereby making it that much more difficult for Kremlin propagandists to get their desired photos and videos of "spontaneous" anti-Western protests.[596]

Estonia has the best Russian counterintelligence program in Europe, according to journalist Edward Lucas, author of *Deception:*

[590] "Latvia Blocks Russian Sputnik Site as Kremlin 'Propaganda Tool'," Radio Free Europe/Radio Liberty, Mar. 30, 2016.
[591] Alex Spence, "Russia Accusses Latvia of 'Blatant Censorship' After Sputnik News Site is Shut Down," *Politico*, Mar. 30, 2016.
[592] "US Challenges Kremlin with New Russian TV Channel," *Daily Mail*, Feb. 27, 2017.
[593] Statement of Rolandas Krisciunas, Ambassador of the Republic of Lithuania, *Russian Policies & Intentions Toward Specific European Countries*, Hearing before the U.S. Senate Committee on Appropriations Subcommittee on State, Foreign Operations, and Related Programs, Mar. 7, 2017, at 6.
[594] Reid Standish, "Russia's Neighbors Respond to Putin's 'Hybrid War,'" *Foreign Policy*, Oct. 12, 2017.
[595] "Baltic Centre for Media Excellence," *European Endowment for Democracy*, 2017.
[596] Michael Weiss, "The Baltic Elves Taking on Pro-Russian Trolls," *The Daily Beast*, Mar. 20, 2016.

Spies, Lies, and How Russia Dupes the West. As then Estonian president Toomas Hendrik Ilves told *Foreign Affairs* in 2014: "We caught four moles in the last five years. That means one of two things. Either we're the only country in the EU with a mole problem, or we're the only country in the EU doing anything about it."[597] Estonia has adopted a "zero tolerance" approach to illegal activities by Russian intelligence operatives and does not downplay their capture or trade them back to Russia. Instead, it prosecutes them to the maximum extent of the law and publicizes an annual report that reviews major cases and publicly names organizations and individuals that are suspected of working with the Russian intelligence services.[598]

Estonia's intelligence service, known as Kapo, publishes annual reviews that detail activities by Russian intelligence services and the government's responses (as do Latvia and Lithuania).[599] Perhaps the most egregious case it documented in recent years was the incursion into sovereign Estonian territory and the alleged kidnapping of an Estonian Kapo officer by Russian security operatives in 2014.[600] The officer had been investigating cross-border cigarette smuggling by Russian smugglers, and some assert that he was kidnapped because he had threatened the FSB's lucrative collaboration with criminal traffickers.[601] Smugglers have also reportedly been recruited by the security services as spies and informants to assist the Kremlin's efforts to destabilize Estonia. Similar to the recruiting method the FSB uses with hackers, traffickers are reportedly threatened with jail time if they refuse to cooperate with Russia's security services.[602]

These comprehensive intelligence reports also help to inform the general public as well as civil society and journalists, who can use the information pursue their own investigations. For example, *re:Baltica* reporters used a clue from Kapo's 2014 report to trace the ownership of three Baltic Russian-language news sites, collectively known as *Baltnews*, through a chain of holding companies that ultimately linked them to Russia's state-sponsored propaganda network.[603]

Kapo's reports also make clear the intentions and capabilities of the Kremlin's influence operations, especially when it comes to economic corruption, and how that knowledge informs its own work. For example, in its 2016 report, the agency noted that "Because of the link between Russian power structures, criminal circles and corruption, we especially focus on corruption that may strengthen Russia's hold on our state. We have noted attempts by the Kremlin to use business contacts and business influence in shaping Estonia's policy. Relevant in this context is the business continuity and

[597] Michael Weiss, "The Estonian Spymasters: Tallin's Revolutionary Approach to Stopping Russian Spies," *Foreign Affairs*, June 3, 2014.
[598] *Ibid.*
[599] "Annual Reviews," Kaitsepolitseiamet, https://www.kapo.ee/en/content/annual-reviews.html (visited on Dec. 31, 2017)
[600] Andrew Higgins, "Tensions Surge in Estonia Amid a Russian Replay of Cold War Tactics," *The New York Times*, Oct. 5, 2014.
[601] *Ibid.*
[602] Holger Roonemaa, "These Cigarette Smugglers Are On The Frontlines Of Russia's Spy Wars," *BuzzFeed News*, Sept. 13, 2017.
[603] Inga Springe & Sanita Jemberga, "Sputnik's Unknown Brother," *re:Balitca*, Apr. 6, 2017,

supply security of energy, where the role of corruption can secretly and considerably influence the country's energy independence."[604]

The Baltic states have thus made it a priority to reduce their historical dependence on energy supplies from Russia. After independence, their legacy gas infrastructure was only connected to countries of the former Soviet Union, not Europe. Russia's state-owned Gazprom and other Russian gas companies held large stakes—up to 50 percent—in Baltic states' natural gas companies, though new EU regulatory requirements led Gazprom to start selling its shares in those companies in 2014. To diversify its supplies, Lithuania opened an LNG regasification terminal in 2014, which has also allowed it to negotiate much better prices for its purchases from Russia (in 2013 Gazprom charged Lithuania $460-$490 per 1,000 cubic meters, compared to an average of $370-$380 for the EU).[605] At the opening ceremony of the terminal, Lithuania's president remarked, "Nobody else, from now on, will be able to dictate to us the price of gas, or to buy our political will."[606] There is also the potential for Lithuania to export some of the LNG it has imported and regasified to its Baltic neighbors, though such infrastructure is not in place yet.

As one of the most connected countries in the world, Estonia has long been a leader in the realm of internet innovation and cyber security. In 2004, Estonia proposed a NATO cyber defense center, which was established in Tallinn in 2008 and consists of six branches focused on technology, strategy, operations, law, education and training, and support.[607] Estonia is also working to strengthen the security of its online voting system by overhauling its software and adding new anti-tampering features that will help guard against potential hacking attacks directed by the Kremlin or other malicious actors.[608]

Latvia, Lithuania, and Estonia are clearly on the front line of the Kremlin's malign influence operations, and have suffered from some of the most egregious cyberattacks and disinformation campaigns yet seen in Russia's near abroad. As members of NATO and the EU that share borders both with Russia and its exclave of Kaliningrad, and which collectively host large Russian-speaking populations, the Baltic states are both primary targets and uniquely susceptible to Russian active measures campaigns. The United States should therefore make it a high priority to study the experiences of the Baltics and apply lessons learned to its own defenses and those of allies and partners around Europe, as well as increase support to the Baltics, in both word and deed, to further deter Kremlin aggression.

[604] Estonian Internal Security Service, *Estonian Internal Security Service Annual Review 2016*, at 35 (Apr. 17, 2017).

[605] Aija Krutaine & Andrius Sytas, "Baltics Can Keep Lights On If Russia Turns Off the Gas," *Reuters*, May 7, 2014.

[606] Georgi Kantchev, "With U.S. Gas, Europe Seeks Escape From Russia's Energy Grip," *The Wall Street Journal*, Feb. 25, 2016.

[607] NATO Cooperative Cyber Defence Centre of Excellence, "About Us," https://ccdcoe.org (visited Dec. 31, 2017).

[608] Ott Ummelas, "World's Most High-Tech Voting System to Get New Hacking Defenses," *Bloomberg Politics*, July 18, 2017.

108

Lessons Learned

- *Public Reporting of Intelligence Findings is Effective:* Exposing and publicizing the nature of the threat of Russian malign influence activities can be an action-forcing event that not only boosts public awareness, but also drives effective responses from the private sector, especially social media platforms, as well as civil society and independent media, who can use the information to pursue their own investigations.

- *Strong Cyber Defenses are Critical:* Estonia was one of the first states to experience cyberwar operations, and the Baltic states are under constant threat from Russia-based hackers. Strong cyber defenses are therefore key to building resilience against the Kremlin's influence operations. The United States can assist the Baltic states to improve their cyber defenses against malicious hacking by Kremlin-sponsored entities. One method would be to work with the EU to train and support emergency cyber response teams that can be immediately deployed to assist allies that are under cyberattack from malicious state or non-state actors. The United States can also learn from Estonia's experience in dealing with cyberattacks on critical infrastructure targets, including the energy grid and electoral systems.

- *Cultural Exports & Exchanges Can Enhance Resilience:* To assist the Baltics, Lithuania's ambassador to the United States believes that more American popular culture in Lithuania would help neutralize the Kremlin's active measures. *Voice of America and Radio Free Europe/Radio Liberty* programs are increasingly well-known in the Baltics, and combining popular entertainment programming with respected and independent news reporting would further their reach and influence. Lithuania's ambassador has also called for more and better-funded cultural exchange programs, including study abroad and journalist training. These measures should be supported by the U.S. government.[609]

---

[609] Statement of Rolandas Krisciunas, Ambassador of the Republic of Lithuania, *Russian Policies & Intentions Toward Specific European Countries,* Hearing before the U.S. Senate Committee on Appropriations Subcommittee on State, Foreign Operations, and Related Programs, Mar. 7, 2017, at 6.

NORDIC STATES: DENMARK, FINLAND, NORWAY, AND SWEDEN

When it comes to asserting that the West is in a state of moral decline, a favorite target of the Kremlin's propaganda machine are the Nordic states of Finland, Sweden, Denmark, and Norway—all members of the EU, and the latter two also members of NATO. For example, in 2017, one of Russia's largest TV stations broadcast a story that claimed Denmark's government had permitted the opening of an animal brothel in Copenhagen. The story, which included an image of a dog dressed up as a street prostitute, evolved in classic "ping pong" fashion, moving from a fringe online publication before being picked up in periphery countries like Belarus and Georgia and several marginal Russian media outlets. Ironically, this false report had first been published as just that—the original source was a satirical French website that posted the story as parody.[610]

But when it comes to exhibiting strong immunity against Russian malign influence operations, the Nordic states are also exemplary. Several factors contribute to their resilience. First, Russia's favorability ratings among the populations of the Nordic countries are lower than anywhere else in the EU.[611] In addition, the Nordic states have extraordinary educational systems that emphasize critical thinking skills, as well as relatively high levels of interpersonal trust and extremely low levels of corruption (of the 176 countries ranked in Transparency International's 2016 corruption index, all four Nordic countries ranked within the six least corrupt countries).[612] While correlation does not prove causation, it would not be surprising if the absence of Russian corrupt influences, as well as strong critical thinking skills that inoculate against the effects of disinformation, are major contributing factors to the low opinion of Russia held among Nordic populations. In addition, the Nordic states have dealt with Moscow's aggression for decades, and their populations arguably have a built-in skepticism of and resistance to the Kremlin's disinformation campaigns and other malign influence operations.

Due to these factors, the Kremlin's traditional propaganda operations have had very little success in the Nordic countries. Sputnik closed its Danish, Finnish, Swedish, and Norwegian language services in 2016. Some analysts attributed the withdrawal to economic conditions in Russia, while others attributed it to the poor performance of outlets, which had poor command of the Nordic languages and found that conspiracy theories and attacks on European values did not have much traction among Nordic audiences.[613]

With the disappearance of traditional propaganda outlets, internet trolls are now the primary pro-Russia disinformation actors in Nordic countries, and they primarily focus on individual targets. Russia-affiliated activists have gone to great lengths to intimidate journalists who report on Russia, especially those carrying out in-

610 "No, Denmark is Not Legalising Sexual Abuse of Animals," *EU vs. Disinfo*, Sept. 9, 2017.
611 "How EU Members View Russia," *Radio Free Europe/Radio Liberty*, https://www.rferl.org/a/28200070.html (visited Dec. 31, 2017) (citing Special Eurobarometer 451—Future of Europe, Oct. 2016).
612 Esteban Ortiz-Ospina & Max Roser, "Trust," Our World in Data, https://ourworldindata.org/trust#note-2 (visited Dec. 31, 2017); Transparency International, *Corruption Perceptions Index 2016*, (Jan. 25, 2017).
613 European External Action Service, "Disinformation Digest," Mar. 18, 2016.

vestigations on the trolls themselves, like Finnish reporter Jessikka Aro, who "has been peppered with abusive emails, vilified as a drug dealer on social media sites and mocked as a delusional bimbo in a music video posted on YouTube."[614] The head of Norway's national police has also accused Russia's intelligence services of targeting Norwegian individuals, especially those with dual citizenship or family members in Russia.[615]

In Finland, which shares an 830-mile border with Russia, Russian disinformation campaigns intensified in 2012, when Kremlin-linked media outlets used doctored photos to accuse Finnish authorities of child abduction in custody battles between Finnish-Russian couples.[616] And in the lead up to its 2015 parliamentary elections, several Twitter accounts, all with official-sounding names that appeared to be linked to Finland's parliament, began tweeting about popular political topics.[617] Initially, the tweets contained content that was considered reasonable and contributed to mainstream discussion, which earned the accounts a relatively large following among people who reportedly thought they were official parliament accounts. Then, just before the election, the accounts took a sharp turn and began tweeting misinformation and fringe viewpoints in an attempt to "muddy the waters," according to Finnish government officials. The officials noted that the attempt was somewhat clumsy and did not accomplish its aims, however they also pointed out that "genuine clumsiness should not lead to complacency."[618]

In that vein, Finnish government officials report that the country is strengthening its "whole-of-society preparedness system ... to take into account the new hybrid challenges," including by focusing on media literacy skills.[619] With the Ukraine crisis and refugee and migrant issues in mind, the government recently recruited two U.S. experts from Harvard and MIT to work with over 100 Finnish officials on how to best counter disinformation campaigns. Jed Willard from Harvard emphasized to participants that the focus should not be on the Kremlin's narrative, but the Finnish narrative—that "the best way to respond ... is with a positive Finnish story."[620] Finland has also recognized the challenge of providing immigrant populations, who may not speak the national language, with news outlets in their native language that can serve as alternatives to outlets from their countries of origin. To that end, in May 2013, Finland's state-owned television station, *Yle*, began a daily Russian-language TV news broadcast to offer a Finnish perspective to its Russian-speaking minority of approximately 70,000 people.[621] *Yle* has a reported viewership of about 200,000 for its five-minute broadcast, which can also be seen in Russia.[622] Finland has also

[614] Andrew Higgins, "Effort to Expose Russia's 'Troll Army' Draws Vicious Retaliation," *The New York Times*, May 30, 2016.
[615] Thomas Nilsen, "Norway's PST Says Russian Intelligence Targets Individuals," *The Independent Barents Observer*, Feb. 3, 2017.
[616] Reid Standish, "Why is Finland Able to Fend off Putin's Information War?" *Foreign Policy*, Mar. 1, 2017.
[617] Committee Staff Discussion with Finnish Government Officials, 2017.
[618] *Ibid.*
[619] Embassy of Finland, Information Provided in Response to Questions from U.S. Senator Ben Cardin, Sept. 20, 2017.
[620] "US Experts Gird Finnish Officials for Information War," *Yle News*, Jan. 22, 2016.
[621] Yle Uutiset, "Yle's Russian Service: A Quarter-Century of News and Controversy," Oct. 10, 2015.
[622] *Ibid.*

led the establishment of the European Centre of Excellence for Countering Hybrid Threats, based in Helsinki, which will serve as think tank and fusion center for EU and NATO efforts across several lines of effort, including disinformation (see Chapter 7).

The Nordic states continue to raise their populations' awareness of and resiliency to Kremlin disinformation campaigns. In advance of a military exercise in Sweden, which also included the other Nordic states, the Baltics, and the United States, the defense ministries of Sweden and Denmark released a joint statement announcing their intention to team up to deter Russian government cyberattacks and disinformation operations.[623] And Sweden, which will hold elections in 2018, has begun ramping up its defenses against disinformation operations through its Swedish Civil Contingencies Agency (MSB). The agency has picked up on fake news stories that push narratives claiming that Sweden is a war zone and the rape capital of Europe, and that it has banned Christmas lights and the eating of bacon on trains.[624] Echoing the U.S. experts hired by Finland, the head of MSB's global analysis and monitoring section, Mikael Tofvesson, has emphasized that the MSB's strategy is not to fight fire with fire, noting that:

> "It's like mudwrestling a pig. You'll both get dirty, but the pig will think it's quite nice. This plays into their hands, whereas for us getting dirty is just a pain. Instead, we have to try to stay clean and focus on the part of our society that has to work: democracy and freedom of expression, to make sure that giving the citizens correct information becomes our best form of resistance."[625]

Sweden has also introduced curriculum into its primary schools to teach "digital competence," including how to differentiate between reliable and unreliable sources.[626] Even Bamse the Bear, one of Sweden's most popular cartoon characters, has been recruited to help children learn about the dangers of fake news and the need to cross check sources of information.[627]

Denmark is also working to counter the Russian government's malign influence operations, with the country's Ministry of Foreign Affairs noting that "the threat [from the Kremlin] against Denmark and Europe is significantly different and more serious than at any other time following the fall of the Berlin Wall" and disinformation campaigns aimed at the public illustrate "how elements of domestic and foreign policy are inextricably linked and require close cooperation across various Danish authorities."[628] To that end, the Ministry of Foreign Affairs has recently established a new unit dedicated to countering pro-Kremlin disinformation

---

[623] Morgan Chalfant, "Denmark, Sweden Team Up to Counter Russian 'Fake News,'" *The Hill*, Aug. 31, 2017.

[624] Emma Lofgren, "How Sweden's Getting Ready for the Election-Year Information War," *The Local*, Nov. 7, 2017.

[625] *Ibid.*

[626] Lee Roden, "Swedish Kids to Learn Computer Coding and How to Spot Fake News in Primary school," *The Local*, Mar. 13, 2017.

[627] Lee Roden, "Why This Swedish Comic Hero Is Going To Teach Kids About Fake News," *The Local*, Jan. 16, 2017.

[628] Ministry of Foreign Affairs of Denmark, *Foreign and Security Policy Strategy, 2017-2018*, at 14, 15 (June 2017).

campaigns.[629] The unit will also lead an interagency task force that includes the Ministry of Defense and the intelligence services. Denmark is also actively promoting cyber defense cooperation among the EU, UN, and NATO, and has begun training its soldiers that participate in NATO exercises like Enhanced Forward Presence on disinformation threats.[630]

The Nordic societies also function with extremely low levels of corruption, and their people have high trust in both their government and fellow citizens—all significant factors in their relative immunity to the Kremlin's efforts. Yet the Nordic states have also clearly recognized the new nature of the hybrid threats they face from the Russian government and other malicious actors, and have taken admirable and effective steps to address these threats not just in their own countries, but also among their allies and partners around in the EU and NATO. The United States government should work closely with the Nordic states both to assist with their efforts and to learn how their actions and methods might be applied to build resiliency here in the United States.

Lessons Learned

- *Disinformation is Ineffective Against a Well-Educated Citizenry:* By essentially inoculating the population against fake news, education efforts have the greatest long-term potential to neutralize the effects of the Kremlin's disinformation operations, especially when combined with an "all of the above" approach that includes monitoring and reporting fake news, promoting alternative positive narratives, and supporting independent media and investigative journalism. Furthermore, this approach tackles the problem at the root; Kremlin-backed disinformation stories are just an outgrowth of the rise of false stories on the internet—even if the Kremlin were to order an end to all of its disinformation operations tomorrow, the problem of fake news stories would still exist. The Kremlin's internet trolls did not invent fake news, but they recognized and exploited it, using new technologies to have far greater reach than past efforts.

---

[629] *Ibid.* at 16; Embassy of Denmark, Information Provided in Response to Questions from U.S. Senator Ben Cardin, Sept. 14, 2017.
[630] Ministry of Foreign Affairs of Denmark, *Foreign and Security Policy Strategy 2017-2018,* at 15; "Denmark to Educate Soldiers in Combatting Disinformation," *EU v.Disinfo,* July 25, 2017.

THE NETHERLANDS

The Kremlin has launched multiple disinformation campaigns in the Netherlands and made attempts to interfere in its elections, and the Dutch government has taken several steps to build both national and regional resilience.

As with the Baltics, the Dutch government has adopted a very visible and public approach to exposing Russian government interference efforts, with the security services producing annual reports which describe both the broad scope and specific activities of those efforts. The Dutch General Intelligence and Security Service noted in 2016 that "the Russian intelligence services have their sights firmly set on the Netherlands" and that "Russia's espionage activities seek to influence decision-making processes, perceptions and public opinion ... [and] the dissemination of disinformation and propaganda plays an important role."[631] The Dutch Military Intelligence and Security Service reports that the Kremlin's propaganda portrays Russia's engagement in various theaters as humanitarian and de-escalating, while Western actions are depicted as anti-Russian, hysterical, hypocritical, and escalating.[632]

In April 2016, the Netherlands held a referendum on whether to approve a trade agreement between the EU and Ukraine. A left-wing member of the Dutch parliament, Harry von Bommel, recruited a "Ukrainian team" to campaign against the agreement. The team used public meetings, television appearances, and social media to portray the Ukrainian government as a "bloodthirsty kleptocracy."[633] Notably, the most active members of the team were from Russia or separatist areas of Ukraine.[634] Other campaigners, including one from the Forum for Democracy (a research group turned political party that won two seats in its first election in 2017 and often promotes the Kremlin's narrative on issues), retweeted a false report that Ukrainian soldiers crucified a three year-old Russian-speaking boy.[635] That piece of propaganda got its start on Russia's primary state-controlled TV station and was based on an interview with a Russian actress posing as a Ukrainian witness.[636] And a false video created by the Internet Research Agency, the troll factory in St. Petersburg, purported to show a group of Ukrainian volunteer soldiers burning a Dutch flag and threatening to launch terrorist attacks against the Netherlands if they voted against the referendum.[637] In addition, many of the themes, headlines, and photographs used by the "no" campaign were reportedly borrowed from RT and Sputnik.[638]

[631] Netherlands Ministry of the Interior and Kingdom Relations, General Intelligence Security Service, *Annual Report 2016*, at 7.
[632] Netherlands Military Intelligence and Security Service, *Annual Report 2016* (translated from Dutch).
[633] Andrew Higgins, "Fake News, Fake Ukrainians: How a Group of Russians Tilted a Dutch Vote," *The New York Times,* Feb. 16, 2017.
[634] *Ibid.*
[635] Dutch News, "Support for Government Parties Slips in New Poll of Polls, FvD Rises," Dutch News, Nov. 8, 2017; Andrew Higgins, "Fake News, Fake Ukrainians: How a Group of Russians Tilted a Dutch Vote," *The New York Times,* Feb. 16, 2017.
[636] Andrew Higgins, "Fake News, Fake Ukrainians: How a Group of Russians Tilted a Dutch Vote," *The New York Times,* Feb. 16, 2017.
[637] *Ibid.*
[638] Anne Applebaum, "The Dutch Just Showed the World How Russia Influences Western European Elections," *The Washington Post, "* Apr. 8, 2016.

Ultimately, the referendum saw a relatively low turnout of 32 percent of the Dutch population, with about two-thirds of those voting against the agreement.[639] One Ukrainian foreign ministry official cited a poll which reported that 59 percent of those voting "no" said that their perception of Ukraine as corrupt was an important motivation for their vote; 19 percent believed that Ukraine was responsible for the shooting down of Malaysia Air Flight 17 (a common and proven false theme of Russian propaganda), which killed 298 people, including 193 Dutch citizens; and 34 percent thought that the agreement would guarantee Ukraine's accession to the EU (the latter two points are demonstrably false).[640] While anti-establishment sentiments and increasing voter skepticism of the EU were viewed as important reasons for the referendum's outcome, the potential effect of the disinformation campaign, not just on voters' choices but also on their understanding of Ukraine, cannot be ignored.[641] When it perceives its interests are at stake, the Kremlin can be expected to carry out similar disinformation efforts during other referendums in Europe and beyond.

The Netherlands has since worked to strengthen the integrity of its electoral process and systems, especially after the Kremlin's attack on the 2016 U.S. presidential election. The Dutch National Coordinator for Security and Counterterrorism described in its annual report how the Dutch government, after noting the hack of the Democratic National Committee in 2016, sought to enhance digital resilience before and during their country's March 2017 election by raising awareness among political parties and organizations.[642] Nonetheless, some Dutch organizations and platforms were subject to distributed denial of service (DDoS) attacks, including websites that helped voters compare the platforms of different political parties.[643] Following rumors that election software was potentially vulnerable to cyberattacks and that Russian hackers could view the Dutch elections as "good practice" before the French and German elections, the month before the election the Minister of Interior and Kingdom Relations decided to switch to paper ballots only and count all votes by hand.[644] According to the U.S. State Department, the Netherlands also requested U.S. government assistance for its March 2017 general election.[645] The election appears to have occurred without any voting issues, and some observers noted that disinformation did not appear to play a large role during the campaign period, with fake news stories posted to Facebook and Twitter being quickly debunked by commentators.[646]

[639] Ibid.
[640] Ibid.
[641] James McAuley, "Dutch Voters Reject Trade Deal Out of Anger Against EU," The Washington Post, Apr. 6, 2016; "Netherlands Rejects EU-Ukraine Partnership Deal," BBC News, Apr. 7, 2016.
[642] Netherlands Ministry of Security and Justice, National Coordinator for Security and Counterterrorism, Cyber Security Assessment Netherlands 2017, at 7 (Aug. 2017).
[643] Ibid. at 12.
[644] Thessa Lageman, "Russian Hackers Use Dutch Polls as Practice," Deutsche Welle, Oct. 3, 2017; Ministry of Security and Justice, National Coordinator for Security and Counterterrorism, Cyber Security Assessment Netherlands 2017, at 35.
[645] U.S. Department of State, Report to Congress on Efforts by the Russian Federation to Undermine Elections in Europe and Eurasia, at 3 (Nov. 7, 2017).
[646] Thomas Escritt, "Dutch Will Hand Count Ballots Due to Hacking Fears," Reuters, Feb. 1, 2017; Peter Teffer, "Fake News or Hacking Absent in Dutch Election Campaign," EUobserver, Mar. 15, 2017.

Like other countries in Europe, the Netherlands is also supporting independent Russian-language journalism. For example, Netherlands-based Free Press Unlimited Foundation manages a $1.4 million government grant to help develop a regional platform for Russian-language media organizations to exchange news items (see Chapter 7).[647] When announcing the program, the Minister of Foreign Affairs, Bert Koenders, noted that the Dutch government was explicitly supporting independent media and not counterpropaganda, saying "misinformation from Moscow is a threat to media diversity in all countries in which Russian is spoken. However, counterpropaganda is ineffective and goes against our democratic principles. We wish to support the work of independent media initiatives without dictating what they should write or broadcast."[648]

Lessons Learned

- *The Kremlin's Disinformation Campaigns are Selective and Opportunistic:* While disinformation appears to have been an important factor in the 2016 referendum on the EU-Ukraine trade agreement, it did not seem to play a role in the 2017 parliamentary election. That suggests that concerted disinformation campaigns are not simply launched at every opportunity, but targeted and scaled depending on the expected success of their efforts.
- *Threat Awareness and Quick Adaptability are Effective Resilience Measures:* The Dutch government's efforts to help raise awareness of and respond to potential cyber threats during the 2017 election period, especially by switching to paper ballots, protected the validity of the election and likely deterred efforts to interfere.

---

[647] Government of the Netherlands, Ministry of *Foreign Affairs,* "The Netherlands to Support Independent Russian-Language Media," Nov. 19, 2015.
[648] *Ibid.*

UNITED KINGDOM

The Russian government has sought to influence democracy in the United Kingdom through disinformation, cyber hacking, and corruption. While a complete picture of the scope and nature of Kremlin interference in the UK's June 2016 referendum is still emerging, Prime Minister Theresa May and the UK government have condemned the Kremlin's active measures, and various UK government entities,[649] including the Electoral Commission and parliamentarians, have launched investigations into different aspects of possible Russian government meddling.[650] The UK government also worked to harden cyber defenses, particularly before the June 2017 election.

The June 2016 referendum in which British voters opted for their country to leave the EU, famously dubbed "Brexit," was a watershed moment for Western countries grappling with a resurgent wave of populism and nationalism in their political systems. Headlines the morning after the vote reflected the world's—and many Britons'—shock. *The Washington Post* assessed it in stark terms: "British voters have defied the will of their leaders, foreign allies and much of the political establishment by opting to rupture this country's primary connection to Europe in a stunning result that will radiate economic and political uncertainty across the globe."[651] What was missing, however, in the morning-after news roundup was discussion of the Russian government and what role it may have played in helping to influence British voters' decisions.

Indeed, the picture of potential Russian meddling in the June referendum vote has only begun to come into sharper focus as subsequent elections around the world revealed common elements—false or inflammatory stories circulated by bots and trolls, allegations of cyber hacking, stories in Russian state-sponsored media outlets playing up fears of migration and globalization, and allegations of corrupt foreign influence on political parties and candidates—that suggested a possible Russian hand. The Kremlin has long aimed to undermine European integration and the EU, in addition to its aims to sow confusion and undermine confidence in democratic processes themselves, making Brexit a potentially appealing target.

The allegations that have emerged of Russian interference prior to the Brexit referendum are all the more stunning given the innate resilience within British society to the Kremlin's anti-democratic agenda.[652] A brief viewing of the lively sessions in Britain's House of Commons is a reminder of the country's traditions of popular representation, robust debate, and transparent governance. Nevertheless, analysts have cited pockets within the UK political system that are relatively more vulnerable to Russian influence.

British campaign finance laws generally focus on restricting expenditures by political parties more than limiting donations,

---

[649] Rowena Mason, "Theresa May Accuses Russia of Interfering in Elections and Fake News," *The Guardian,* Nov. 14, 2017.

[650] Jeremy Kahn, "UK Proves Russian Social Media Influence in Brexit Vote, *Bloomberg Politics,* Nov. 2, 2017.

[651] Griff Witte et al., "In Stunning Decision, Britain Votes to Leave the E.U.," *The Washington Post,* Jun. 24, 2016.

[652] Neil Barnett, *The Kremlin's Trojan Horses: Russian Influence in France, Germany, and the United Kingdom,* The Atlantic Council, at 18 (2016).

though foreign donors are not considered "permissible donors" under UK law.[653] However, the beneficial owners of non-British companies that are incorporated in the EU and carry out business in the UK are immaterial under the law; this opacity may have enabled Russian-related money to be directed with insufficient scrutiny to various UK political actors.[654] Investigative journalists have also raised questions about the sources of sudden and possibly illicit wealth that may have been directed to support the Brexit "Leave" campaign; the UK Electoral Commission has subsequently begun to investigate.[655] Meanwhile, experts have pointed to the role of the far-right UK Independence Party (UKIP) and its leader, Nigel Farage, in fanning anti-EU sentiment, criticism of the European sanctions on Russia, and flattering assessments of Russian President Putin as well as far left wing views as conducive to alignment with Russia's anti-EU and NATO-skeptic positions.[656]

More broadly, there are concerns about vulnerabilities to Russian government influence on various UK actors, including political parties, civil society, and think-tanks, through extensive Russian financial ties and possibly illicit financial activity.[657] While unrecorded inflows of cash may not necessarily be illicit, market research done in 2015 by Deutsche Bank confirmed through balance of payments data "the popular belief that Russian money has flooded into the UK in recent years," particularly into the real estate market, and that a "considerable chunk" of unrecorded inflows into the country are the result of Russian capital flight.[658] In March 2015, UK Metropolitan Police noted that a total value of 180 million British pounds in properties in the UK had been put under investigation as possibly purchased with corrupt proceeds by secretive offshore companies, in arrangements akin to "putting money in a Swiss bank," according to one investigator.[659] Documents gathered and released to numerous media outlets in March 2017 by the Organized Crime and Corruption Reporting Project and Russian newspaper *Novaya Gazeta* detailed a "global laundromat" scheme involving an estimated 500 Russian oligarchs, bankers, or individuals with connections to the FSB who moved at least $20 billion in stolen or illicit money out of Russia from 2010-2014.[660] The documents showed that British banks processed nearly $740 million of this allegedly laundered money, drawing questions about the lack of scrutiny applied to suspicious money transfers and the anonym-

[653] The Political Parties, Elections and Referendum Act 2000, c. 41, § 54 (UK).
[654] *Ibid.*; Barnett, *The Kremlin's Trojan Horses: Russian Influence in France, Germany, and the United Kingdom,* at 18.
[655] Alastair Sloan & Iain Campbell, "How Did Arron Banks Afford Brexit?" Open Democracy UK, Oct. 19, 2017; Holly Watt, "Electoral Commission to Investigate Arron Banks' Brexit Donations," *The Guardian,* Nov. 1, 2017.
[656] Barnett, The Kremlin's Trojan Horses: Russian Influence in France, Germany, and the United Kingdom, at 18.
[657] *Ibid.* at 20-23.
[658] Deutsche Bank Markets Research, "Dark Matter: The Hidden Capital Flows that Drive G-10 Exchange Rates," Mar. 2015.
[659] Robert Booth, "UK Properties Held by Offshore Firms Used in Global Corruption, Say Police," *The Guardian,* Mar. 3, 2015.
[660] Organized Crime and Corruption Reporting Project, The Russian Laundromat, Aug. 22, 2014; Luke Harding et al., "British Banks Handled Vast Sums of Laundered Russian Money," *The Guardian,* Mar. 20, 2017.

118

ity afforded under UK law to the beneficial owners of British-registered companies.[661]

With regard to cyberspace, in February 2017 the head of the UK's National Cyber Security Centre (NCSC), Ciaran Martin, asserted that the Russian government had stepped up its online aggression against Western countries.[662] He cited 188 major cyberattacks over a three-month period against the UK government, most of which were reportedly attributable to Russian and Chinese actors; the NCSC reportedly blocked 34,450 attacks over a six-month period against UK entities more broadly (although not all of these attacks are necessarily attributable to the Russian government).[663] In a November 2017 public speech, he indicated that Russian interference over the past year "included attacks on the UK media, telecommunications and energy sectors."[664]

The Russian government has also apparently sought to seize on populist sentiments and economic frustrations, exploiting the UK's generally open marketplace for free speech and political competition by introducing fake or misleading news. Officially, the Russian government asserted its neutrality on the question of the Brexit referendum, but its English-language media outlets RT and Sputnik covered the referendum campaign extensively and offered "systematically one-sided coverage" supporting a British departure from the European Union and frequently broadcasted statements from UKIP head Farage.[665]

Reporting in November 2017 on cached material from Twitter accounts tied to the Internet Research Agency, the Russia-based troll farm that generated false stories around the 2016 U.S. elections, *CNN* alleged that numerous accounts had also blasted out pro-Brexit messages before the UK referendum.[666] Two researchers from the University of Edinburgh ultimately asserted that more than 400 of the Internet Research Agency Twitter accounts that had been active in the U.S. election had also been actively posting about Brexit.[667] Meanwhile, research conducted by a joint team of experts from the University of California at Berkeley and Swansea University in Wales reportedly identified 150,000 Twitter accounts with various Russian ties that disseminated messages about Brexit before the referendum—interestingly, a combination of messages both supporting and criticizing Britain's membership in the European Union, which may signal that the broader aim was to magnify societal discord.[668] In contrast, however, Twitter representatives reported in November 2017 that the company found only six Tweets on its platform—all generated by RT, which spent roughly

---

[661] Luke Harding et al., "British Banks Handled Vast Sums of Laundered Russian Money," *The Guardian,* Mar. 20, 2017.

[662] Richard Kerbaj, "Russia Steps Up Cyber-Attacks on UK," *The Times,* Feb. 12, 2017.

[663] Pierluigi Paganini, "Britain's Security Has Been Threatened by 188 Major Cyber Attacks in the Last Three Months, According to the Head of the National Cyber Security Centre," *Security Affairs,* Feb. 13, 2017.

[664] United Kingdom National Cyber Security Centre, "Cyber Security: Fixing the Present So We Can Worry About the Future," Nov. 15, 2017.

[665] Ben Nimmo, "Putin's Media are Pushing Britain for the Brexit," *The Interpreter,* Feb. 12, 2016; Ministry of Foreign Affairs of the Russian Federation, Tweet, https://twitter.com/mfa—russia/status/748231648936869888, June 29, 2016.

[666] Donie O'Sullivan, "Russian Trolls Pushed Pro-Brexit Spin on Day of Referendum," *CNN,* Nov. 10, 2017.

[667] Karla Adam & William Booth, "Rising Alarm in Britain Over Russian Meddling in Brexit Vote," *The Washington Post,* Nov. 17, 2017.

[668] *Ibid.*

$1,000 to promote them—constituting Russian-sponsored misinformation during the Brexit campaign; the parliamentarian chairing the select committee to whom the information was reported called the Twitter report a "completely inadequate" response that was overly narrow in scope.[669] In addition, Facebook reports that the accounts they "attribute to the Internet Research Agency ran three ads that delivered to the UK during the relevant electoral period. Those ads delivered around 200 total impressions and were associated with a total spend of $0.97 USD."[670] However, in limiting their investigation to just the Internet Research Agency, Facebook missed that it is only one troll farm which "has existed within a larger disinformation ecosystem in St. Petersburg," including Glavset, an alleged successor of the Internet Research Agency, and the Federal News Agency, a reported propaganda "media farm," according to Russian investigative journalists.[671]

With the deepening realization of the threat of Russian government interference, the UK government has stepped up its scrutiny of possible Russian intrusions into its democratic system and heightened its responses, from which helpful lessons can be drawn.

Lessons Learned

- *Consolidating and Enhancing Cyber Security Can Preempt Disclosure of Hacked Material:* In 2016, the UK established the NCSC as a "one-stop shop" for cybersecurity within its government to protect critical services from cyberattacks, manage major incidents, and pursue technological improvements to bolster Internet security.[672] The UK government also recently announced a $2.3 billion increase in spending on cybersecurity to counter emerging threats and "hostile foreign actors." Some observers suggest this funding increase is linked to growing concerns about Russian activity.[673] Prior to the UK's general election in June 2017, the NCSC contacted political party leaders and offered to help strengthen their network security in light of the potential for hostile foreign state action against the UK political system.[674] British officials stated after the poll that there was "no successful Russian cyber intervention" into the election process seen and asserted that systems were in place to protect against electoral fraud at all levels, though it is unclear the extent to which the lack of meddling may have also been due to a shift in the Kremlin's approach.[675]

- *A Diverse, Visible Response by Government and Parliamentary Actors Helps Raise Awareness of the Threat:* Growing revela-

[669] Alex Hern, "Twitter's Response to Brexit Interference Inquiry Inadequate, MP Says," *The Guardian*, Dec. 14, 2017.

[670] Email from Facebook Official to Committee Staff.

[671] Diana Pilipenko, "Facebook must 'follow the money' to uncover extent of Russian meddling," *The Guardian*, Oct. 9, 2017.

[672] National Cyber Security Centre of the United Kingdom Government Communications Headquarters, *Annual Review* (2017).

[673] Henry Ridgwell, "Britain Invests Billions in Cybersecurity in Face of Russian Threat," Voice of America, Nov. 4, 2016; Jamie Grierson, "UK Hit by 188 High-Level Cyber-Attacks in Three Months," *The Guardian*, Feb. 12, 2017.

[674] William James & Robin Pomeroy, "UK Political Parties Warned of Russian Hacking Threat," *Reuters*, Mar. 12, 2017; Richard Kerbaj, "Russia Steps Up Cyber-Attacks on UK," *The Times*, Feb. 12, 2017.

[675] Paul Shinkman, "British Say Election Was Free of Russian Meddling," *U.S. News & World Report*, June 16, 2017.

120

tions of possible Russian government interference into the Brexit referendum and UK democracy were met with a sharp warning from Prime Minister May in an address in November 2017 in which she told the Kremlin, "We know what you are doing ... and you will not succeed," and described Russian state actions as "threatening the international order."[676] In mid-November 2017, Prime Minister May suggested that a prominent intelligence and security parliamentary committee would be re-formed soon to investigate Russian meddling in the British election, a development called for by senior parliamentarians from both the Labour and Conservative parties. Meanwhile, the Commons' Digital, Culture, Media, and Sport Select Committee opened an inquiry in January 2017 to investigate the scope and role of disinformation and propaganda in Britain.[677] As mentioned earlier, the Electoral Commission opened investigations into possible campaign finance violations and the source of funding for the Brexit "Leave" campaign. On the corruption front, in May 2016 the United Kingdom hosted an anti-corruption summit in which 43 governments and six international organizations participated, resulting in a Global Declaration Against Corruption and 648 commitments by participating states and entities to strengthen various aspects of transparency and accountability for corruption.[678] The government of Former Prime Minister David Cameron announced at the summit, among other steps, the launch of "the UK's public central register of company beneficial ownership information for all companies incorporated in the UK" as well as for "foreign companies who already own or buy property in the UK, or who bid on UK central government contracts."[679] The United Kingdom in April 2017 also passed into law the Criminal Finances Act, which strengthens provisions against tax evasion and includes a section modeled after the U.S. Global Magnitsky Rule of Law and Accountability Act enabling the freezing of assets of foreign officials who have committed gross human rights violations.[680]

[676] David Kirkpatrick, "British Cybersecurity Chief Warns of Russian Hacking," *The New York Times*, Nov. 14, 2017.
[677] Robert Booth & Alex Hern, "Intelligence Watchdog Urged to Look at Russian Influence on Brexit Vote," *The Guardian*, Nov. 15, 2017; United Kingdom House of Commons Select Committee Digital, Culture, Media and Sport Committee, "'Fake News' Inquiry Launched," Jan. 30, 2017.
[678] Transparency International, 3 Things We've Learned Since the Anti-Corrutpion Summit in London 2016, Sept. 19, 2017.
[679] Anti-Corruption Summit London 2016, United Kingdom Country Statement, at 1, May 12, 2016.
[680] UK Parliament, Summary of the Criminal Finances Act of 2017, https://services.parliament.uk/bills/2016-17/criminalfinances.html (visited Dec. 30, 2017); "Magnitsky Bill Turns UK into 'Hostile Environment' for Kleptocrats," *BBC*, Feb. 21, 2017.

FRANCE

The Russian government has sought to influence democracy in France through the use of cyberattacks, disinformation, and cultural and political influence. Despite relatively strong historical, political, and cultural ties to Russia compared to other European powers, France and its new president Emmanuel Macron—himself a target of cyber hacking and disinformation—are emerging as strong voices against Russian government interference and have played a leading role in Europe to resist Kremlin meddling.

Barely three weeks after he was elected with nearly twice the votes of his far-right, pro-Kremlin challenger Marine Le Pen, French President Emmanuel Macron stood next to Russian President Vladimir Putin for a press conference at Versailles.[681] An exhibition inside the Palace was celebrating the 1717 visit to Paris of Russian tsar Peter the Great, a figure to whom Russia's modern-day strongman is often compared.[682] But that day it was Macron, after being asked why certain Russian media outlets were not given access to his campaign, who projected a forceful stance. "I will yield nothing on this. Nothing, madam. So let's set things straight ... Russia Today and Sputnik did not act as news outlets and journalists, but they acted as organs of influence, of propaganda, and of deceptive propaganda. It's that simple."[683] Reports disseminated by these outlets and on pro-Kremlin social media had variously decried Macron as a puppet of U.S. political and business leaders, alleged he held an offshore account in the Bahamas to evade taxes, and fueled rumors of an extra-marital gay relationship, which Macron publicly denied.[684]

For his part, Putin used the press conference to dismiss the notion of Russian government meddling in the French election, claiming Macron "did not show any interest [in discussing it] and I even less."[685] But investigations by government and non-government researchers have pointed to a myriad of Russian malign influence tools that were deployed in France prior to its 2017 election. The French response was multi-faceted and quick, animated by a desire to avoid falling victim to meddling similar to what was seen in the Brexit referendum and U.S. presidential election in 2016.[686] And if, as it appeared, the Kremlin's goal was to undermine Macron's candidacy, then the French response successfully stymied that goal.

In recent years, the French government's posture has become increasingly critical toward Russian aggression in Ukraine and Syria. Macron's predecessor Francois Hollande in 2014 stopped delivery of two French warships ordered by the Kremlin and, in 2016, suggested Russian complicity in war crimes in Aleppo—an allegation

[681] Gregor Aisch, et al., "How France Voted," *The New York Times,* May 7, 2017; Nicholas Vinocur, "Macron, Standing by Putin, Calls RT and Sputnik 'Agents of Influence,'" *Politico,* May 29, 2017.
[682] Nicholas Vinocur, "Macron and the Czar at Versailles," *Politico,* May 29, 2017.
[683] James McAuley, "French President Macron Blasts Russian State-Owned Media as 'Propaganda,'" *The Washington Post,* May 29, 2017.
[684] Andrew Osborn & Richard Balmforth, "Macron Camp Bars Russian News Outlets, Angers Moscow," *Reuters,* Apr. 27, 2017; Charles Bremmer, "Websites Pump Out Fake News Minutes After Offshore Claims," *The Times,* May 5, 2017.
[685] James McAuley, "French President Macron Blasts Russian State-Owned Media as 'Propaganda,'" *The Washington Post,* May 29, 2017.
[686] James McAuley, "French President Macron Blasts Russian State-Owned Media as 'Propaganda,'" *The Washington Post,* May 29, 2017; Committee Staff Discussion with French Foreign Ministry Officials, Nov. 2017.

that prompted Putin to cancel a planned official visit to Paris.[687] The French Foreign Ministry has also maintained that EU sanctions on the Russian Federation must remain in place until the Minsk Agreements are fully implemented.[688] Among Western European powers, however, broader French society provides relatively fertile ground for Russian influence. The country has a long historical relationship with Russia, as evidenced by Franco-Russian ties that exist in political parties, universities, think tanks, and journalist circles.

Pro-Kremlin sentiment has been demonstrated by actors across the French political spectrum, especially on the far right, far left, and center right. The Front National (FN), Marine Le Pen's Eurosceptic and ultra-nationalist party, has staunchly defended Russian actions in Ukraine and Syria, calling for "balanced" relations between Russia and the Western powers, particularly against an Islamist "menace."[689] FN publicly acknowledged it took a loan of nine million euros from the First Czech-Russian Bank in Moscow, reportedly owned by pro-Kremlin oligarchs, after French banks refused to loan money to the party because of its historically anti-Semitic and extremist positions.[690] In the month prior to the first round of the 2017 presidential election, Le Pen traveled to Moscow to meet with Putin and endorse the lifting of European sanctions on Russia, while Putin told the assembled press that Russia did not seek to "influence" the French poll but simply "reserve the right to talk to all of the country's political forces."[691] Far-left and Communist parties in France have been sympathetic to the Russian government, based on skepticism toward Europe and a shared penchant for statism.[692] Meanwhile, some center-right elements in France have viewed Russia through the prism of business and industry interests—during the 2016 campaign, Republican party candidate Francois Fillon cautioned against a European hard line on sanctions and a military build-up along NATO's eastern flank, and dismissed assertions by U.S. government officials of Russian meddling in the French poll as "fantasies."[693]

The Kremlin has also cultivated ties with French civil society and religious actors it can exploit to influence French policies in Russia's favor. For example, Vladimir Yakunin, the former head of Russian Railways who is under U.S. sanctions, is the co-president of Association Dialogue Franco-Russe in Paris, which, in the wake of European sanctions on Russia, has advocated for "normal" ties between France and Russia to be promptly re-established.[694] The

[687] Michael Stothard, et al., "France Suspends Delivery Of Mistral Warship to Russia," *Financial Times*, Nov. 25, 2015; Kim Willsher & Alec Luhn, "Vladimir Putin Cancels Paris Visit Amid Syria Row," *The Guardian*, Oct. 11, 2016.

[688] "France Says Russia Sanctions to Remain in Place," *Associated Press*, Mar. 9, 2017.

[689] Vivienne Walt, "Why France's Marine Le Pen is Doubling Down on Russia Support," *TIME*, Jan. 9, 2017.

[690] *Ibid.*; Anne-Claude Martin, "National Front's Russian Loans Cause Uproar in European Parliament," EURACTIV.fr, Dec. 5, 2014; Sanita Jemberga, et al, "How Le Pen's Party Brokered Russian Loans," *EUobserver*, May 3, 2017.

[691] "Le Pen Meets Putin Ahead of French Presidential Election," *France 24*, Mar. 24, 2017.

[692] Alina Polyakova et al., *The Kremlin's Trojan Horses*, Atlantic Council, at 7-8 (Nov. 15, 2016).

[693] John Irish, "Russia Not Interfering in French Elections, Says Candidate Fillon," *Reuters*, Mar. 31, 2017.

[694] Association Dialogue Franco-Russe, "Board, Vladimir Yakunin," http://dialoguefrancorusse.com/en/association-uk/board/557-vladimir-yakunin.html (visited Dec. 30, 2017); U.S. Department of the Treasury, "Treasury Sanctions Russian Officials, Members Of

123

Paris-based Institute for Democracy and Cooperation is led by a former Duma deputy, Natalia Narochnitskaya, and according to one expert "toes a blatantly pro-Kremlin line," with its representatives regularly appearing on Russian state-controlled media.[695] The Russian Orthodox Church has a significant presence in France and recently completed construction on a new church and community center near the Eiffel Tower—seen as a visible display of Russian might in the heart of Europe and part of the Kremlin's attempts to influence France's 200,000-strong Russian diaspora.[696] The facility has been accorded diplomatic status and the community center's activities are opaque, amidst concerns held by some government and civil society interlocutors in Paris that the space could be used to house Russian intelligence activities.[697]

Against this backdrop of carefully fostered cultural, media and political ties, the Kremlin ramped up the use of additional information warfare tools to seize on anti-European sentiment around the 2017 French presidential election and discredit Macron in particular. For example, a study released in April by a UK-based firm noted that nearly one in four website links shared by French social media users before the French election "come from sources which challenge traditional media narratives."[698] In April, a Macron campaign spokesman said that "2,000 to 3,000 attempts have been made to hack the campaign, including denial-of-service attacks that briefly shut down Macron's website and more sophisticated efforts to burrow into email accounts of individual campaign workers."[699] Research by a private cybersecurity firm indicated that the Macron campaign was a target of APT28, the same Russian government-linked hackers behind the World Anti-Doping Agency (WADA) and DNC doxing attacks.[700] Just days before the runoff vote, hacked emails and documents from Emmanuel Macron's campaign were leaked online. The hack was first announced by an alt-right activist in the United States, whose tweet promoting the leak was reportedly spread with the help of bots and a network of alt-right activists before being picked up by Wikileaks, which ultimately published a searchable archive of tens of thousands of emails and documents hacked from the Macron campaign.[701]

Indications of Russian state-sponsored cyberattacks against French entities date back to before the 2017 presidential election, starkly illustrated by the massive cyberattack against French global broadcaster TV5Monde in 2015. In a swift assault, 12 of the net-

The Russian Leadership's Inner Circle, And An Entity For Involvement In The Situation In Ukraine," Mar. 20, 2014; Association Dialogue Franco-Russe, "The Franco-Russian Dialogue is in Favor of the Imminent Resumption of Normal Cooperation with Russia," Mar. 29, 2016.
[695] Natalya Kanevskaya, "How The Kremlin Wields Its Soft Power In France," *Radio Free Europe/Radio Liberty*, June 24, 2014.
[696] Antoine Blua, "Russian 'Spiritual Centre' Set to Open in the Heart of Paris," *The Guardian*, Oct. 19, 2016.
[697] Antoine Blua, "Russia Unveils Cultural, Orthodox Jewel On The Seine," *Radio Free Europe/Radio Liberty*, Oct. 17, 2016.
[698] The Role and Impact of Non-Traditional Publishers in the 2017 French Presidential Election, Bakamo, 2017; Andrew Rettman, "Russia-Linked Fake News Floods French Social Media," *EUobserver*, Apr. 20, 2017.
[699] Rick Noack, "Cyberattack on French Presidential Front-Runner Bears Russian 'Fingerprints', Research Group Says," *The Washington Post*, Apr. 25, 2017.
[700] John Leyden, "Kremlin-Backed DNC Hackers Going After French Presidential Hopeful Macron," *The Register*, Apr. 25, 2017.
[701] "Macron Leaks: The Anatomy of a Hack," *BBC News*, May 9, 2017; "Wikileaks Publishes Searchable Archive of Macron Campaign Emails," *Reuters*, July 31, 2017.

work's channels suddenly went dark on the night of April 9. Within nine hours, an on-site technical team was able to identify and disable the malicious server (a more protracted delay to return to the airwaves could have resulted in the cancellation of contracts by satellite carriers, endangering the company). While messages posted on the company's Twitter and Facebook pages at the onset of the attack alleged to be from a group calling itself the "Cyber Caliphate" that espoused the Islamic State, French officials who investigated the attack subsequently linked it to APT28.[702] The seeming aim of the attack—not to disable, but to destroy—suggested that it may have been "an attempt to test forms of cyber weaponry as part of an increasingly aggressive posture," and the company's profits and staff were hampered for months until the extent of the breach could be addressed and more rigorous security protocols put into place.[703]

On May 9, Admiral Mike Rogers, Director of the U.S. National Security Agency and Commander of the U.S. Cyber Command acknowledged in a hearing before the Senate Armed Services Committee that Washington had become "aware of Russian activity" to hack French election-related infrastructure in the months prior to the French election and had signaled this to French counterparts, with an offer to assist in building resilience.[704] The broader response that the French government pursued to counter Russian election meddling reflected engagement and cooperation with not only other governments but also media and political parties, and provides a helpful, comprehensive model from which the United States and other countries can draw.

Lessons Learned

- *Swift Engagement with Political Parties and on Electoral Infrastructure Can Blunt Effects of Meddling:* In response to what French authorities viewed as possible Russian efforts to hack the digital infrastructure of political campaigns, France's main cybersecurity agency, the French Network and Information Security Agency (ANSSI), warned all political parties about the Russian cyber threat in the fall of 2016.[705] ANSSI subsequently offered cybersecurity awareness-raising and training seminars for all French political parties ahead of French elections this past spring; all parties participated except for Front National, which declined.[706] ANSSI itself, created in 2007 after the emergence of massive denial-of-service attacks in Estonia which that government had attributed to Russian-backed hackers, was the focus of increased French government investment—with a 93 percent jump in its budget between 2010 and

---

[702] Sam Jones, "Russia Mobilises an Elite Band of Cyber Warriors," *Financial Times,* Feb. 23, 2017.

[703] Gordon Corera, "How France's TV5 Was Almost Destroyed By 'Russian Hackers'," *BBC,* Oct. 20, 2016.

[704] Testimony of Admiral Michael S. Rodgers, Commander of the U.S. Cyber Command, *United States Cyber Command,* Hearing before the Senate Armed Services Committee, May 9, 2017.

[705] Mehdi Chebil, "France Takes Steps to Prevent an Election Hack Attack," *France24,* Jan. 16, 2017.

[706] Laura Daniels, "How Russia Hacked the French Election," *Politico,* Apr. 23, 2017.

2014.[707] And France's 2015 National Digital Security Strategy identified spreading disinformation and propaganda "an attack on defence and national security" to be met with a response.[708] In advance of June 2017 parliamentary elections, the French government also discontinued electronic voting by French citizens abroad.[709]

- *Direct Diplomatic Engagement Clearly Pointing to Malicious Actors and the Consequences of Their Actions Can Act as a Deterrent:* In a February speech to the French parliament, then Foreign Minister Jean-Marc Ayrault stated that France "will not accept any interference whatsoever in our electoral process, no more from Russia than from any other state. This is a question of our democracy, our sovereignty, our national independence."[710] Ayrault's warning included a pledge to carry out retaliatory measures against any such interference.[711] French government officials reiterated this warning privately to Russian officials in France, which may have prompted overt Russian interference in the campaign and comments on specific candidates to apparently subside.[712] Since then, the Macron Administration has stressed the importance of boosting international cooperation to prevent and respond to cyberattacks.[713]

- *Encouraging Vigilance by Non-Government Actors and Collective Discipline in Media, the Private Sector, and Civil Society is a Critical Ingredient in an Effective Response:* Subsequent to the dump of hacked material from the Macron campaign less than 48 hours before the runoff vote, the French electoral commission issued an instruction to news media in France not to publish the contents of the leaked information or risk criminal charges.[714] For its part, the media effectively complied with the government ban, but also took steps on its own to exercise collective discipline and increase its scrutiny of information before publication to avoid spreading fake news. Mainstream news organizations increased their fact-checking efforts as signs of Russian disinformation emerged.[715] *Le Monde's* Decodex project, for example, enabled a suite of fact-checking products based on a database of more than 600 websites, both French and international, which its fact checkers had identified as unreliable because the site could not be verified as legitimate or was deemed to manipulate information.[716] Perhaps

[707] Nicholas Vinocur, "France At Risk of Being Next Election Hacking Victim," *Politico,* Jan. 5, 2017.
[708] Office of the Prime Minister of France, *French National Digital Security Strategy 2015,* at 20.
[709] "France Drops Electronic Voting for Citizens Abroad Over Cybersecurity Fears," *Reuters,* Mar. 6, 2017. The French government had previously allowed its citizens abroad to vote electronically in legislative elections, but not presidential elections.
[710] "France Warns Russia Against Meddling in Election," *Reuters,* Feb. 15, 2017.
[711] *Ibid.*
[712] Committee staff discussion with French foreign ministry officials, Nov. 2017.
[713] Press Statement, "Cybersecurity: Attacks Against Private and Public Actors," Ministry of Europe and Foreign Affairs of the French Republic, May 15, 2017.
[714] Lizzie Dearden, "Emmanuel Macron Hacked Emails: French Media Ordered by Electoral Commission Not to Publish Content of Messages," *The Independent,* May 6, 2017.
[715] Dana Priest & Michael Birnbaum, "Europe Has Been Working to Expose Russian Meddling for Years," *The Washington Post,* June 25, 2017.
[716] Jessica Davies, "Le Monde Identifies 600 Unreliable Websites in Fake-News Crackdown," *Digiday,* Jan. 25, 2017.

drawing from lessons learned in the 2016 U.S. election, Facebook stated publicly in April 2017 that it had suspended 30,000 accounts for promoting propaganda or election-related spam before the French poll, though subsequent press reporting on private meetings between company officials and congressional staff indicate the number of accounts ultimately suspended could have been as many as 70,000.[717] This reporting also cited evidence connecting Russian intelligence to approximately two dozen fake Facebook accounts that were used to conduct surveillance specifically on Macron campaign staff, which the company deactivated.[718] The Macron campaign, mindful it was a hacking target, also took defensive steps to furnish false logins and information in response to spearphishing emails; while hackers ultimately were able to break into campaign materials, the effort may have helped to delay the release of the information until late in the campaign, at which point it gained limited traction with a forewarned, and vigilant, French audience.[719]

---

[717] Eric Auchard & Joseph Menn, "Facebook cracks down on 30,000 fake accounts in France," *Reuters*, Apr. 13, 2017; Joseph Menn, "Russia Used Facebook to Try to Spy on Macron Campaign—Sources," *Reuters*, July 27, 2017.
[718] *Ibid.*
[719] Rachel Donadio, "Why the Macron Hacking Attack Landed With a Thud in France," *The New York Times*, May 8, 2017.

GERMANY

The Russian government has sought to influence democracy in Germany through energy ties, cultural and political influence, disinformation, and cyberattacks. The German government and its Chancellor Angela Merkel are regarded as indispensable leaders in sustaining a united, democratic Europe. This has particularly been the case since the Russian military aggression into Ukraine in 2014. Nevertheless, historical business and political ties between Russia and some camps in Germany, as well as relationships forged in the energy sector, have presented opportunities for the Kremlin to attempt to meddle.

A 2007 meeting between German Chancellor Angela Merkel and Russian President Vladimir Putin at the latter's summer residence in Sochi, Russia—in which Putin let his black Labrador into the room to approach Merkel, who has a fear of dogs—has been widely hailed as a sign of Putin's cunning statecraft.[720] But Merkel's assessment of the situation in an interview later dismissed the Russian leader's power play: "I understand why he has to do this—to prove he's a man," she told a group of reporters. "He's afraid of his own weakness. Russia has nothing, no successful politics or economy. All they have is this."[721] Indeed, Merkel has proven to be a formidable obstacle to Putin in achieving his goals to undermine a democratic Europe, particularly in the leading diplomatic role Merkel and Germany have played in projecting a united—and firm—European response to the Russian invasion of Ukraine and the imposition of EU sanctions. Ten years after the infamous dog incident, Merkel held firm in a tense May 2017 meeting on EU sanctions imposed against Russia for its annexation of Crimea and support for Ukrainian separatists, and raised concerns about human rights abuses inside Russia and the Kremlin's election meddling abroad.[722]

Even before the Ukraine conflict, however, the Russian government has used energy politics as a key lever of influence in Germany. In 2005, former chancellor Gerhard Schröder became the chairman of the shareholders' committee of Nord Stream AG, a consortium led by Gazprom to bring Russian gas to Germany under the Baltic Sea via two pipelines.[723] The first was inaugurated in 2011, but completion of the second, dubbed Nord Stream 2, has faced considerable obstacles from European Union members and littoral states who fear it will increase European reliance on Russian gas and undermine stability in Ukraine, which currently receives transit payments for the gas that runs through its territory

---

[720] Tim Hume, "Vladimir Putin: I Didn't Mean to Scare Angela Merkel with My Dog," *CNN*, Jan. 12, 2016.

[721] Thomas Johnson, "Merkel Appears to Roll Her Eyes at Putin, and the Internet Can't Get Enough," *The Washington Post*, July 7, 2017.

[722] Patrick Donahue & Ilya Arkhipov, "In Tense Encounter, Merkel Tells Putin Sanctions Must Remain," *Bloomberg*, May 2, 2017; Andreas Rinke & Denis Pinchuk, "Putin, Merkel Struggle to Move Past Differences in Tense Meeting," *Reuters*, May 2, 2017.

[723] Nord Stream, "Who We Are," https://www.nord-stream.com/about-us/ (visited Dec. 31, 2017); "Former German Chancellor Gerhard Schroder Nominated to Russia's Rosneft Board," *Deutsche Welle*, Aug. 12, 2017.

to Europe.[724] In September 2017, the Russian state-controlled oil company Rosneft named Schröder its board chairman.[725]

Meanwhile, Russia has also cultivated ties with both extreme ends of the political spectrum in Germany. The Alternative for Germany (AfD) party, which ascended to third place in the September 2017 elections and is the first far-right party to enter the Bundestag since World War II, has reportedly sought close ties with Russian state-backed media.[726] It has reportedly also forged alliances between its youth wing and leaders of United Russia's Yunarmiya (Young Guard) and former Nashi youth movement, and courted ethnic Russian voters in Germany.[727] The German newspaper *Bild* alleged that Russia had directed funds to the AfD ahead of the September elections through the sale of gold to the AfD via middlemen at under-market values, a scenario through which the party may not have realized it was being subsidized with Russian cash.[728] Both the AfD and the Kremlin have fervently denied any such financial ties.[729] Meanwhile, the far-left Die Linke party has proven sympathetic ground for the Kremlin's interests, with party leaders positing that the Ukraine conflict is the result of American actions and traveling to the separatist "Donetsk People's Republic" in eastern Ukraine to express solidarity and provide humanitarian relief.[730]

Civil society and popular movements have also been used as influence tools to promote a pro-Kremlin worldview. For example, the Dialogue of Civilizations Research Institute, founded in 2016 in Berlin and financed by Putin ally Vladimir Yakunin, with reported investments from other Russian businessmen, sponsors research and events with the reported aim to make Russia's world view "popular."[731] The Patriotic Europeans Against the Islamization of the West movement in Germany has displayed Russian flags and pro-Kremlin slogans at its protests decrying Germany's hospitality to migrants and refugees, which have also been broadcast live on RT's German language channel, RT Deutsch.[732] A few German media outlets also reported in the run-up to the September 2017 election on concerns that increasingly popular "systema clubs" established throughout the country to teach a martial art form used

[724] "U.S. Diplomat Says Nord Stream 2 Pipeline Probably Won't Be Built," *Radio Free Europe/Radio Liberty,* Nov. 29, 2017; "Denmark Passes Law to Block Nord Stream 2," *Newsbase,* Dec. 7, 2017; Statement of Dr. Constanze Stelzenmuller, "The Impact of Russian Interference on Germany's 2017 Elections," *Russian Intervention in European Elections,* Hearing before the U.S. Senate Select Committee on Intelligence, June 28, 2017. For more on Nord Stream 2, see Chapter 4.

[725] Rosneft, "Corporate Governance; Board of Directors," https://www.rosneft.com/governance/board (visited Dec. 31, 2017); Geoffrey Smith, "Vladimir Putin Just Gave Ex-German Chancellor Gerhard Schroeder A Plum Oil Job," *Fortune,* Sept. 29, 2017.

[726] Simon Shuster, "How Russian Voters Fueled the Rise of Germany's Far-Right," *TIME,* Sept. 25, 2017.

[727] Melanie Amann & Pavel Lokshin, "German Populists Forge Ties with Russia," *Spiegel Online,* Apr. 27, 2016.

[728] Andrew Rettman, "Illicit Russian Money Poses Threat to EU Democracy," *EUobserver,* Apr. 21, 2017.

[729] Simon Shuster, "How Russian Voters Fueled the Rise of Germany's Far-Right," *TIME,* Sept. 25, 2017.

[730] Alina Polyakova et al., *The Kremlin's Trojan Horses,* Atlantic Council, at 15 (Nov. 2016).

[731] Ben Knight, "Putin Associate Opens Russia-Friendly Think Tank in Berlin," *Deutsche Welle,* July 1, 2016.

[732] Roman Goncharenko, "In Dresden, Russian Flags of Protest Against Islam and Merkel," *Deutsche Welle,* Nov. 22, 2015; Alina Polyakova et al., *The Kremlin's Trojan Horses,* at 16.

by Russian special security services were potentially being used to recruit new agents for the Russian state.[733]

Indeed, as Merkel's Germany has led the defense of transatlantic values that underlie open, democratic societies, playing on fears of migrants has become a durable theme of Russian disinformation and political influence in an effort to undermine the German government's standing with its own population. A well-known example of this is the "Lisa case" of January 2016, a fabricated story initiated on a Russian state-run television broadcaster and circulated widely on social media of a 13 year-old Russian-German girl who was kidnapped and sexually assaulted by "Southern-looking," presumably Muslim, migrants.[734] Police interviewed the alleged victim and quickly determined the story to be false, but even Russian Foreign Minister Sergei Lavrov joined the fray in publicly highlighting the case and suggesting an official cover-up.[735] The case sparked protests by thousands of Russian-German citizens who decried Germany's acceptance of migrants.[736] Ironically, the Lisa case was essentially a victim of its own success, as it piqued awareness in German society of Russian-sponsored disinformation and helped contribute to a healthy skepticism of fake news as Germany entered a hotly contested election season.

The use of bots and trolls in the 2016 German election appears to have been less extensive than in the recent elections in France and the United States and the Brexit referendum in the United Kingdom. Nevertheless, social media analyses by U.S. and European-based researchers suggested that prior to the German election, pro-Kremlin and primarily Russian-language "bot" accounts on Twitter combined commercial and pornographic posts and retweets with pro-AfD content, concerns about electoral fraud, and attacks on Russian anti-corruption campaigner Alexey Navalny—though it was unclear who was managing or directing these sporadic posts.[737] A purported Russian hacker told *BuzzFeed News* that he and thirty other hackers were amplifying non-official, pro-AfD content prior to the poll; the party itself had stated it would not use Twitter bots as part of its campaign.[738] Meanwhile, Russian state-sponsored media outlets RT and Sputnik crafted and pushed out stories carefully framed to undermine Merkel and her party. RT ran positive articles on the AfD and amplified German nationalists who railed on the country's perceived failures in European integration and counter-terrorism, while Sputnik put out stories that played up Russian and German interests allegedly being

[733] Andrew Rettman, "Fight Club: Russian Spies Seek EU Recruits," *EUobserver,* May 23, 2017.
[734] Damien McGuinness, "Russia Steps into Berlin 'Rape' Storm Claiming German Cover-Up," *BBC,* Jan. 27, 2016; Ben Knight, "Teenage Girl Admits Making Up Migrant Rape Claim That Outraged Germany," *The Guardian,* Jan. 31, 2016.
[735] Damien McGuinness, "Russia Steps into Berlin 'Rape' Storm Claiming German Cover-Up," *BBC,* Jan. 27, 2016.
[736] Statement of Melissa Hooper, Director of Human Rights and Civil Society, Human Rights First, *The Scourge of Russian Disinformation,* Hearing before the U.S. Commission on Security and Cooperating in Europe, Sept. 14, 2017, at 3.
[737] "#ElectionWatch: Russian Botnet Boosts German Far-Right Posts," Digital Forensic Research Lab, Sept. 21, 2017; Anne Applebaum et al., *'Make Germany Great Again:' Kremlin, Alt-Right, and International Influences in the 2017 German Elections,* Institute for Strategic Dialogue and LSE Institute for Global Affairs, at 13.
[738] Henk Van Ess & Jane Lytvynenko, "This Russian Hacker Says His Twitter Bots Are Spreading Messages to Help Germany's Far Right Party In The Election," *BuzzFeed News,* Sept. 24, 2017.

undermined by Europe and the United States, as well as the countries' mutual hardships during the Second World War.[739]

Germany's domestic intelligence agency also alleged that Kremlin-linked hackers were behind a 2015 hack of the lower house of the Bundestag that exfiltrated thousands of documents, and were responsible for subsequent hacks of Merkel's Christian Democratic Union party and other political foundations and organizations affiliated with it.[740] The head of German domestic intelligence said in comments to reporters that the attacks were part of a campaign directed by Russia to "generate information that can be used for disinformation or for influencing operations . . . . Whether they do it or not is a political decision . . . that I assume will be made in the Kremlin."[741] German officials determined that the attacks had been likely carried out by APT28, the hacker group also known as Fancy Bear that has been linked to the Russian government, and which was connected to several high-profile cyberattacks in the United States, France, Ukraine, and elsewhere.[742] Interestingly, by the September 24 election in Germany, a data dump of hacked information similar to those in the United States and France did not take place—perhaps out of concern for Merkel's reaction in the event that she won the election.[743]

In meetings with Committee staff in the months before the German election, most German interlocutors seemed sanguine that Russia would not interfere in a significant way, but political party representatives did express growing apprehension about their lack of preparation for a Russian attack. But time and the experience of other countries had afforded the German government, political parties, and the media the opportunity to build defenses against Russian meddling before election day. These defenses included a mix of government and non-government steps to boost resilience, from which the United States and others can draw important lessons.

Lessons Learned

- *Disincentivizing the Sharing of Disinformation Must be Balanced with Freedom of Expression Concerns:* In late 2016, with the encouragement of the Interior Ministry, all German political parties except for the AfD agreed not to use bots or paid trolls in their campaigning, while Chancellor Merkel warned in a major address of the threat of fake news and disinformation tactics and signaled a willingness to explore increased government regulation of this space.[744] The Interior Ministry also proposed the creation of a "Center of Defense Against Misinformation," noting that Russian-Germans and people of Turkish origins are especially susceptible to disinformation and rec-

---

[739] Donald N. Jensen, "Moscow's New Strategy in Berlin," Center for European Policy Analysis, Oct. 4, 2017.

[740] Andrea Shalal, "Germany Challenges Russia Over Alleged Cyberattacks," *Reuters*, May 4, 2017.

[741] *Ibid.*

[742] FireEye iSight Intelligence, *APT28: At the Center of The Storm, Russia Strategically Evolves Its Cyber Operations*, at 4 (Jan. 2017).

[743] Michael Schwirtz, "German Election Mystery: Why No Russian Meddling?" *The New York Times*, Sept. 21, 2017.

[744] Jefferson Chase, "Experts Say Laws Not Enough as Germany Fights Bots and Fake News," *Deutsche Welle*, Nov. 25, 2016.

ommending "an intensification of political education work" with those groups.[745] In June 2017, the German parliament passed legislation that enabled fines of up to €50 million for social media companies that failed to remove obviously illegal content within 24 hours, or that failed to assess likely false content and remove it within seven days. While the law increased incentives for social media companies like YouTube, Facebook, and Twitter to police the content on their platforms, critics of the law called it a concerning legal model that possibly infringes on free speech and places too much power in the hands of companies to curb content simply to avoid fines.[746] The government also relied on Germany's already relatively stringent laws on defamation and hate speech that promotes violence against minorities.[747] Facebook reported that it increased its efforts throughout the German parliamentary election campaign period, providing candidates with cybersecurity training, working directly with the Federal Office for Information Security (BSI) national cybersecurity office, and removing tens of thousands of fake accounts.[748] While German government, business, and civil society actors have deployed "vigorous action" against the causes and effects of information manipulation and dissemination, some experts have noted difficulties enforcing strengthened legal regimes and the risk they pose to freedom of expression, and have urged that the German government couple its monitoring and oversight of online propaganda with increasing media literacy among the population.[749]

- *Prioritize Cybersecurity Rapid-Response Capacity and Information Sharing* German efforts to bolster cyber capabilities included adopting a new cyber security strategy in November 2016 that outlines a plan to confront a range of emerging cyber threats, including the kind of threats many analysts have attributed to Russia. Under this new cyber strategy, overseen by the BSI, rapid reaction cyber teams have been created across the government to respond quickly to cyber threats against government institutions and critical infrastructure.[750] The German government has also created a new "Cyber Command" within its armed forces, staffed by about 13,500 military and other personnel.[751] A 2015 information technology security law established minimum standards for companies to protect critical cyber infrastructure and requires them to inform authorities about any critical incidents, in response to which BSI analyzes the threat and informs other companies who may be at

---

[745] "Germany Plans Creation of 'Center Of Defense' Against Fake News, Report Says," *Deutsche Welle*, Dec. 23, 2016.

[746] Carla Bleiker & Kate Brady, "Bundestag Passes Law to Fine Social Media Companies for not Deleting Hate Speech," *Deutsche Welle*, June 30, 2017.

[747] Thorsten Severin & Emma Thomasson,"German Parliament Backs Plan to Fine Social Media Over Hate Speech," *Reuters*, June 30, 2017.

[748] Richard Allan, Vice President for Public Policy EMEA, Facebook Ireland,"Update on German Elections," Facebook blog post, Sept. 27, 2017, https://de.newsroom.fb.com/news/2017/09/update-zu-den-wahlen (visited Dec. 30, 2017).

[749] Lisa-Maria N. Neudert, *Computational Propaganda in Germany: A Cautionary Tale*, University of Oxford, at 23 (June 2017).

[750] German Federal Ministry of the Interior, *Cyber Security Strategy for Germany*, Nov. 2016.

[751] "German Army Launches New Cyber Command," *Deutsche Welle*, Apr. 1, 2017.

risk of a similar attack.[752] BSI also advises parliamentary groups on how to protect themselves, and German political campaigns have agreed not to exploit any information that was the result of cyber hacking.[753]

- *Direct Diplomatic Warnings Can Deter Kremlin Aggression:* In their tense May 2017 meeting, Chancellor Merkel publicly warned that there would be "decisive measures" taken against any attempts to interfere in the German election through cyberattacks or disinformation. She pointed to the hybrid warfare techniques as a hallmark of Russian military doctrine, but also underscored that she was "not anxious" about possible Russian interference.[754]

---

[752] Janosch Delcker,"Germany's Cybersecurity Chief on Hacking, Russia and Problems Hiring Experts," *Politico EU,* Mar. 20, 2017; Act to Enhance the Security of Information Technology Systems (IT Security Act) (Gesetz zur Erhohung der Sicherheit informationstechnischer Systeme), German Federal Law Gazette 2015, Part I, No. 31, 1324, July 25, 2015.

[753] Delcker, "Germany's Cybersecurity Chief on Hacking, Russia and Problems Hiring Experts," Politico EU; Michael Schwirtz, "German Election Mystery: Why No Russian Meddling?" *The New York Times,* Sept. 21, 2017.

[754] Roland Oliphant, "'There's No Proof': Putin Denies Hacking Elections as Angela Merkel Visits for Summit on 'Problematic' Differences," *The Telegraph,* May 2, 2017.

133

In Spain, the authorities have grappled with the pernicious activities of Russian-based criminal organizations for decades. Their efforts have revealed direct ties between the Russian mafia and senior members of Putin's regime, as well as links between Putin himself and entities that have allegedly engaged in money laundering in Europe. Russia-based criminal organizations have reportedly been active in Catalonia for years, building their influence in politics and business and working to exploit rivalries between regional and national law enforcement entities. There is also an increasing body of evidence that Kremlin-run news outlets like RT and Sputnik, reinforced by bots and fake social media accounts, carried out a disinformation campaign during Catalonia's independence referendum in October 2016.

According to an extensive report by Sebastian Rotella published in *ProPublica*, a nonprofit investigative journalism organization, the Russian mafia landed in Spain in the late 1990s, when a high-ranking figure from St. Petersburg's notorious Tambov gang, Gennady Petrov, made his home on the island of Mallorca, from where he ran a worldwide network of the gang's businesses, including cobalt and cigarette smuggling through Finland, money laundering operations in Germany, Belgium, Cyprus, and the Czech Republic, and an embezzlement scheme in Germany that stole more than $100 million and resulted in thousands of shipyard workers losing their jobs.[755]

Spanish law enforcement grew curious about the source of Petrov's wealth—he had reportedly amassed $50 million in Spain alone—and began to monitor his phone calls.[756] They found that Petrov had active ties to senior officials throughout the Russian government.[757] He reportedly plotted with a senior justice ministry official in Moscow, who promised to intimidate a shipbuilder who was behind schedule in building a yacht for Petrov. A few days later, the shipbuilder was back on schedule.[758] And in a conversation with his son, Petrov boasted of meeting with Russia's then defense minister, Anatoly Serdiukov, with whom he reportedly made deals involving real estate, airplanes, and energy investments (Serdiukov was sacked by Putin in 2012 during an anti-corruption campaign, and granted amnesty in 2014).[759]

Spanish prosecutors met with Alexander Litvinenko—the former Russian spy who some suspect was assassinated on orders from Putin—in June 2006 and persuaded him to testify against Russian mobsters in Spain about information he had from his time in Russia's intelligence services.[760] But Litvinenko's killers got to him be-

---

[755] Sebastian Rotella, "A Gangster Place in the Sun: How Spain's Fight Against the Mob revealed Russian Power Networks," *ProPublica*, Nov. 10, 2017.

[756] *Ibid.*

[757] *Ibid.*

[758] *Ibid.*

[759] *Ibid.*; Jason Bush & Baczynska, "Russia Grants Amnesty to Former Defence Minister Anatoly Serdyukov—Report," *Reuters*, Mar. 6, 2014.

[760] An inquiry by the UK's House of Commons concluded that order to kill Litvinenko was likely approved by Putin. United Kingdom House of Commons, *The Litvinenko Inquiry: Report into the Death of Alexander Litvinenko*, at 244 (Mar. 2015); see Appendix B; Sebastian Rotella, "A Gangster Place in the Sun: How Spain's Fight Against the Mob revealed Russian Power Networks," *ProPublica*, Nov. 10, 2017.

134

fore he could testify at trial. Jose Grinda Gonzalez, Spain's leading law enforcement expert on Russian organized crime, told reporters, "We had accepted the idea that the world of the Russian mafia was like that. But it's true that the case made other people think this gentleman had told the truth, because now he was dead." [761]

Through their investigations of Petrov's gang, Spanish law enforcement authorities found enough evidence linking the criminal organization to Russian government officials that they named over a dozen of them in the indictments, including the former defense minister.[762] Petrov was arrested in 2008 in a massive crackdown on Russian organized crime that eventually resulted in pretrial indictments against 27 suspects on charges of criminal association and money laundering.[763] Vladislav Reznik, a senior Duma member and leader of Putin's United Russia party, is among the accused, and the indictment alleges that he operated at "the highest levels of power in Russia on behalf of Mr. Petrov and his organization." [764] Petrov's trial is set to begin in February 2018, though he is unlikely to attend: he disappeared to Russia on bond in 2012 and the Russian government has not taken any action to return him to Spain.[765] But the Petrov case has led to more progress in Spain's fight against Russian organized crime: in 2009, while pursuing a lead from the case, Spanish police entered the office of a lawyer suspected of money laundering, only to see him grab a document from his desk, crumple it up, and begin to eat it.[766] The document, after being forcibly spat out, led investigators to a new group of alleged money launderers in Barcelona who have suspected ties to Kremlin-linked organized crime.[767]

The suspected money laundering ring in Barcelona is indicative of long-running efforts by Russian organized crime groups to set up shop in Catalonia. Russian mobsters have reportedly been active in Catalonia for years, building influence among politicians and businesspeople and seeking to exploit the rivalry between regional and national law-enforcement agencies.[768] According to *ProPublica,*

> Suspected underworld figures also surfaced as representatives of a major Russian oil company, Lukoil, that was proposing to join with a Spanish firm to open 150 gasoline stations in [Barcelona]. The deal ultimately fell through, but information from Spanish and Russian law enforcement cited in court documents suggested that organized crime figures with ties to both Lukoil and the Russian spy agencies planned to use the deal to launder illicit funds.[769]

And in 2013, the Catalan regional government appointed Xavier Crespo, a former mayor belonging to the Convergence and Union (CiU) party, to the post of security secretary, which controls the

---

[761] Sebastian Rotella, "A Gangster Place in the Sun: How Spain's Fight Against the Mob revealed Russian Power Networks," *ProPublica,* Nov. 10, 2017.
[762] While mentioned in court documents, the officials were not actually charged. *Ibid.*
[763] *Ibid.*
[764] *Ibid.*
[765] *Ibid.*
[766] *Ibid.*
[767] *Ibid.*
[768] Sebastian Rotella, "A Gangster Place in the Sun: How Spain's Fight Against the Mob revealed Russian Power Networks," *ProPublica,* Nov. 10, 2017.
[769] *Ibid.*

Catalan police.[770] However, the appointment was rescinded when intelligence services based in Madrid presented evidence that Crespo was involved in money laundering, and in 2014 he was indicted for accepting bribes from Petrov.[771] The CiU also allegedly received funds laundered by Russian crime syndicates through Catalonian banks and shell companies.[772]

A faction of the CiU joined with two leftist parties to form the coalition that held the referendum on October 1, 2017 for Catalonia's independence from Spain. The referendum was driven by decades-long domestic political, cultural, and economic issues, but it also presented Moscow with an opportunity to promote an outcome that would weaken a major EU state. And there is now an increasingly large body of evidence showing that the Kremlin, at least through its state-run media outlets, directed a significant disinformation campaign targeting the referendum. The U.S. State Department reported that:

> Russian state news outlets, such as Sputnik, published a number of articles in the run up to the poll that highlighted alleged corruption within the Spanish government and driving an overarching anti-EU narrative in support of the secessionist movement. These Russian news agencies, as well as Russian users on Twitter, also repeatedly promoted the views of Julian Assange, the founder of WikiLeaks, who has taken to social media to call for Spanish authorities to respect the upcoming vote in Catalonia. Spanish newspapers have also reported that Russian bots attempted to flood social media with controversial posts in support of Catalonian independence prior to the referendum.[773]

One analysis looked at more than five million social media messages on Catalonia posted between September 29 and October 5, and found that 30 percent of the messages came from anonymous accounts that exclusively post content from *RT* and Sputnik, while 25 percent came from bots and 10 percent from the official accounts of the two propaganda platforms.[774] Another analysis found that, just before the referendum took place, pro-Kremlin Twitter accounts increased their mentions of the Catalan crisis by 2,000 percent.[775]

The Kremlin's interests in Catalonia's referendum were likely varied. First, Moscow has recently favored independence and secessionist movements that occur beyond Russia's borders and weaken the EU. For example, before Brexit, Kremlin-linked disinformation campaigns were pro-Scottish independence. But after the UK decided not to be in the EU, and many voters in Scotland indicated

[770] Martin Arostegui, "Officials: Russia Seeking to Exploit Catalonia Secessionist Movement," *VOA News*, Nov. 24, 2017.
[771] *Ibid.*
[772] *Ibid.*
[773] U.S. Department of State, "Report to Congress on Efforts by the Russian Federation to Undermine Elections in Europe and Eurasia," Pursuant to the Countering America's Adversaries through Sanctions Act of 2017 (P.L. 115-44), Nov. 7, 2017.
[774] Itxu Diaz, "Venezuela and Russia Teamed Up to Push Pro-Catalan Fake News," *The Daily Beast*, Nov. 28, 2017.
[775] David Alandete, "Pro-Russian Networks See 2,000% Increase in Activity in Favor of Catalan Referendum," *El Pais*, Oct. 1, 2017.

a desire to stay in the EU, the Kremlin changed its stance to anti-Scottish independence.[776] And as Spanish Prime Minister Mariano Rajoy told reporters, after noting that over half of the fake profiles involved in spreading fake news came from Russia, "What is clear is that there are people who may be interested in things not going well in Europe."[777] But there were also other, darker motives likely at work. According to Spanish intelligence analysts, Russian companies would look to fill the vacuum created by the exit of Catalan and Spanish companies that left because of instability.[778] In addition, the Kremlin could "see an independent Catalonia as a possible base from which to penetrate other parts of Europe, where their business activities are restricted by sanctions enforced by the United States and the European Union."[779]

While the referendum did not result in Catalonia's independence from Spain, it showed that Spain is a growing target of the Kremlin's malign influence operations. Spain can strengthen its resiliency by studying the experiences of and cooperating with other similarly-targeted European countries, and the U.S. government should take steps to help shore-up ongoing efforts.

Lessons Learned

- *Aggressive Investigations of Money Laundering Can Reduce the Kremlin's Influence:* Spain's investigations and prosecutions are targeting and removing bad actors who have spread corruption throughout Europe and likely here in the United States. The U.S. government has assisted with these investigations, and should continue to do so to the greatest extent possible. Furthermore, the U.S. government should establish a task force dedicated to investigating money laundering by Russian entities, and should also designate Russia as a jurisdiction of primary money laundering concern, which would subject Russian financial institutions to additional reporting requirements. Spanish authorities should also be commended and used as an example for the complicated and courageous work that its law enforcement officials are carrying out against Russia-based organized criminal organizations.

- *The Kremlin Will Pursue Targets of Opportunity:* As shown in other elections and referendums among Western democracies, the Kremlin's disinformation operations will not pass up on opportunities to sow chaos and confusion in an attempt to undermine the democratic process and weaken European institutions. The United States and its partners and allies, as well as the private sector and civil society, must proactively identify potential next targets and launch efforts to build resiliency against Kremlin influence operations well in advance of elections and referendums.

[776] Chris Green, "Russia 'Set to U-turn on Support for Scottish Independence," *The Scotsman,* May 11, 2017.

[777] William Booth & Michael Birnbaum, "British and Spanish Leaders Say Russian Trolls Meddled in Their Elections," *The Washington Post,* Nov. 14, 2017.

[778] Martin Arostegui, "Officials: Russia Seeking to Exploit Catalonia Secessionist Movement," *VOA News,* Nov. 24, 2017.

[779] *Ibid.*

In recent years, Italy has seen a resurgence of anti-establishment, populist parties that have garnered appeal among the population and achieved some electoral success. Some of these parties are strong advocates of pro-Kremlin foreign policies, and have extensively used fake news and conspiracy theories in their media campaigns, often drawn from Russian state-owned media outlets. With national elections coming up in 2018, Italy could be a target for electoral interference by the Kremlin, which will likely seek to promote parties that are against renewing EU sanctions for Russia's aggression in Ukraine.

The Five Star Movement (M5S), which was formed in 2009 and surged to popularity in recent years with its anti-establishment message, seeks to end sanctions on Russia and normalize relations with the regime of Syrian dictator Bashar al-Assad, and recognizes the annexation of Crimea, opposes Italian participation in NATO exercises, and has called for a referendum on Italy's inclusion in the Eurozone.[780] The chairman of M5S's foreign affairs committee, Manlio Di Stefano, has stated that NATO is secretly preparing a "final assault" on Russia and that "there's a limit" to the alliance that Italy and the United States forged in the aftermath of World War II.[781]

During a failed 2016 constitutional referendum, M5S used a "sprawling network of websites and social media accounts that [were] spreading fake news, conspiracy theories, and pro-Kremlin stories to millions of people," according to an analysis by *BuzzFeed News*. A video created by *RT* and promoted by M5S's network claimed to show thousands of people protesting against the referendum, when in fact they were at a rally that was supporting the referendum (*RT* later claimed that this was due to a production error). And one M5S parliament member promoted a conspiracy theory on Facebook that asserted Italy's government had colluded with the media to report that an earthquake which hit the country was not as powerful as it actually was, thereby allowing the government to reduce payments for damage.[782] A former M5S communications advisor has said that spreading conspiracy theories is not just a tactic of the party, but "akin to a policy."[783]

The Kremlin has also worked to establish formal political ties and influence with extremist Italian political parties. For example, the United Russia party and the Northern League, a radical right-wing populist party, signed a cooperation agreement in 2017, where they agreed to develop ties in the Council of Europe and the OSCE, as well as promote business links between their coun-

---

[780] Alberto Nardelli & Craig Silverman, "Italy's Most Popular Political Party Is Leading Europe in Fake News and Kremlin Propaganda," *BuzzFeed News*, Nov. 29, 2016; Jason Horowitz, "With Italy No Longer in U.S. Focus, Russia Swoops to Fill the Void," *The New York Times*, May 29, 2017.
[781] Jason Horowitz, "With Italy No Longer in U.S. Focus, Russia Swoops to Fill the Void," *The New York Times*, May 29, 2017.
[782] Alberto Nardelli & Craig Silverman, "Italy's Most Popular Political Party Is Leading Europe in Fake News and Kremlin Propaganda," *BuzzFeed News*, Nov. 29, 2016.
[783] Jason Horowitz, "In Italian Schools, Reading, Writing, and Recognizing Fake News," *The New York Times*, Oct. 18, 2017.

tries.[784] Some observers also suspect that the Northern League may have received funds from the Kremlin's security services.[785]

While there is no known evidence of M5S receiving funding from Kremlin-linked sources, one Italian national security official told *Business Insider* that "I think some of our political parties are vulnerable to infiltration. They don't have the experience, the antibodies, to fend off such formidable intelligence services."[786] Estonia's ambassador to Italy, Celia Kuningas-Saagpakk, who in a previous role monitored the Kremlin's malign influence operations in Ukraine and elsewhere, noted to the *The New York Times,* that the Russian government "has invested a lot in influencing public opinion in [Italy]."[787]

State-owned Russian energy firms also exert influence through Italian energy firms such as ENI, which is currently a partner of Gazprom in the Nord Stream 2 pipeline (see Chapter 4).[788] At the request of Gazprom, though unbeknownst to its attendees, an ENI subsidiary reportedly sponsored a foreign policy conference at a think tank in Italy, where "it was stressed that Russia could be an important ally for the EU."[789] It is worth noting that Russia is Italy's biggest supplier of natural gas, and Italian oil major ENI's policy is to give priority to its relationship with Gazprom over Algerian suppliers. ENI has also signed a strategic partnership agreement with Gazprom, and pledged to cooperate with Gazprom both on the now-cancelled South Stream pipeline and the under-consideration Nord Stream 2 pipeline.[790]

Since the 2016 referendum, Italy's government has begun to take actions to better inoculate its population against fake news and disinformation campaigns. The president of Italy's Chamber of Deputies, Laura Boldrini, has spearheaded a project with Italy's Ministry of Education to train students at 8,000 high schools across the country on how to verify news stories and recognize fake news and conspiracy theories that they see on social media platforms. Facebook is reportedly contributing to the initiative by promoting it with targeted ads aimed at high-school-age users in Italy.[791] The program should help to mitigate fake news stories that originate both at home and from abroad, and should be studied by other countries as they develop their own school curriculums to counter fake news.

According to the now-confirmed U.S. Ambassador to Italy, Lewis Eisenberg, Italy is aware of the Kremlin's tactics in Italy and the country "shares our concerns about Russian aggression in Europe,

[784] Max Seddon & James Politi, "Putin's Party Signs Deal with Italy's Far-Right Lega Nord," *Financial Times,* Mar. 6, 2017.

[785] Peter Foster & Matthew Holehouse, "Russia Accused of Clandestine Funding of European Parties as US Conducts Major Review of Vladimir Putin's Strategy," *The Telegraph,* Jan. 16, 2016.

[786] Jason Horowitz, "With Italy No Longer in U.S. Focus, Russia Swoops to Fill the Void," *The New York Times,* May 29, 2017; Sebastian Rotella, "Russia is Engaged in a Full-Scale Shadow War in Europe," Business Insider, Apr. 20, 2017.

[787] Jason Horowitz, "With Italy No Longer in U.S. Focus, Russia Swoops to Fill the Void," *The New York Times,* May 29, 2017.

[788] Warsaw Institute, "Italians with Gazprom Again," Russia Monitor, Sept. 1, 2017.

[789] Vladislava Vojtiskova et al., *The Bear in Sheep's Clothing: Russia's Government-Funded Organisations in the EU,* Wilfried Martens Centre for European Studies, at 25 (July 2016).

[790] Angelantonio Rosato, "A Marriage of Convenience? The Future of Italy-Russia Relations," *European Council on Foreign Relations,* July 15, 2016.

[791] Jason Horowitz, "In Italian Schools, Reading, Writing, and Recognizing Fake News," *The New York Times,* Oct. 18, 2017.

including Russian disinformation campaigns and malign influence activities." During his Senate confirmation hearing, Eisenberg told the U.S. Senate Foreign Relations Committee that he will "work to strengthen our coordination with Italian partners, across relevant agencies, to detect and counter these activities that seek to undermine democratic institutions and principles" and to "make U.S.-Italian cooperation on this issue a priority, particularly in advance of Italian national elections that are likely to take place in 2018."[792]

The U.S. government must follow through on these commitments and help Italy secure its democratic process against foreign interference. Italy is an essential NATO ally and a key member of the EU, which will vote in 2018 on whether to uphold sanctions related to the Russian government's activities in Ukraine.[793] Italy has at times been skeptical of imposing and strengthening EU sanctions on Russia, and in 2015 delayed a sanctions renewal decision, arguing that more discussion was needed.[794] In the Veneto region of Italy, a local assembly controlled by the Northern League adopted a resolution in 2016 to call for Italy to end the sanctions on Russia, arguing that counter-sanctions are damaging the Venetian economy (the region also voted in late 2017 in favor of greater autonomy from Rome).[795]

Lessons Learned

- *Italy May be a Target of Opportunity for the Kremlin:* Given the opportunity to promote an outcome that could weaken the EU's united stance on sanctions, the Russian government could seek to interfere in Italy's elections in early 2018. Along with other important elections around Europe, the United States and our partners and allies must maintain the highest levels of cooperation and vigilance to ensure that our electoral processes remain free from undue foreign influence.

- *Disinformation Comes From Domestic Sources Too:* The Kremlin is not the only source of disinformation and conspiracy theories that seek to undermine European institutions like the EU and NATO. Domestic political parties, especially populist ones, can also make effective use of the same tactics that the Kremlin employs. As Italy also shows, educating the population on media literacy and how to discern fake news can be one of the most important steps toward strengthening the resilience of the democratic process.

---

[792] Responses to Additional Questions for the Record, Lewis M. Eisenberg, Nominee for Ambassador to Italy & San Marino, *Nomination of Lewis M. Eisenberg to be Ambassador Extraordinary and Plenipotentiary of the United States of America to the Italian Republic,* Hearing before the U.S. Senate Committee on Foreign Relations, July 20, 2017.

[793] Connor Murphy, "EU Extends Russia Sanctions through January 2018," *Politico,* June 28, 2017.

[794] James Kanter, "Italy Delays E.U.'s Renewal of Sanctions Against Russia," *The New York Times,* Dec. 14, 2015.

[795] Angelantonio Rosato, "A Marriage of Convenience? The Future of Italy-Russia Relations," European Council on Foreign Relations, July 15, 2016. "Northern Italy Regions Overwhelmingly Vote for Greater Autonomy," *The Guardian,* Oct. 22, 2017. Italy's exports to Russia did fall significantly after the sanctions were implemented, dropping around 40 percent in the first half of 2015. European Parliament, Directorate-General for External Policies, Policy Department, *Russia's and the EU's Sanctions: Economic and Trade Effects, Compliance, and the Way Forward,* at 9 (Oct. 2017).

Chapter 7: Multilateral & U.S. Efforts to Counter the Kremlin's Asymmetric Arsenal

In addition to the measures that individual states have taken to build resiliency against malign influence operations within their own borders (see Chapters 5 and 6), many countries, especially those that belong to the EU and NATO, have also launched or joined multilateral efforts. These efforts include building collective defenses against disinformation and cyberattacks, improving cross-border cooperation on energy diversification, applying sanctions on malicious actors, and more. Although the United States participates in some of these multilateral efforts and has taken a few steps on its own to address Russian government hybrid warfare, its response lags far behind what is necessary to defend against and deter the threat.

Over the past several years, European governments and institutions have recognized that Russia's disinformation operations are a challenge that requires increased attention and resources. In response, they have launched several multilateral and regional initiatives to improve Europe's resilience, with varying levels of success. One of the first such organizations was the NATO Strategic Communications Center of Excellence, established by seven NATO member states in July of 2014, and headquartered in Riga, Latvia. The Center provides analysis, advice, and support to the NATO alliance, including research into identifying the early signs of hybrid warfare and the study of Russia's disinformation operations in Ukraine.[796] The EU's External Action Service, which works under the EU's foreign affairs chief, launched a similar operation in 2015, known as the EU East StratCom Task Force. The Task Force uses a wide volunteer base from around the EU and elsewhere to collect examples of pro-Kremlin disinformation and analyze and publicize them in a searchable database.[797] While the Task Force has only about a dozen full-time employees, its volunteer network has over 400 experts from more than 30 countries. It publishes news and analysis on the website *EU vs. Disinfo,* and is responsible for communicating EU policies toward the Eastern Partnership countries of Armenia, Azerbaijan, Belarus, Georgia, Moldova, and

---

[796] NATO Strategic Communications Centre of Excellence, "About Us," https://www.stratcomcoe.org/about-us (visited Dec. 14, 2017).
[797] EU vs. Disinfo, "Disinformation Cases," https://euvsdisinfo.eu/disinformation-cases (visited Dec. 14, 2017).

Ukraine.[798] To promote a positive narrative of the EU, the Task Force constructs simple messages meant to resonate in each country about the benefits of cooperation with the EU. The Task Force has a very broad mandate, but relatively little funding.[799]

To combine the efforts of both EU and NATO countries and broaden the scope beyond disinformation, Finland launched the European Center of Excellence for Countering Hybrid Threats in Helsinki in July 2017. Currently comprised of 12 EU and NATO countries, including the United States, it uses research and training to improve participants' readiness to respond to cyberattacks, disinformation, and propaganda.[800] Finland started the Center after it experienced Russian attempts to use social media to interfere in it 2015 elections.[801] After the election, the Finnish government ordered all of its ministries to imagine worst-case scenarios of foreign interference, which they compiled into a report and shared with EU and NATO partners.[802] The report led to the creation of the Center, which has three work strands, also known as "communities of interest": (1) hybrid influencing, led by the UK; (2) terrorism and radicalism; and (3) vulnerabilities and resilience, led by Finland.[803] The Center's officials also hope to work with Google, Facebook, and other social media companies to track online content and identify threats.[804] NATO's Cooperative Cyber Defense Center of Excellence, based in Tallinn, Estonia, also focuses on helping member states secure their cyber infrastructure. The Center draws on experts with military, government, and private industry experience from 20 nations to provide training and expertise to NATO nations and partners.[805]

Although these initiatives were conceived and launched on an ad hoc basis, collectively they form a network of institutions that address overlapping threats and vulnerabilities facing Europe and its allies, including the United States.

A number of NGOs and think tanks have also launched their own regionally focused programs to counter disinformation. One of the first such operations was the Kremlin Watch Monitor, launched by the European Values Think Tank in 2015 and headquartered in Prague. With the support of private and public donors, including several European governments, this initiative focuses on fact checking and analysis of Russian government-backed

[798] European Union External Action Service, "Questions and Answers about the East StratCom Task Force," https://eeas.europa.eu/headquarters/headquarters-homepage/2116/-questions-and-answers-about-the-east-stratcom-task-force—en (visited Dec. 14, 2017).

[799] The head of the EU's External Action Service, Federica Mogherini, has come under fire from scores of analysts and academics for keeping the team "absurdly understaffed" and underfunded. See European Values, Open Letter from European Security Experts to Federica Mogherini, Mar. 20, 2017, http://www.europeanvalues.net/mogherini/. One EU official told Politico that Mogherini "is considered to be soft on Russia compared to others in the Commission, or what some Eastern countries would like. Officials who work on these issues get no support from her." Ryan Heath, "Federica Mogherini 'Soft' on Disinformation, Critics Say," Politico, Mar. 22, 2017.

[800] European Centre of Excellence for Countering Hybrid Threats, "About Us," https://www.hybridcoe.fi/about-us (visited Dec. 15, 2017).

[801] See Chapter 6, Finland.

[802] Committee Staff Discussion with Finnish Government Officials.

[803] European Centre of Excellence for Countering Hybrid Threats, "About Us," https://www.hybridcoe.fi/about-us (visited Dec. 15, 2017). As of publication, there was no designated country lead for the work strand on terrorism and radicalism.

[804] Committee Staff Discussion with Finnish Government Officials.

[805] NATO Cooperative Cyber Defence Centre of Excellence, "About Cyber Defence Centre," https://www.ccdcoe.org/about-us.html (visited Dec. 15, 2017).

disinformation. It also provides regular monitoring reports and policy recommendations, publishes case studies, conducts trainings, and convenes practitioners and policymakers in both open and closed forums.[806] A similar effort, the Information Warfare Initiative, is run by the Center for European Policy Analysis (CEPA), an American think tank with offices in Europe. The program monitors the content and techniques of Russian disinformation in Belarus, Estonia, Latvia, Lithuania, Poland, and Romania. In addition to monitoring, the initiative works to help policymakers develop strategies to counter disinformation.[807]

European countries have also begun to develop multilateral efforts to produce and support accurate, independent Russian-language media that can serve as an alternative to Kremlin propaganda for Russian-speaking audiences. In response to a 2015 report by the European Endowment for Democracy, European governments are working to develop a Russian-language regional news hub and a multimedia distribution platform, as well as other initiatives.[808] For example, the Netherlands and Poland are supporting the development of an independent Russian-language regional news agency.[809] In addition, the British Broadcasting Corporation (BBC) is developing a blueprint for a "content factory" to help Central and Eastern European countries create Russian-language entertainment programs.[810]

European governments' joint efforts to promote investigative journalism have already proven effective. One positive example is the Russian Language News Exchange Program, launched in 2016 with support from the government of the Netherlands and other European governments and institutions. The program supports and trains journalists in the EU Eastern Partnership countries on Russia's periphery. In 2016, the program's participants produced and exchanged more than 500 stories, and each story produced by the exchange garnered at least one million views across multiple platforms. Analysts attribute the program's strong success to its focus on unique local reporting rather than covering the international stories that dominate Russian disinformation.[811] The program, currently funded through 2019, should be continued and expanded in future years.

Finally, efforts to improve media literacy on Russia's periphery have also shown a large return on investment. For example, the Learn to Discern Program, funded by the Canadian government, operated in Ukraine from July 2015 to March 2016. The program trained 15,000 Ukrainians in "safe, informed media consumption techniques," including avoiding emotional manipulation, verifying sources, identifying hate speech, verifying expert credentials, de-

---

[806] European Values, "Kremlin Watch, What We Do," http://www.europeanvalues.net/kremlinwatch/what-we/ (visited Dec. 31, 2017).

[807] Center for European Policy Analysis, "Information Warfare Initiative," http://infowar.cepa.org/About (visited Dec. 15, 2017).

[808] European Endowment for Democracy, "Bringing Plurality & Balance to Russian Language Media—Final Recommendations," https://www.democracyendowment.eu/news/bringing-plurality-1/ (visited Dec. 15, 2017).

[809] Andrew Rettman, "Dutch-Polish 'Content Factory' to Counter Russian Propaganda," EUobserver, July 21, 2015.

[810] Government Accountability Office, *U.S. Government Takes a Country-Specific Approach to Addressing Disinformation Overseas*, at 62 (May 2017).

[811] Nina Jankowicz, *Assessing the Western Response to Russian Disinformation in Europe: How Can We Do Better?*, at 11 (2016-2017).

144

tecting censorship, and debunking news, photos, and videos. In a survey, 89 percent of participants reported using their new skills and 91 percent reported sharing their new skills with an average of six people each, reaching 90,000 Ukrainians in total. Furthermore, 54 percent of the 2.3 million Ukrainians who viewed the program's information campaign in its first two weeks reported a need for greater skills in discerning disinformation.[812]

EUROPEAN ENERGY DIVERSIFICATION AND INTEGRATION

While Europe has been slow to recognize and respond to the Kremlin's weaponization of energy, some countries have begun taking steps to mitigate their dependence on Russian energy supplies and therefore reduce the Kremlin's influence. The EU has traditionally had little, if any, influence over the energy policies of its member states. Since energy policy in European countries is set by national governments, with each EU member state making its own decisions regarding energy mix, suppliers, and contracts, the Kremlin has been able to pursue and implement its "divide and conquer" strategy by dealing with states on a bilateral basis. Over the past decade, however, EU member states, concerned about reliance on Russian energy and facing pressure to combat climate change, have begun to gradually increase cooperation and work toward developing a unified EU energy policy. In March 2015, the EU's member state governments endorsed a European Commission proposal for a "European Energy Union." Among other things, the proposal focuses on energy security and solidarity, and an integrated European energy market.[813]

Several European countries have also come out in strong opposition to the Nord Stream 2 pipeline, which could make Europe more dependent on Russian energy supplies and would significantly diminish Ukrainian government revenues collected from pipeline transit fees in its territory. In the summer of 2016, the leaders of Croatia, the Czech Republic, Estonia, Hungary, Latvia, Lithuania, Poland, Slovakia, and Romania wrote to the European Commission president about their concerns that the Nord Stream 2 pipeline (NS2) could create "destabilizing geopolitical consequences" and "pose certain risks for energy security," especially by increasing Central and Eastern European countries' reliance on Russian gas supplies.[814] And in late November 2017, the Danish government passed a law that would allow it to block NS2 for security or foreign policy reasons (the pipeline requires approval from Denmark, Sweden, and Finland, as it would traverse their territories).[815]

The EU has also supported several projects to improve energy integration and reduce reliance on Russian energy supplies. These infrastructure projects, especially cross-border ones, are known as "Projects of Common Interest," and are supported by an EU fund

---

[812] IREX, "Learn to Discern," https://www.irex.org/project/learn-discern (visited Dec. 15, 2017).
[813] See European Commission, Energy Strategy and Energy Union, https://ec.europa.eu/energy/en/topics/energy-strategy-and-energy-union (visited Dec. 31, 2017); Michael Ratner et al., *Europe's Energy Security: Options and Challenges to Natural Gas Supply Diversification,* Congressional Research Service, at 7 (Nov. 2015).
[814] Andrew Rettman, "Eastern EU Leaders to Warn Juncker on Nord Stream II," *EUobserver,* Mar. 17, 2016.
[815] Erik Matzen & Stine Jacobsen, "Denmark Passes Law That Could Ban Russian Pipeline from Going Through its Waters," *Reuters,* Nov. 30, 2017; Henry Roy et al., "Gazprom to Receive Funding for Nord Stream 2 Pipeline," *Financial Times,* Apr. 24, 2017.

that aims to boost energy, transport, and digital infrastructure.[816] One project, the development of a liquid natural gas (LNG) terminal in Croatia, would provide new opportunities for energy supply diversification throughout the Balkans.[817] Similar LNG terminals in Lithuania and Poland have had transformational effects in reducing dependence on Russian pipelines for natural gas supplies.[818] LNG terminals allow for the development of spot markets for natural gas, ensuring that market forces keep prices in check, and reduce the Kremlin's bargaining power by increasing supplier options. After it built an LNG import terminal, Lithuania was able to leverage a fair market price for its natural gas imports from Russia, ending years of paying the highest rates for gas in Europe. Lithuania's president summarized the benefits of new sources of LNG upon the first delivery of U.S. LNG to her country in 2017: "U.S. gas imports to Lithuania and other European countries is a game changer in the European gas market. This is an opportunity for Europe to end its addiction to Russian gas and ensure a secure, competitive and diversified supply."[819]

The EU has also made market liberalization and integration a key part of its energy strategy, launching the "Third Energy Package" in 2011 to work towards a single EU gas and electricity market. The Package included key provisions on "unbundling," or separating the activities of energy transmission from production and supply interests. Subsequently, the EU concluded that Gazprom had to unbundle its plans for the South Stream pipeline, leading Gazprom to effectively cancel the project.[820] A smart grid development between Slovenia and Croatia, as well as the development of improved Romania-Bulgaria electricity interconnections will also have positive effects. In northern Europe, several ongoing developments will also reduce dependence on Gazprom, including: a gas pipeline from Norway to Poland, via Denmark (Baltic Pipe); a Poland-Lithuania gas interconnector project; the construction of a Finland-Estonia gas pipeline; upgrades to make the Estonia-Latvia gas interconnector bi-directional; Baltic state participation in the "Nordpool" wholesale market for electricity; and plans for all Baltic states to desynchronize from the Russia-Belarus electricity grid and integrate into the European energy grid. All of these developments show the importance of improving intra-EU connectivity and moving away from monopoly suppliers and companies, especially state-driven monopoly suppliers, which bring along with them entrenched oligarchies and other bad actors.[821]

EU AND U.S. EFFORTS TO SANCTION MALICIOUS ACTORS

The Russian government's malign influence and hybrid warfare operations have led to a strong sanctions regime jointly imple-

816 European Commission, "Funding for Projects of Common Interest," https://ec.europa.eu/energy/en/topics/infrastructure/projects-common-interest/funding-projects-common-interest (visited Dec. 15, 2017).
817 European Commission, "EU Invests in Energy Security and Diversification in Central and South Eastern Europe," https://ec.europa.eu/info/news/eu-invests-energy-security-and-diversification-central-and-south-eastern-europe-2017-dec-18—en (visited Jan. 4, 2018).
818 Robbie Gramer, "First U.S. Natural Gas Shipped to Poland," Foreign Policy, June 8, 2017.
819 Agnia Grigas, "U.S. Natural Gas Arrives in Lithuania," Foreign Affairs, Sep. 12, 2017.
820 "South Stream Bilateral Deals Breach EU Law, Commission Says," EURACTIV.com, Dec. 4, 2013.
821 U.S. Department of State, Information Provided to Committee Staff.

mented by Europe and the United States. Many of these sanctions were put in place as a consequence for Russia's illegal annexation of Ukraine's Crimea and its support for separatists in eastern Ukraine. Other sanctions, especially those unilaterally implemented by the United States, punish malicious actors who are engaged in cyberattacks, human rights violations, or significant acts of corruption.

The EU's sanctions require the unanimous agreement of all 28 EU member states to implement, and unanimity is required to extend the sanctions every six months.[822] The EU's sanctions against Russia fall in to three categories:

1. Restrictive measures on individuals and entities in Russia and Ukraine believed to be involved in the annexation of Crimea and efforts to destabilize eastern Ukraine;

2. Economic sanctions targeting Russia's finance, defense, and energy sectors; and

3. Restrictions on trade, investment, and tourism services with the occupied Crimea region.[823]

In early 2014, shortly after Russia's annexation of Crimea, U.S. and EU sanctions mostly focused on visa bans and asset freezes, but under pressure from the U.S. Congress, the Obama Administration applied additional sectoral sanctions in July 2014.[824] After intelligence sources indicated that separatists using a Russian-supplied missile shot down Malaysia Airlines Flight MH17 over Ukraine, the EU also expanded its sanctions list and added sectoral sanctions.[825] The EU has tied the removal of sanctions on Russia with the full implementation of the Minsk peace agreements for Ukraine, and appears to be committed to maintaining the sanctions until then.

U.S. sanctions on Russia for Ukraine-related and cyber-related matters were codified into law in August 2017 with the passage (by a vote of 98-2 in the Senate and 419-3 in the House of Representatives) and signing of the Countering America's Adversaries Through Sanctions Act of 2017, also known as CAATSA.[826] The law codified Russia-related sanctions imposed by executive orders under the Obama Administration, and the cyber-related sanctions designating both the FSB and the GRU (Russia's military intelligence agency) as institutions threatening U.S. cybersecurity.[827] CAATSA enlarged the scope of the sanctions to prohibit a range of cyber-related activities conducted on behalf of the Russian government that undermine the cybersecurity of any U.S. or foreign per-

[822] Kristin Archick et al., *EU Sanctions on Russia Related to the Ukraine Conflict*, Congressional Research Service, at 1 (Sept. 2017).

[823] *Ibid.*

[824] *Ibid.*; U.S. Treasury Department, Office of Foreign Assets Control, "Directives 1 and 2 Issued Pursuant to Executive Order 13662 (Blocking Property of Additional Persons Contributing to the Situation in Ukraine)," July 16, 2014.

[825] Julian Borger et al., "EU Announces Further Sanctions on Russia After Downing of MH17," *The Guardian*, July 22, 2017; European Council of the European Union, "EU Restrictive Measures in Response to the Crisis in Ukraine," http://www.consilium.europa.eu/en/policies/sanctions/ukraine-crisis (visited Jan. 4, 2018).

[826] Countering America's Adversaries Through Sanctions Act (CAATSA), P.L. 115-44, Enacted Aug. 2, 2017 (originally introduced by Senator Ben Cardin as the Counteracting Russian Hostilities Act of 2017, S. 94, Jan.11, 2017).

[827] Executive Order 13757, "Taking Additional Steps to Address the National Emergency with Respect to Significant Malicious Cyber-Enabled Activities," (Annex), Dec. 29, 2016.

147

son.[828] In addition, CAATSA mandated sanctions on U.S. or foreign persons that engage in significant transactions with persons related to Russia's defense or intelligence sectors.[829] Furthermore, CAATSA targets corruption inside Russia by mandating sanctions on people who make or facilitate investments of at least $10 million that contribute to the privatization of Russian state-owned assets "in a manner that unjustly benefits" government officials, relatives, or associates.[830]

Beyond CAATSA, the Sergei Magnitsky Rule of Law Accountability Act and the Global Magnitsky Human Rights Accountability Act also allow, respectively, for the sanctioning of Russian individuals who are complicit in human rights abuses or corruption (see Chapter 2).[831] Canada and some European countries, notably the United Kingdom, Lithuania, and Estonia, have also passed similar Global Magnitsky Act legislation to sanction human rights abusers and corrupt actors.[832]

While it is difficult to differentiate the economic impact of sanctions from the drop in oil prices and other macroeconomic effects, the International Monetary Fund (IMF) estimated in 2015 that U.S. and EU sanctions and Russia's retaliatory ban on agricultural imports reduced GDP in Russia over the short term by up to 1.5 percent.[833] Over the medium term, IMF models suggest that sanctions could reduce output by up to 9 percent, as lower capital accumulation and reduced technology transfers further weaken productivity growth.[834] Economists from the U.S. State Department calculated that, relative to non-sanctioned firms, the average sanctioned company in Russia saw decreases of one-third of its operating revenue, over one-half of its asset value, and about one-third of its employees. Their research also suggested that lower oil prices had a larger impact on Russia's overall economy than sanctions.[835]

Even though Mr. Putin has complained that sanctions are "severely harming Russia," when it comes to accessing international financial markets, the sanctions mostly affect state-owned companies and do not prohibit the government from selling bonds to Western investors. Furthermore, the Russian government can ease sanctioned firms' access to financing by lending them money raised from bond sales in international capital markets.[836] The U.S. Treasury Department is required to report in early 2018 on the possible effects on Russia's economy of sanctions on sovereign debt, which could have the potential to foreclose external sources of funds. While the head of Russia's central bank believes that "there won't be any seriously negative consequences" from such sanctions,

[828] CAATSA, P.L. 115-44, § 224.
[829] *Ibid.* § 231.
[830] *Ibid.* § 233.
[831] Sergei Magnitsky Rule of Law Accountability Act, P.L. 112-208, Title IV (enacted Dec. 14, 2012); The Global Magnitsky Human Rights Accountability Act, P.L. 114-328, Subtitle F, Title XII (enacted Dec. 23, 2016).
[832] Stratfor, "Russia Won't Sit Still for Additional U.S. Sanctions," Dec. 28, 2017.
[833] International Monetary Fund, *Russian Federation: Staff Report for the 2015 Article IV Consultation,* at 5 (Aug. 2015).
[834] *Ibid.*
[835] Daniel Ahn & Rodney Ludema, "Measuring Smartness: Understanding the Economic Impact of Targeted Sanctions," Office of the Chief Economist, U.S. Department of State, Working Paper 2017-01, Dec. 2016.
[836] Max Seddon & Elaine Moore, "Russia Plans First Bond Issuance Since Sanctions," *Financial Times,* Feb. 7, 2016.

economists have warned that such sanctions "may totally stop other foreign investors, not the U.S. investors only, from buying the new government debt, fiercely pushing up borrowing costs for Russia."[837]

U.S. EFFORTS TO CREATE ALTERNATIVE
AND ACCURATE QUALITY PROGRAMMING

The U.S. Broadcasting Board of Governors (BBG) seeks to "inform, engage, and connect people around the world in support of freedom and democracy," and it has pursued that goal with several efforts throughout Russian-speaking parts of the world.[838] The BBG's regional strategy for Russia is to confront anti-American propaganda and misinformation in Russian media, demonstrate the value and role of free media, and counter the Kremlin's narrative. The BBG operates Voice of America (VOA) and Radio Free Europe/Radio Liberty (RFE/RL), the only alternative to Russian-owned or supported media outlets in many former Soviet Union countries.[839]

In October 2014, RFE/RL, in cooperation with VOA, launched a 30-minute daily show called *Current Time,* to provide Russian-speaking audiences with objective reporting and analysis of important events in the region and the United States (its motto: "be truthful, be credible, be interesting").[840] The show has been successful, and in October 2016, building on the *Current Time* brand, RFE/RL and VOA launched a 24-hours-a-day, 7-days-a-week Russian-language news network, which broadcasts in Ukraine, Moldova, Georgia, Estonia, Latvia, Lithuania, and Russia, as well as several countries in Central Asia.[841] *Current Time* also produces an hour-long Russian-language newscast about the United States, which provides in-depth interviews with high-profile figures, features about life in America (for example a 26-part series on the life of the Russian diaspora in America), and the perspectives of American officials and subject experts on current events, including simultaneous interpretation of high-profile U.S. political and breaking news events.[842]

As a sign of its influence, Russian state media has labeled *Current Time's* reporting part of a "U.S. information war" and a threat to Russia's national security. RFE/RL officials note that with just twice as much funding (the current budget is about $22 million) they could produce four times as much content, allowing for

[837] Andre Tartar & Anna Andrianova, "Bond Sanctions Could Hurt Russia More Than It's Letting On," *Bloomberg Markets,* Nov. 27, 2017; Andrew Biryukov & Natasha Doff, "Russia Says Its Debt Markets Can Withstand the Shock of Sanctions," *Bloomberg,* Nov. 16, 2017.

[838] Broadcasting Board of Governors, "Mission," https://www.bbg.gov/who-we-are/mission (visited Jan. 4, 2018).

[839] Government Accountability Office, *U.S. Government Takes a Country-Specific Approach to Addressing Disinformation Overseas,* at 32 (May 2017).

[840] In November 2017, as retaliation for the U.S. Department of Justice's request that *RT* register under the Foreign Agents Registration Act (FARA), the Duma passed a law that allows Russia's Ministry of Justice to add foreign media outlets to Russia's registry of foreign agents, so long as the organizations are based outside of Russia and receive funds from abroad. Shortly thereafter, Russia's Ministry of Justice sent a letter to *Current Time* threatening to restrict its activities because it "shows the signs of performing the function of a foreign agent." Russian officials also suggested that VOA, CNN, and Germany's Deutsche Welle could face similar treatment. "Russia's Justice Ministry Warns the U.S.-Government-Funded Media Outlet 'Current Time' That Will Be Treated As A Foreign Agent," *Meduza,* Nov. 15, 2017; "Russia's Federation Council Passes 'Foreign Agents' Media Bill," *Radio Free Europe/Radio Liberty,* Nov. 22, 2017.

[841] *Current Time* TV, https://www.currenttime.tv/p/6018.html (visited Dec. 31, 2017). *Current Time* also includes programs on fact-checking, culture, and entertainment.

[842] Committee Staff Discussion with VOA Officials.

around-the-clock breaking news coverage and original programming.

RFE/RL and VOA also produce other regionally-focused programming, such as *Crimea Realities*, a weekly show that features news and stories on life in Crimea under increasingly authoritarian governance; *Schemes*, a weekly investigative news program that reports on corruption throughout Ukraine; and *See Both Sides*, a weekly show that explores the differences in how media in different regions—especially Russian state-owned media—cover the same news stories.[843] BBG has also contracted with PBS to bring almost 400 hours of U.S. public media programming to Estonia, Lithuania, and Ukraine.[844] Bringing more high-quality U.S. educational and entertainment content to broadcasters in Russia's periphery can help displace Russian television content, which is licensed for next-to-nothing but often comes with obligations to also broadcast Kremlin-sponsored "news" programs.

In addition to TV programming, RFE/RL and VOA create Russian-language video content for social media and mobile platforms, mostly aimed at youth, and operate a fact-checking website, Polygraph.info.[845] Polygraph focuses on fact-checking statements on relations between Russia and the West, however, the website is only in English, severely limiting its ability to reach Russian-speaking audiences in Europe.[846]

ASSESSING THE STATE DEPARTMENT'S GLOBAL ENGAGEMENT CENTER

In contrast to many European countries, especially the Baltic and Nordic states, the U.S. government still lacks a coherent, public strategy to counter the Kremlin's disinformation operations abroad and at home. Instead, it has a patchwork of offices and programs tasked with mitigating the effects of Kremlin disinformation operations.[847] At the direction of the U.S. Congress, the central hub for these activities is the Global Engagement Center (GEC), within the State Department.[848] In December 2016, Congress expanded the GEC's mandate from countering terrorist communications to include "foreign state and non-state propaganda and

---

[843] Josh Lederman, "US-Funded News Channel in Russian Offers Kremlin Alternative," Associated Press, Feb. 8, 2017; "RFE/RL's Ukrainian Service: Radio Svoboda," *Radio Free Europe/Radio Liberty*, https://pressroom.rferl.org/p/6139.html (visited Jan. 4, 2017).

[844] Statement of Benjamin G. Ziff, Deputy Assistant Secretary, Bureau of European and Eurasian Affairs, U.S. Department of State, *Putin's Invasion of Ukraine and the Propaganda that Threatens Europe,* Hearing before the U.S. Senate Subcommittee on Europe and Regional Security Cooperation, Nov. 3, 2015, at 7.

[845] Office of Inspector General, U.S. Department of State and Broadcasting Board of Governors, "Inspection of Radio Free Europe/Radio Liberty," at 4 (May 2014); Government Accountability Office, *U.S. Government Takes a Country-Specific Approach to Addressing Disinformation Overseas,* at 16 (May 2017).

[846] Government Accountability Office, *U.S. Government Takes a Country-Specific Approach to Addressing Disinformation Overseas,* at 16 (May 2017).; Polygraph.info, "About," https://www.polygraph.info/p/5981.html (visited Dec. 15, 2017).

[847] These efforts include monitoring, fact-checking, promoting objective news content, and providing training and grants to improve skills in media literacy and investigative journalism. The National Endowment for Democracy (NED), for example, has increased support for media literacy programs in the Baltics and Eastern Europe that address Russian disinformation.

[848] The GEC is tasked with coordinating counter-disinformation efforts across the U.S. government and includes personnel from the Department of Defense, Department of Treasury, Central Intelligence Agency, National Security Agency, National Counterterrorism Center, and the Broadcasting Board of Governors.

disinformation efforts" that target the U.S. and its interests.[849] However, a lack of urgency and self-imposed constraints by the current State Department leadership has left the effort in limbo.

Launched in March 2016, the GEC is the latest in a line of State Department attempts to coordinate interagency counter-messaging efforts.[850] Recognizing the severity of the disinformation threat and the additional resources needed to counter it, Congress increased the GEC's budget by nearly three-fold by enabling the State Department to request up to $60 million a year from the Department of Defense (DoD), and gave the GEC new hiring and grant-making authorities. GEC officials planned to use about half of those new funds on countering Kremlin disinformation, and a quarter of the new funds to increase the organization's data science capability (currently the GEC works across four lines of effort: messaging partnerships, content planning, government coordination, and data analysis). But Secretary of State Rex Tillerson was slow to approve the additional funding, with one of his top aides reportedly concerned that the extra money would anger Moscow.[851] After coming under pressure from Congress, Tillerson eventually approved $40 million, but inexplicably rejected another $20 million that could have been used to counter Russian disinformation.[852] The GEC was also hamstrung by the Department's hiring freeze, kept in place by Tillerson, which prevented the hiring of new personnel to meet the office's expanded mandate and mission.

In the State Department, the GEC reports to the Under Secretary for Public Diplomacy and Public Affairs, a position for which the Trump Administration waited nearly eight months to announce a nominee. As of publication of this report in January 2018, the Administration has yet to fill the Special Envoy and Coordinator of the GEC, suggesting that the Administration does not consider the GEC's new mission of countering foreign state propaganda a priority. The Administration's lackadaisical approach to staffing these positions and providing leadership to U.S. efforts to fight Kremlin disinformation stands in sharp contrast to the accelerating nature of the threat. As one GEC official put it, "every week we spend on process is a week the Russians are spending on operations."[853]

The GEC has a critical role to play in closing the gaps in the U.S. government's efforts to counter the Kremlin's disinformation operations. New funding and grant-making authorities delegated to the GEC should be used to support existing, effective organizations in Russia's periphery engaged in monitoring disinformation, promoting media literacy, and producing objective news content and investigative journalism. These organizations would benefit greatly from additional funding that would enable them to expand operations and reach larger audiences. To ensure that the GEC is fulfilling its objectives and funds are used as intended, Congress must be vigilant in monitoring the GEC's progress and effectiveness if

---

[849] National Defense Authorization Act for Fiscal Year 2017, P.L. 114-328, Section 1287, Enacted Dec. 23, 2016.

[850] The GEC's state-sponsored propaganda mandate includes Russia, China, North Korea, and Iran, with different teams dedicated to each.

[851] Nahal Toosi, "Tillerson Spurns $80 Million to Counter ISIS, Russian Propaganda," *Politico,* Aug. 2, 2017.

[852] Nahal Toosi, "Tillerson Moves Toward Accepting Funding for Fighting Russian propaganda," *Politico,* Aug. 31, 2017.

[853] Committee Staff Discussion with GEC Officials (2017).

the United States is to achieve the level of engagement needed to counter foreign state propaganda and disinformation.

In addition to the GEC, the State Department and USAID support a number of other assistance programs that can help build resilience in democratic institutions, to include projects to monitor and counter disinformation, promote independent media and investigative journalism, and strengthen civil society and civic education. State Department officials overseas closely monitor local media stories and distribute them throughout the Department and U.S. embassies.[854] The U.S. government conducts or commissions polls of foreign audiences to get a read on their perceptions of Russian media, as well as their reactions to different types of messages. The State Department and the Department of Defense's European Command (EUCOM) have launched a joint effort called the Russian Information Group (RIG), which grew out of a small social media group called the Ukraine Task Force that the State Department set up to counter Russian disinformation in Ukraine in 2014. RIG seeks to support a "credible counter-Russian voice in the region," according to a former senior State Department official.[855] In testimony before the Senate Armed Services Committee, the head of EUCOM, General Curtis Scaparrotti, noted that the RIG "has to be reinforced, it has to be financed, they have to have the authorities that they need to lead that forward."[856] Finally, State Department exchange programs, such as the International Visitor Leadership Program (IVLP), can be highly effective counter measures to Russian state media disinformation campaigns. IVLP brings media professionals to the United States and trains them on investigative journalism skills and the role of a free press in democracies.[857]

To their credit, mid-level officials at the State Department have given some thought to crafting a "multi-faceted approach to push back against the Russian [government's] malign influence." In congressional testimony, Deputy Assistant Secretary for European and Eurasian Affairs, Hoyt Yee, outlined the State Department's approach to combatting Kremlin propaganda, which includes "amplifying our messages, correcting false statements, and engaging decision makers," to support independent media and investigative jour-

[854] Two offices in the State Department conduct audience research around the world to inform public diplomacy messaging efforts: The Office of Opinion Research, located within the Bureau of Intelligence and Research, and the Office of Policy, Planning, and Resources, located within the Office of the Undersecretary for Public Diplomacy and Public Affairs. The Department of State also launched a Russian-language Twitter feed in 2015 to enable U.S. diplomats to share official statements directly with Russian-speaking audiences (some analysts report that this Twitter account only appeals to a very limited audience). Government Accountability Office, *U.S. Government Takes a Country-Specific Approach to Addressing Disinformation Overseas,* (May 2017).

[855] Rick Stengel, "What Hillary Knew About Putin's Propaganda Machine," *Politico,* Nov. 15, 2017.

[856] Testimony of General Curtis Scaparrotti, Commander, U.S. European Command and NATO Supreme Allied Commander Europe, U.S. Department of Defense, *United States European Command,* Hearing before the U.S. Senate Committee on Armed Services, Mar. 23, 2017.

[857] U.S. Department of State, "IVLP," https://eca.state.gov/ivlp (visited Jan. 4, 2018). Although beyond the scope of this report, the U.S. has made considerable investments in enhancing the military capabilities of our partners in Europe to deter Russia since 2014. For 2018, the U.S. is seeking a $1.4 billion increase, to $4.8 billion, for the European Deterrence Initiative (EDI). As part of EDI, the U.S. deploys on average 7,000 servicemembers to Europe. The U.S. also plays a leading role in NATO's "Enhanced Forward Presence" which deploys multi-national battlegroups to Estonia, Lithuania, Latvia and Poland. As of May 9, 2017, 4,530 troops from 15 countries participate in the EFP effort. U.S. European Command Public Affairs Office "2018 European Deterrence Initiative (EDI) Fact Sheet," Oct. 2, 2017; NATO Enhanced Forward Presence Factsheet, May 2017.

nalists with small grants.[858] In its December 2017 National Security Strategy, the White House admitted that the United States has done too little to deter Putin's assaults, noting, "U.S. efforts to counter the exploitation of information by rivals have been tepid and fragmented. U.S. efforts have lacked a sustained focus and have been hampered by the lack of properly trained professionals." [859] While recognizing these shortcomings is an important first step, the Administration has unfortunately failed to put forward a plan to rectify them. Notably, the Strategy states only that "the United States and Europe will work together to counter Russian subversion and aggression." [860] Yet coordination is only one piece of the aggressive strategy that the United States needs.

[858] Testimony by Hoyt Yee, Deputy Assistant Secretary, Bureau of European and Eurasian Affairs, U.S. Department of State, The Balkans: Threats to Peace and Stability, Hearing before the U.S. House of Representatives Foreign Affairs Subcommittee on Europe, Eurasia, and Emerging Threats, May 17, 2017, at 3.
[859] The White House, National Security Strategy of the United States of America, at 35 (Dec. 2017).
[860] Ibid. at 48.

Chapter 8: Conclusions and Recommendations

The Russian government, under Putin's leadership, has shown that it is both capable of and willing to assault democratic and transatlantic institutions and alliances. These assaults take many forms, including the use of disinformation, cyberattacks, military invasions, alleged political assassinations, threats to energy security, election interference, and other subversive tactics that fuel corruption, employ organized crime, and exploit both far-right and far-left ideologies to sow discord and create confusion. Putin also seeks to repress the exercise of human rights and political participation both at home and abroad, to promote a climate more conducive to the Russian government's corrupt and anti-democratic behavior.

There are multiple lines of effort across the West—at the local, national, and supranational level—working to counter the Kremlin's malign influence operations and build resiliency in democratic institutions. The United Kingdom's leadership has made resolute, public statements that Russian meddling is unacceptable and will be countered. The French government has worked with independent media and political parties to expose and blunt the dissemination of fake news. The German government has bolstered domestic cybersecurity capacities, particularly after the 2015 hack of the Bundestag. Estonia has strengthened counterintelligence capabilities and exposed the intelligence operations of its eastern neighbor. The Lithuanian government has made progress in diversifying its supplies of natural gas, and all the Baltic governments have worked to integrate their electricity grids to reduce dependence on Soviet-era electrical infrastructure. The Nordic countries have built resiliency across all elements of society, especially in their education systems. And the Spanish government has investigated, exposed, and cut off significant money laundering operations by Russia-based organized crime groups.

In the disinformation sphere, current multilateral efforts run the gamut from monitoring and fact-checking to promoting investigative journalism and media literacy. Monitoring and fact-checking initiatives are a necessary and logical first step—the problem has to be identified and understood before it can be addressed. And as the Kremlin continues to change its methods and tactics in response to growing awareness and adaptation by its targets, it will be necessary to continue existing monitoring efforts to inform responses.

However, monitoring and countering propaganda alone will never be sufficient. While a whole-of-government approach is necessary to identify the threat and sound the trumpet, a whole-of-society approach is necessary to neutralize it. The EU, NATO, and member states' ministries of defense, foreign affairs, and interior may develop tactical responses to the threat of disinformation, but it will ultimately be the education ministries, civil society, and independent news organizations that are most effective in inoculating their societies against fake news.

In addition, no single country or institution has yet stepped forward to be the leader in coordinating efforts to build resilience against the Kremlin's asymmetric arsenal and identifying and filling any gaps. The U.S. government has a unique capacity to lead the formulation and implementation of a grand strategy with individual countries and multilateral groups in Europe, like NATO and the EU, to counter and deter hybrid threats emanating from the Kremlin. While the Global Engagement Center (GEC) has begun outreach to allies in Europe, the U.S. government appears not to have a strategic plan to comprehensively counter Russian government influence and interference, including but not limited to disinformation. There are several institutions in Europe working on countering disinformation that could benefit from additional U.S. engagement, and U.S. leadership and coordination among donors could also help maximize the effectiveness of existing assistance.

Yet despite the growing intensity of Russian government interference operations, President Trump has largely ignored this threat to democracy in the United States and Europe. The Trump Administration has also proposed cuts to assistance across Europe that could help counter the Kremlin's malign influence, especially in the areas of good governance, anti-corruption, and independent media efforts. President Trump is squandering an opportunity to lead America's allies and partners to build a collective defense against the Kremlin's global assault on democratic institutions and values. But it is not too late.

By implementing the recommendations below, the United States can better deter and defend against the Kremlin's use of its asymmetric arsenal, while also strengthening international norms and values to blunt the effects of malign influence operations by any state actor, including Russia.

1. Assert Presidential Leadership and Launch a National Response: President Trump has been negligent in acknowledging and responding to the threat to U.S. national security posed by Putin's meddling.

a. *Declare the Policy:* The President should immediately declare that it is U.S. policy to counter and deter all forms of the Kremlin's hybrid threats against the United States and around the world. This policy should be a visibly prominent component of the administration's agenda—policymakers should discuss these issues publicly and regularly raise the threat posed by the Russian government in their diplomatic interactions. The President should also present to Congress a comprehensive national strategy to counter these grave national security threats and work with the Congress and our allies to get this strategy implemented and funded.

b. *Establish an Inter-Agency Fusion Cell:* The President should establish a high-level inter-agency fusion cell, modeled on the National Counterterrorism Center (NCTC), to coordinate all elements of U.S. policy and programming in response to the Russian government's malign influence operations. This fusion cell should include representatives from the FBI, CIA, and Departments of Homeland Security, State, Defense, and Treasury and it should immediately produce a strategy, plan, and robust budget that coordinates all current and projected government programming to counter Russian government interference and malign influence.

c. *Build U.S. Expertise:* The U.S. government should increase funding for programs administered by the State Department's Intelligence and Research Bureau that aim to educate and develop Europe and Eurasia experts in the United States. Programming and training at the State Department's Foreign Service Institute should also be expanded to include courses on the Russian government's malign influence activities. Such courses should also be accessible to relevant officials from other U.S. agencies represented on the inter-agency fusion cell described above.

d. *Increase Funding to Counter Disinformation:* The U.S. government should increase the funding dedicated to countering Russian disinformation, working primarily though partners in vulnerable countries. The GEC should also accept all funding from the Defense Department made available through congressional appropriations and use it to increase the capacity of existing organizations in Russia's periphery that are engaged in monitoring disinformation, promoting media literacy, and producing objective news content and investigative journalism with local impact. Grants should also provide multi-year funding to allow these organizations to formulate and implement long-term strategic plans. The BBG should expand funding for sophisticated Russian-language VOA programming like *Current Time* and find more creative ways to bring high-quality U.S. educational and entertainment programming to media markets vulnerable to Kremlin propaganda.

2. *Support Democratic Institution Building and Values Abroad, and with a Stronger Congressional Voice:* The executive and legislative branches have a responsibility to show leadership on universal values of democracy and human rights. A lack of U.S. leadership risks undermining or endangering democratic activists and human rights defenders around the world—including within Russia—who are working to advance these values in their own societies. It also risks weakening democratic institutions, including independent media and civil society, that are critical actors in overcoming disinformation, shining a light on corruption and abuses, and building resiliency against Kremlin attempts to divide and weaken democratic societies. Furthermore, democracies with transparent governments, the rule of law, a free media, and engaged citizens are naturally more resilient to Putin's asymmetric arsenal.

a. *Increase Assistance:* The U.S. government should provide democracy and governance assistance, in concert with allies in

Europe, to build resilience in democratic institutions among those European and Eurasian states most vulnerable to Russian government interference. Using the funding authorization outlined in CAATSA as policy guidance, the U.S. government should increase this spending in Europe and Eurasia to at least $250 million over the next two fiscal years.

b. *Clear Messaging:* To reinforce these efforts, the U.S. government should demonstrate clear and sustained diplomatic leadership in support of the individual human rights that form the backbone of democratic systems. U.S. and European government officials at the highest levels should message clearly and regularly in support of universal principles of human rights and accountable governance in Europe and Eurasia, and, in particular, speak out regularly regarding Russian government abuses against its own citizens. These messages should be delivered through public statements as well as in private, high-level diplomatic engagements. U.S. and European officials should also utilize the Organization for Security and Cooperation in Europe (OSCE), the United Nations Human Rights Council, and other multilateral fora to deliver these messages and to hold the Russian government and other governments in Europe and Eurasia accountable to their international human rights obligations and commitments.

c. *Legislative Branch Leadership:* Members in the U.S. Congress have a responsibility to show U.S. leadership on values by making democracy and human rights a central part of their agendas. They should conduct committee hearings and use their platforms to publicly advance these issues. This would include using the Senate confirmation process to elicit commitments from nominees on democracy and human rights. Congress should also institutionalize platforms for regular dialogue with parliaments across Europe and Eurasia on issues of democracy and human rights, to include multilateral bodies such as the OSCE Parliamentary Assembly, as well as bilateral parliamentary engagements. Members of Congress should also regularly visit countries in the region to further solidify transatlantic bonds; such visits should include engagement with civil society.

d. *Leverage Legacy Enterprise Foundations:* The U.S. government established a series of enterprise funds across Central and Eastern Europe which exhibited varying degrees of success and spun off into legacy foundations that provide grants to civil society actors and independent media across the region. The U.S. government should require those foundations to strategically focus their investments on efforts to counter the Russian government's malign influence. In particular, tens of millions of dollars associated with the U.S. Russia Foundation have been dormant for years due to "congressional holds" by the House Foreign Affairs Committee and Senate Foreign Relations Committee. The issues associated with those holds should be resolved so those funds can be unlocked and used to counter Russian government aggression.

e. *Support for Democratic Institutions and Processes in Russia:*
The U.S. government and its European partners should maintain a lifeline of support to non-governmental organizations
and independent media outlets in Russia that are promoting
respect for human rights, transparency, and accountability in
their country, and follow these entities' lead in determining the
contours of such support. This work is not meant to interfere
in the affairs of another country, but simply supports those
values enshrined in the Helsinki Final Act, to which Russia is
a signatory.

f. *People to People Exchanges:* The U.S. State Department should,
to the extent possible, seek to expand programs and opportunities that increase interaction between American and Russian
citizens, as well as other European countries, and should work
to ensure that such people-to-people ties are not used as
grounds for persecution of Russian citizens by their government. It should also increase cultural exchanges, especially
study abroad semesters, Fulbright scholarships, International
Visitor Leadership Program exchanges, Peace Corps, and other
programs that increase interaction between Americans and
citizens that live in the countries on Russia's periphery or that
are particularly vulnerable to Russian malign influence.

g. *Strengthen Use of International Monitoring and Accountability
Mechanisms:* The OSCE's Moscow Mechanism, invoked by a
group of OSCE participating States or requested by the state
in question itself, can enable a mission of experts to investigate
and facilitate resolution to questions related to human rights
in a particular OSCE participating State. Since it was agreed
to in 1991, the Moscow Mechanism has been used seven
times—both with and without the cooperation of the state in
question. This mechanism should be activated more frequently
and used to the fullest extent possible, and with respect to
Russia, to respond to demands from within that country for
scrutiny of the Kremlin's domestic human rights record and
providing specific recommendations for remedying abuses.

3. *Expose and Freeze Kremlin-Linked Dirty Money:* Corruption
provides the motivation and the means for many of the Kremlin's
malign influence operations. Under President Putin, the Kremlin
has nationalized organized crime and cybercrime, and now uses
Russia-based organized crime groups and cybercriminals for operational purposes abroad. The United States remains a prime destination for illicit financial flows from Russia, especially through
the purchase of real estate and luxury goods by anonymous shell
companies. The U.S. capability to constructively assist countries in
the region remains weak due to an inadequate number of U.S. embassy personnel focused on these issues.

a. *Expose High-Level Individual Corruption:* The Treasury Department should make public any intelligence related to
Putin's personal corruption and wealth stored abroad, and take
steps with European allies to cut off Putin and his inner circle
from the international financial system.

b. *Expose Energy Sector Corruption:* The U.S. government should also expose corrupt and criminal activities associated with Russia's state-owned energy sector.

c. *Impose Sanctions:* The U.S. government should implement the Global Magnitsky Human Rights Accountability Act and the Countering America's Adversaries Through Sanctions Act (CAATSA) provisions, which allow for sanctions against corrupt actors in Russia and abroad.

d. *Russia Financial Task Force:* The U.S. Treasury Department should form a high-level unit within its Office of Financial Crimes Enforcement Network (FinCen) that is tasked solely with investigating and prosecuting Russian-linked illicit financial flows. The unit should also place liaison officers in select U.S. embassies throughout Europe, and the U.S. government should encourage our European partners to set up similar units.

e. *Corruption Reporting:* The U.S. government should issue yearly reports that assign tiered classifications based on objective third-party corruption indicators, as well as governmental efforts to combat corruption.

4. Subject State Hybrid Threat Actors to an Escalatory Sanctions Regime: The Kremlin and other regimes hostile to democracy must know that there will be consequences for their actions.

a. *Create a New Designation:* The U.S. government should designate countries that employ malign influence operations to assault democracies as State Hybrid Threat Actors.

b. *Establish an Escalatory Sanctions Regime:* Countries that are designated as such would fall under a preemptive and escalatory sanctions regime that would be applied whenever the state uses asymmetric weapons like cyberattacks to interfere with a democratic election or disrupt a country's vital infrastructure. Existing sanctions included within the CAATSA legislation can be used to target those involved with cyberattacks.

c. *Coordinate sanctions with the EU:* The U.S. government should work with the EU to ensure that these sanctions are coordinated and effective.

5. Publicize the Kremlin's Global Malign Influence Efforts: Exposing and publicizing the nature of the threat of Russian malign influence activities, as the Baltic states regularly do and the U.S. intelligence community did in January 2017, can be an action-forcing event that not only boosts public awareness, but also drives effective responses from the private sector, especially social media platforms, as well as civil society and independent media, who can use the information to pursue their own investigations.

a. *Issue Public Malign Influence Reporting:* The Director of National Intelligence should produce yearly public reports that detail the Russian government's malign influence operations in the United States. The Department of State should similarly produce annual reports on those operations around the world.

b. *Declassify Assassination Intelligence:* The Director of National Intelligence should also update and consider declassifying its report to Congress on the use of political assassinations as a form of statecraft by the Russian government.

c. *Establish Independent Commissions to Investigate Election Meddling:* The U.S. Congress should pass pending legislation to create an independent, nonpartisan commission to comprehensively investigate Russian government interference in the 2016 U.S. election. Countries across Europe that have held elections over the past two years should also consider comprehensive governmental or independent investigations into the nature and scope of Russian government interference.

6. Build an International Coalition to Counter Hybrid Threats: The United States is stronger and more effective when we work with our partners and allies abroad.

a. *Build the Coalition:* The U.S. government should lead an international effort of like-minded democracies to build awareness of and resilience to the Kremlin's malign influence operations. Specifically, the President should convene an annual global summit on hybrid threats, modeled on the Global Coalition to Counter ISIL or the Countering Violent Extremism (CVE) summits that have taken place since 2015. Civil society and the private sector should participate in the summits and follow-on activities.

b. *Harness the OSCE:* The OSCE should be a central forum for exposing Russian government attacks on democracy and directly challenging its actions. As part of her Senate confirmation hearing, the nominee for U.S. Ambassador to the OSCE should commit to using every tool and forum to advance this goal, working with like-minded countries in the organization. The U.S. should also expand its extra-budgetary support to OSCE projects aimed at building resilience to external threats to democratic institutions and processes in OSCE participating states.

c. *Share Successful Techniques:* The State Department and USAID should conduct a comprehensive assessment of the most successful efforts to counter Russian government interference in all of its forms and partner with relevant governments, aid agencies, and NGOs to ensure that these lessons are shared with the most vulnerable countries in Europe and Eurasia. For example, based on constructive measures taken during the recent French and German election periods, the United States could work closely with their Ministries of Foreign Affairs, the French Agence Francaise de Developpement (AFD) and the German Gesellschaft fur Internationale Zusammenarbeit (GiZ) to implement specific joint programs in vulnerable democracies on cyber defense, media training, and other areas.

d. *Participate in Centers of Excellence:* The U.S. government should provide funding and seconded U.S. government employees for the Finnish Hybrid Center of Excellence and NATO

Centers of Excellence related to strategic communication, cyber
security, and energy independence.

  e. *Deploy FBI Investigators to Key Embassies in Vulnerable European Countries:* The U.S. Department of Justice should deploy FBI investigators to vulnerable countries in Europe with a mandate to address Russian government and oligarchic efforts to corrupt economies, societies, and governments. Countries across the region contend with corruption, but some U.S. embassies across the region lack the capacity to fully assist and coordinate with these anti-corruption efforts at a diplomatic level. These positions should be on par with Defense Attaches from the Pentagon and prioritized as such.

  f. *Promote Passage of Magnitsky Laws Abroad:* The 2012 Sergei Magnitsky Rule of Law Accountability Act calls on the U.S. government to engage in diplomatic efforts to lobby other governments to pass similar laws. The U.S. government should report to Congress on their efforts to persuade countries in Europe and Eurasia to pass legislation modeled after the U.S. Magnitsky Laws (both the Russia-specific and the Global Magnitsky Human Rights Accountability laws) that enable targeted, individual sanctions against gross violators of human rights and perpetrators of significant acts of corruption. Furthermore, these laws must be strongly implemented by the U.S. executive branch.

  7. *Uncover Foreign Funding that Erodes Democracy:* Foreign illicit money corrupts the political, social, and economic systems of democracies.

  a. *Pass Legislation on Campaign Finance Transparency and Shell Companies:* The United States and European countries must make it more difficult for foreign actors to use financial resources to interfere in democratic systems, specifically by passing legislation to require full disclosure of shell company owners and improve transparency for funding of political parties, campaigns, and advocacy groups.

  8. *Build Global Cyber Defenses and Norms:* The United States and our European allies remain woefully vulnerable to cyberattacks, which are a preferred asymmetric weapon of state hybrid threat actors. While the threat posed by cyberattacks from state and non-state actors has grown, the international community has not developed rules of the road which could establish norms that govern behavior over the long term. Moreover, the United States and its allies have not defined the contours of cyberattacks in the context of NATO's Article 5. In addition to the strategic-level discussion on cyber threats, the U.S. government does not have an institution capable of robustly engaging and assisting non-governmental entities under pressure from cyberattacks. The administration has tools, like the CAATSA legislation, which authorized sanctions on those who conduct cyberattacks on democratic institutions. It has yet to exercise these authorities, despite the existence of clear sanctions targets.

  a. *Establish a Cyber Alliance:* The U.S. government and NATO should lead a coalition of countries committed to mutual de-

161

fense against cyberattacks, to include the establishment of rapid reaction teams to defend allies under attack.

b. *Discuss Article 5:* The U.S. government should also call a special meeting of the NATO heads of state to review the extent of Russian government-sponsored cyberattacks among member states and develop formal guidelines on how the Alliance will consider such attacks in the context of NATO's Article 5 mutual protection provision.

c. *Negotiate an International Treaty:* The U.S. government should lead an effort to establish an international treaty on the use of cyber tools in peace time, modeled on international arms control treaties.

d. *Implement Existing Cyber-related Sanctions:* The administration should fully implement Section 224 of CAATSA, which mandates sanctions on individuals acting on behalf of the Russian government who undermine the cybersecurity of any government or democratic institution. The administration should also work to build support in Europe for a similar package of EU cyber sanctions.

e. *Increase Transatlantic Cooperation on Combatting Cybercrime:* The U.S. government should work with European partners to raise the priority of investigating and prosecuting Russia-based organized crime groups and cybercriminals, who should be viewed not just as criminal threats, but as threats to national security. Agencies should increase information sharing between intelligence and law enforcement entities, and increase the targeting of criminal assets.

9. Hold Social Media Companies Accountable: Social media platforms are a key conduit of disinformation that undermines democracies.

a. *Make Political Advertising on Social Media Transparent:* U.S. and European governments should mandate that social media companies make public the sources of funding for political advertisements, along the same lines as TV channels and print media.

b. *Conduct Audits on Election Period Interference:* European governments should also increase pressure on and cooperation with social media companies to determine the extent of Russian-linked disinformation operations using fake accounts in recent elections and referendums around the continent. Social media companies should conduct comprehensive audits on how their platforms may have been used by Kremlin-linked entities to influence elections occurring over the past several years.

c. *Convene Civil Society Advisory Councils:* Social media companies should also establish civil society advisory councils to provide input and warnings about emerging disinformation trends. Leaders from the United States and Europe in government, the private sector, and civil society must work to promote a culture where citizens are armed with critical thinking skills. To that end, philanthropic organizations should embark on an initiative to work with educational organizations and social media companies to develop a curriculum on media literacy and critical thinking skills that could be offered free of charge to the public. These tools should also be amplified for the broader public through a large scale media campaign.

d. *Block Malicious Inauthentic and/or Automated Accounts:* While accounting for freedom of speech concerns, social media companies should redouble efforts to prevent, detect, and delete such accounts, especially those that are primarily used to promote false news stories.

10. Reduce European Dependence on Russian Energy Sources: Europe is overly dependent on Gazprom, a Russian state-owned company, for its natural gas supplies. Payments to Gazprom from European states fund military aggression abroad, as well as overt and covert activities that undermine democratic institutions and social cohesion in Europe. The Russian government uses the near monopoly of its state-owned natural gas companies over European gas supplies as leverage in political and economic negotiations with European transshipment countries, especially Ukraine and the Balkans.

a. *Promote Energy Diversification:* OPIC and USTDA should help to finance strategically important energy diversification projects in Europe. This includes supporting new pipeline projects such as the Trans Adriatic Pipeline (TAP) and the Trans Anatolian Natural Gas Pipeline (TANAP), as well as the construction of more liquid natural gas (LNG) regasification terminals to facilitate the import of LNG from non-Russian sources. The U.S. should also support efforts that promote renewable energy options.

b. *Support a Single EU Energy Market:* The U.S. government, through OPIC, USTDA, and other assistance mechanisms, should also support strategic infrastructure projects that support the realization of a single EU gas and electricity market. The U.S. government should also assist EU governments with implementation of the EU's Third Energy Package, which seeks to establish a single energy market.

c. *Oppose Nord Stream 2:* The U.S. should continue to oppose Nord Stream 2. The U.S. government should encourage the European Commission and Parliament to sponsor an independent inquiry into the energy security and geopolitical implications of Nord Stream 2 and its infrastructure in Russia and host countries. The U.S. Departments of Energy and State should assist the independent inquiry in whatever way possible.

APPENDICES

Appendix A: 1999 Apartment Building Bombings

In early September 1999, less than three weeks after Putin was installed as Prime Minister, a large truck bomb destroyed a five-story apartment building in the Russian republic of Dagestan, killing 64 people.[1] A second, far more powerful bomb was found in a truck near a military hospital in the city, but was defused just 12 minutes before it was timed to explode, saving the city's center from being leveled.[2] As the bombings occurred in an ethnically diverse republic thousands of kilometers from Moscow, public outrage in the capital was limited. But five days after the bombing in Dagestan, a bomb struck an apartment building in Moscow, killing 100 and injuring nearly 700.[3] The Moscow unit of the FSB revealed that evidence from the scene showed traces of TNT and a potent military explosive called hexogen (a substantial investigation of the crime scene was never carried out because the authorities razed the building just days after the blast and discarded its remnants at the municipal dump).[4]

Just four days later, another bomb went off in Moscow at 5 a.m., destroying a nine-story apartment building and killing 124 sleeping residents.[5] Later that morning, the speaker of Russia's lower house of parliament, the Duma, Gennady Seleznyov, announced that an apartment building had blown up in the city of Volgodonsk.[6] But the bombing in Volgodonsk did not happen until three days after his announcement, when an apartment block was attacked in the city, again at 5 a.m., killing 18 people and injuring nearly 90.[7] When a Duma member later asked Seleznyov on the Parliament floor to "please explain, how come you told us on Monday about the blast that occurred on Thursday?" his microphone was cut off and the Duma voted to revoke his speaking privileges for one month.[8]

---

[1] David Satter, *The Less You Know, The Better You Sleep: Russia's Road to Terror and Dictatorship under Yeltsin and Putin,* Yale University Press, at 7 (2016); Scott Anderson, "None Dare Call it a Conspiracy," *GQ,* Mar. 30, 2017.

[2] Satter, *The Less You Know, The Better You Sleep,* at 7.

[3] *Ibid.*

[4] Scott Anderson, "None Dare Call it a Conspiracy," *GQ,* Mar. 30, 2017; Satter, *The Less You Know, the Better You Sleep,* at 7.

[5] Satter, *The Less You Know, The Better You Sleep,* at 7.

[6] *Ibid.*

[7] *Ibid.*

[8] Vladimir Zhirinovsky, Remarks before the Russian Duma, Sept. 17, 1999, https://www.youtube.com/watch?v=Lf9r3DEY5UA (translated from Russian). Some observers suggest that someone in the chain of command of the FSB botched the planned sequence of the bombings and gave the news to Seleznyov in the wrong order. Mikhail Trepashkin, a former FSB agent and lawyer who investigated the bombings, claims that Seleznyov was given an erroneous report by an FSB officer. Scott Anderson, "None Dare Call it a Conspiracy," *GQ,* Mar. 30, 2017.

Terrified residents began to spend the night outdoors rather than risk being blown up while sleeping in their apartments.[9] Less than a week later, on September 22, a resident in the city of Ryazan, about 120 miles southeast of Moscow, called the police to report suspicious men going in and out of his apartment building. Police investigated and discovered what appeared to be a large bomb in the building's basement. The head of the local bomb squad disconnected a military-grade detonator and timer and analyzed the sacks of white powder they were connected to, which reportedly tested positive for hexogen.[10]

Two men matching the witnesses' descriptions were arrested; but both were found to be in possession of FSB identification, and the Moscow FSB ordered the Ryazan police to release them.[11] At the Kremlin, FSB director Nikolai Patrushev (now head of Russia's influential Security Council) announced that the whole thing was a training exercise, that the sacks of white powder were in fact only sugar, and that while similar exercises had taken place in other cities around Russia, only the citizens of Ryazan had been vigilant enough to detect the sucrose threat.[12]

Putin blamed the bombings on Chechen terrorists and immediately ordered Russia's armed forces to retaliate.[13] Yet while Russian authorities said that there was a "Chechen trail" leading to the bombings, no Chechen claimed responsibility.[14] In response to questions from the U.S. Senate Foreign Relations Committee in February 2000, then Secretary of State Madeleine Albright wrote that "We have not seen evidence that ties the bombings to Chechnya."[15] A State Department cable from the U.S. Embassy in Moscow relays how a former member of Russia's intelligence services told a U.S. diplomat that the FSB "does indeed have a specially trained team of men whose mission is to carry out this type of urban warfare," and that the actual story of what happened in Ryazan would never come out, because "the truth would destroy the country."[16] The report of the British government's public inquiry into the murder of former FSB agent Alexander Litvinenko refers to the theory in Litvinenko's book that "the bombings had been the work of the FSB, designed to provide a justification for war in Chechnya and, ultimately, to boost Mr. Putin's political prospects."[17] The inquiry's chairman, Sir Robert Owen, wrote that the book was "the product of careful research" and referred to the view that the book had "credibly investigated" the issue and "piled up the evidence pointing a very damaging finger at the FSB and its involvement in those explosions."[18] In addition, U.S. Senators

[9] Satter, *The Less You Know, the Better You Sleep*, at 8.
[10] *Ibid.* at 9-10.
[11] *Ibid.* at 10.
[12] Amy Knight, "Finally, We Know About the Moscow Bombings," *The New York Review of Books*, Nov. 22, 2012.
[13] Scott Anderson, "None Dare Call it a Conspiracy," *GQ*, Mar. 30, 2017.
[14] Satter, *The Less You Know, the Better You Sleep*, at 2 (citing Ilyas Akhmadov & Miriam Lansky, The Chechen Struggle: Independence Won and Lost, Palgrave Macmillan at 162 (2010)).
[15] U.S. Senate Committee on Foreign Relations, 2000 Foreign Policy Overview and the President's Fiscal Year 2001 Foreign Affairs Budget Request (Feb. and Mar. 2000).
[16] U.S. Department of State Cable, Released via Freedom of Information Act to David Satter, Case No. F-2016-08858.
[17] United Kingdom House of Commons, *The Litvinenko Inquiry: Report into the Death of Alexander Litvinenko*, at 57 (Jan. 2016).
[18] *Ibid.*

John McCain and Marco Rubio, who both serve on the Senate Select Committee on Intelligence, have gone on the record pointing to
evidence that alleges the involvement of the Russian security services in the bombings, with Rubio referring to "open source and
other" reporting.[19] The CIA, however, has not released any of its
potential records relating to the bombings, stating that to do so
would reveal "very specific aspects of the Agency's intelligence interest, or lack thereof, in the Russian bombings."[20]
  Attempts to investigate the Ryazan incident and the bombings
were stonewalled by Russian officials or stymied by opponents in
the Duma. Due to uniform opposition from pro-Putin deputies, several efforts in the Duma to investigate the Ryazan incident failed.[21]
Instead, a group of deputies and civilian activists created a public
commission to investigate, led by Sergei Kovalev, a Soviet-era dis-
sident who served for a time as Yeltsin's human rights advisor (he
resigned after accusing Yeltsin of abandoning democratic principles).[22] In 2003, one of the Duma deputies and "most active"
members on the commission, Sergei Yushkenov, was shot dead in
front of his apartment building.[23] Another member of the commission, Yuri Shchekochikhin, died from a mysterious illness three
months later, likely from thallium poisoning, just before he was
scheduled to fly to the United States to meet with investigators
from the FBI.[24] Others investigating the bombings, including
former FSB agent Alexander Litvinenko and journalist Anna
Politkovskaya, were also murdered.[25]
  Russian authorities held two trials in relation to the bombings.
The first trial started in May 2001, and accused five men from the
Karachai-Cherkessian Republic (about 250 miles west of Chechnya)
of preparing explosives and sending them to Moscow "in bags similar to those used to carry sugar produced by a sugar refiner in

---

[19] Senator John McCain, Press Release, "McCain Decries 'New Authoritarianism in Russia,'"
Nov. 4, 2003. McCain said that "there remain credible allegations that Russia's FSB had a hand
in carrying out these attacks." *Ibid.* Senator Rubio said in January 2017 that "there's [an] incredible body of reporting, open source and other, that this was all—all those bombings were
part of a black flag operation on the part of the FSB." Remarks of Marco Rubio, Nomination
of Rex Tillerson to be Secretary of State, Hearing before the U.S. Senate Committee on Foreign
Relations, Jan. 11, 2017.

[20] David Satter, "The Mystery of Russia's 1999 Apartment Bombings Lingers—the CIA Could
Clear It Up," *National Review,* Feb. 2, 2017.

[21] Satter, *The Less You Know, the Better You Sleep,* at 21, 25; "Duma Vote Kills Query on
Ryazan," *The Moscow Times,* Apr. 4, 2000.

[22] Satter, *The Less You Know, the Better You Sleep,* at 25; Sergei Kovalev, "A Letter of Resignation," *The New York Review of Books,* Feb. 29, 1996.

[23] Satter, *The Less You Know, the Better You Sleep,* at 25, 31, 126-27; "Russian MP's death
sparks storm," *BBC News,* Apr. 18, 2003. Russian authorities convicted Mikhail Kodanyov, the
leader of a rival member of Yushkenov's Liberal Russia party, with ordering the assassination.
Prosecutors argued that Kodanyov ordered the murder because he wanted to take control of Liberal Russia's finances. Kodanyov maintained his innocence throughout the trial. Carl Schrek,
"4 Convicted for Yushenkov Murder," *The Moscow Times,* Mar. 19, 2004.

[24] Satter, *The Less You Know, the Better You Sleep,* at 31; Jullian, O'Halloran, "Russia's Poisoning 'Without a Poison,'" *BBC News,* Feb. 6, 2007.
  http://news.bbc.co.uk/2/hi/programmes/file_on_4/6324241.stm; "September 1999 Russian apartment bombings timeline," *CBC,* Sept. 4, 1999.

[25] Satter, *The Less You Know, the Better You Sleep,* at 36, 121, 127. After the 2003 trial, three
years before she was assassinated, Politkovskaya said of the court proceedings that "This investigation hasn't answered the main question: Who ordered the apartment blasts in Moscow and
Volgodonsk. The accusations raised by some politicians that the FSB may have been behind the
explosions have never been seriously considered by this investigation and have never been investigated at all. And it is quite clear that it will never happen. It remains up to independent
journalists and a very small circle of independent politicians to continue to dig up this tragic
riddle. The last politician in Russia who sincerely raised these hard questions was Sergei
Yushenkov. But he was killed." David Holley, "Separatists Tied to '99 Bombings," *Los Angeles
Times,* May 1, 2003.

Karachai-Cherkessian Republic."[26] The trial was held 750 miles south of Moscow and closed to the public, including the press. The men were convicted of plotting terrorist attacks across Russia in 1999, but due to the lack of evidence, the trial investigators dropped the charges that the men were involved in the Moscow and Volgodonsk bombings.[27]

The second trial, which occurred in 2003 and was also closed to the public, charged two other Karachai-Cherkessian men, one of whom said that it was the CIA, not the FSB, that was involved in the Volgodonsk bombing.[28] While he admitted his involvement in the Volgodonsk bombing, he said that he was given heavy narcotics, and he has maintained that he was not involved with the two Moscow bombings.[29]

Two sisters who lost their mother in one of the Moscow bombings hired a lawyer and former FSB agent, Mikhail Trepashkin, to represent them at the second trial.[30] Trepashkin was also an investigator on Kovalev's commission.[31] According to the U.S. State Department, Russian authorities arrested Trepashkin one month after he published claims that the FSB was involved in the bombings and just one week before he was scheduled to represent the sisters in court and present related evidence. He was convicted of disclosing state secrets (Trepashkin maintains that FSB agents planted classified documents in his home during a search) and sentenced to four years in prison.[32] With two members of the public commission dead, others threatened, and Trepashkin imprisoned and his life possibly at risk, its investigation stalled.

The Russian public continued to push for investigations and in 2009, a few dozen protestors held a demonstration demanding a new investigation into the bombings. During the protests against Putin in 2011 and 2012, some demonstrators carried signs referencing the attacks.[33] A public opinion poll conducted in September 2013 found that only 31 percent of Russians thought that any involvement of the special services in the explosions should be excluded.[34] Another poll conducted in 2015 found that only about 6 percent of Russians had clarity about who was behind the 1999

[26] "Five Men Charged with Apartment Bombings in moscow," Strana.ru, May 11, 2001.

[27] Oksana Yablokova & Navi Abdullaev, "Five Men Convicted for Terrorist Plots," *The Moscow Times*, Nov. 15, 2001.

[28] "Terrorist Adam Dekkushev Blames CIA for Preparations of Explosions in Volgodonsk," *Kommersant*, Dec. 19, 2003 (translated from Russian).

[29] Amy Knight, Orders to Kill: The Putin Regime and Political Murder, St. Martin's Press (2017); "Terror Convict Asks Court to Reject $900,000 Claim," *RIA Novosti*, Mar. 3, 2006.

[30] Satter, *The Less You Know, the Better You Sleep*, at 29-30.

[31] *Ibid.*

[32] U.S. Department of State, Bureau of Democracy, Human Rights, and Labor, 2007 *Country Reports on Human Rights Practices: Russia* (Mar. 2008). While imprisoned, Trepashkin complained of improper medical care for severe asthma, which resulted in his transfer to a harsher general prison regime. The European Court of Human Rights ruled in 2007 that the Russian government violated the European Convention on Human Rights due to his poor prison conditions. *Ibid.* As of September 2017, Trepashkin was representing plaintiffs demanding compensation from the Russian government for its use of disproportionate force in ending the Beslan siege in 2004. "Beslan siege: Russia 'Will Comply' with Critical Ruling," *BBC*, Sept. 20, 2017; Scott Anderson, "None Dare Call it a Conspiracy," *GQ*, Mar. 30, 2017.

[33] "Russian Protesters Demand Investigation of 1999 Apartment Bombings," *Radio Free Europe/Radio Free Liberty*, Sept. 10, 2009; Satter, *The Less You Know, the Better You Sleep*, at 38.

[34] Press Release, Levada Center, "Russians About Terrorist Attacks," Sept. 30, 2013, https://www.levada.ru/2013/09/30/rossiyane_o_teraktah/ (translated from Russian).

bombings.[35] To this day, no credible source has ever claimed credit for the bombings and no credible evidence has been presented by the Russian authorities linking Chechen terrorists, or anyone else, to the Moscow bombings. As the public polling results show, there is still considerable doubt among the Russian public about who was responsible for the 1999 apartment building bombings, suggesting that further investigation into the matter is still required.

-----

[35] Press Release, Levada Center, "The Tragedy in Beslan and the Apartment Bombings in Autumn 1999," Sept. 4, 2015 (translated from Russian).

Appendix B: Alleged Political Assassinations

More than two dozen politicians, journalists, activists, and other critics of Mr. Putin's regime have died under mysterious or suspicious circumstances in Russia during his time in power.[1] A number of individuals, including vocal Putin critics, investigative journalists, and others in the Kremlin's crosshairs, have died beyond Russia's borders, often under similar mysterious circumstances. Many observers suspect that these deaths were at the hands or direction of the Russian security services. Such actions are officially allowed under a Russian law passed by the Duma in July 2006 that permits the assassination of "enemies of the Russian regime" who live abroad.[2]

The most infamous case in recent memory was that of Alexander Litvinenko, a career FSB officer. In the early 1990s, he investigated the Tambov group, an Uzbek criminal organization based in St. Petersburg that he found was smuggling heroin from Afghanistan to Western Europe via Uzbekistan and St. Petersburg. His investigation led him to believe that there was "widespread collusion between the Tambov group and KGB officials, including both Vladimir Putin and Nikolai Patrushev."[3] He was also allegedly ordered to kill Mikhail Trepashkin (see Appendix A) after the recently resigned FSB investigator brought a lawsuit against the FSB's leadership and filed complaints that went all the way up to the director, Vladimir Putin. Litvinenko refused to carry out the order, became disenchanted with his assignment on a hit team, and held a press conference with four other colleagues, as well as Mr. Trepashkin, where they exposed the assassination plots they had been ordered to carry out.[4] After the press conference, Litvinenko was fired from the FSB (Putin was then still FSB director), and he fled to the UK, where he was granted asylum and, eventually, British citizenship.[5] He began to investigate the 1999 apartment building bombings and wrote a book, *Blowing up Russia: Terror from*

---

[1] Oren Dorell, "Mysterious Rash on Russian Deaths Casts Suspicion on Vladimir Putin," *USA Today*, May 4, 2017; Committee to Protect Journalists, "58 Journalists Killed in Russia/Motive Confirmed," https://cpj.org/killed/europe/russia/ (visited Dec. 5, 2017).

[2] Terrence McCoy, "With His Dying Words, Poisoned Spy Alexander Litvinenko Named Putin as His Killer," *The Washington Post*, Jan. 28, 2015; Steven Eke, "Russia Law on Killing 'Extremists' Abroad," *BBC News*, Nov. 27, 2006.

[3] United Kingdom House of Commons, *The Litvinenko Inquiry: Report into the Death of Alexander Litvinenko*, at 15 (Jan. 2016).

[4] *Ibid.* at 21.

[5] "Alexander Litvtnenko: Profile of Murdered Russian Spy," *BBC News*, Jan. 21, 2016; Griff Witte & Michael Birnbaum, "Putin Implicated in Fatal Poisoning of Former KGB Officer at London Hotel," *The Washington Post*, Jan. 21, 2016.

(171)

172

Within, which accused the FSB of being behind the attacks on the apartment buildings.[6]

In November 2006, while reportedly investigating the death of Russian investigative journalist Anna Politkovskaya as well as Spanish links to the Russian mafia, Litvinenko met two former FSB colleagues, Andrei Lugovoi and Dmitri Kovtun, for tea in London. Later that day he fell ill, his organs began to fail, and he died within a few weeks, killed by a rare radioactive isotope: Polonium-210.[7] An investigation by the British authorities found that Lugovoi and Kovtun had poisoned Litvinenko. However, the Russian government refused to extradite Lugovoi, which led to a deterioration in bilateral relations, with the UK cutting off links to the Russian security services and diplomatic personnel being expelled by both sides (Putin would later award a state medal to Lugovoi, who is now a member of the Russian Duma).[8] That deterioration of relations made the British government reluctant to accede to the coroner's request for a public inquiry into Litvinenko's death.[9] In 2015, however, the British government began a public inquiry, which one year later concluded that "the FSB operation to kill Mr. Litvinenko was probably approved by [then FSB director] Mr. Patrushev and also by President Putin."[10]

In the decade between Litvinenko's death and the publishing of the results of the public inquiry, a number of potential "enemies of the Russian regime" died in Britain under mysterious circumstances. With decades of practice and the investment of considerable state resources, the Russian security services have reportedly developed techniques that a former Scotland Yard counterterrorism official characterized as "disguising murder" by staging suicides and using chemical and biological agents that leave no trace.[11] A former KGB lieutenant colonel told *The New York Times* that "The government is using the special services to liquidate its enemies. It was not just Litvinenko, but many others we don't know about, classified as accidents or maybe semi-accidents."[12]

One possible target was Alexander Perepilichnyy, a Russian financier who had reportedly helped Russian authorities engage in a $230 million tax fraud scheme that was exposed by Sergei Magnitsky, a Moscow lawyer for the British hedge fund Hermitage Capital Management.[13] After Magnitsky exposed the extent of the

---

[6] *Ibid.*; *see* Appendix A.

[7] *Ibid.* A British physicist who testified at the public inquiry into Litvinenko's death said that the polonium's poisonous effects would have to have been tested in advance to know the proper dosage to kill. He noted two unexplained deaths in Russia that occurred before Litvinenko's and with similar symptoms: the Chechen warlord Lecha Islamov and the one-time Putin associate Roman Tsepov, who both died in 2004. "Plutonium that killed Alexander Litvinenko Came from Russian Plant, UK Court Told," *Financial Times*, Mar. 11, 2015.

[8] "Alexander Litvinenko: Profile of Murdered Russian Spy," *BBC*, Jan. 21, 2016; "Russia's Putin Honors Suspect in Litvinenko Poisoning," *Reuters*, Mar. 9, 2015.

[9] Michael Holden, "Britain Says Ties with Russia Played Part in Litvinenko Ruling," *Reuters*, Jul. 19, 2013.

[10] United Kingdom House of Commons, *The Litvinenko Inquiry*, at 244.

[11] Heidi Blake et al., "From Russia with Blood," *BuzzFeed News*, June 15, 2017.

[12] Andrew Kramer, "More of Kremlin's Opponents Are Ending Up Dead," *The New York Times*, Aug. 20, 2016.

[13] Alan Cowell, "Another Russian Emigre Dies Mysteriously, But It's a Different Britain," *The New York Times*, Sept. 16, 2016; "Alexander Perepilichnyy Death: Russian May Have Talked to UK Spies," *BBC News*, Jan. 13, 2016; The founder of Hermitage Capital Management, Bill Browder, alleges that $30 million of the $230 million stolen in the tax fraud flowed into Britain. U.S. government investigators traced over $7.5 million of the stolen funds to a British bank account tied to a Moscow-based investment. "U.S. Traces US $7.5 Million from Russian Fraud Scheme Uncovered by Magnitsky," Organized Crime and Corruption Reporting Project, Apr. 17,

tax fraud—the largest in Russian history—he was arrested and charged with the crime himself, then tortured and killed in prison by his captors. Magnitsky's death reportedly led Perepilichnyy to turn against his bosses and cooperate with investigations—he fled to Britain and turned over evidence to Swiss prosecutors.[14] In 2012, on the same day he returned from a short trip to Paris, he collapsed while jogging and died from what police said was a heart attack.[15] Perepilichnyy's death occurred shortly before he was apparently due to provide additional evidence to Swiss authorities in a "confrontation" setting with Vladlen Stepanov, the husband of a senior tax official who was a key player in the tax fraud that Magnitsky had uncovered.[16] Because Perepilichnyy had received numerous threats, shortly before his death he had applied for several life insurance policies that required medical checks, the results of which gave him a clean bill of health and did not reveal any heart problems. After his death, one of the insurance companies ordered a new round of tests on his body and an expert in plant toxicology subsequently found that his stomach had traces of gelsemium, a rare Chinese flowering plant that, when ingested, triggers cardiac arrest. It is also "a known weapon of assassination by Chinese and Russian contract killers," according to a lawyer for the insurance company.[17]

A high-profile Russian also died under mysterious circumstances in Washington, D.C. in 2015. Mikhail Lesin, founder of the Russian state-owned television network *RT* and formerly a close adviser to Putin, was found dead in his hotel room in Dupont Circle with "blunt force injuries of the head, neck, torso, upper extremities, and lower extremities."[18] A nearly year-long investigation by D.C. police, the U.S. Attorney's Office for D.C., and the FBI concluded that "Lesin entered his hotel room on the morning of Wednesday, Nov. 4th, 2015, after days of excessive consumption of alcohol and sustained the injuries that resulted in his death while alone in his hotel room."[19] Lesin died the day before he was reportedly going

---

2017, https://www.occrp.org/en/daily/6342-u-s-traces-us-7-5-million-from-russian-fraud-scheme-uncovered-by-magnitsky; Neil Buckley, "Magnitsky Fraud Cash Laundered Through Britain, MPs Hear," *Financial Times,* May 3, 2016.

[14] Mike Eckel, "U.S. Settles Magnitsky-Linked Money Laundering Case on Eve of Trial," *Radio Free Europe/Radio Liberty,* May 13, 2017; Jeffrey Stern, "An Enemy of the Kremlin Dies in London: Who Killed Alexander Perepilichny?" *The Atlantic,* Jan./Feb., 2017.

[15] Alan Cowell, "Another Russian Emigre Dies Mysteriously, but it's a Different Britain," *The New York Times,* Sept. 16, 2016; "Alexander Perepilichny Death: Russian May Have Talked to UK Spies," *BBC News,* Jan. 13, 2016.

[16] *See* United Kingdom Courts and Tribunal Judiciary, Inquest Into the Death of Alexander Perepilichny, Day 4 (Questioning of Russ Whitworth, Legal and General), June 8, 2017.

[17] Jeffrey Stern, "An Enemy of the Kremlin Dies in London," *The Atlantic,* Jan./Feb. 2017.

[18] District of Columbia Office of the Chief Medical Examiner, "Joint Statement from the District of Columbia's Office of the Chief Medical Examiner and the Metropolitan Police Department," Mar. 10, 2016. The manner of death was undetermined.

[19] U.S. Department of Justice, "Investigation into the Death of Mikhail Lesin Has Closed," Oct. 28, 2016. According to the D.C. police report of the incident, on November 4, a hotel security guard checked in on a "stumbling drunk" Lesin in his room at 2:23 p.m. and asked him if he needed medical help, to which Lesin responded "nyet." At 8:16 p.m., another guard found Lesin face down on the floor of his hotel room, breathing but unresponsive. The next day, at 11:30 a.m., a security guard went to Lesin's room to remind him to check out and found him still face down on the floor. The guard called 911 and Lesin was pronounced dead at the scene. Peter Hermann, "Police Report on 2015 Death of Russian Political Aide Details Days of Drinking," *The Washington Post,* Dec. 4, 2017.

174

to meet with officials from the U.S. Department of Justice about
RT's operations.[20]

Some U.S. national security officials are now reportedly concerned that Russia's security services will start "doing here what
they do with some regularity in London."[21] The warning echoes a
much earlier one, given in 2004 after two Russian agents killed a
former president of Chechnya in Qatar, using explosives smuggled
in a diplomatic pouch. In a telephone interview with *The New York
Times,* a Chechen separatist leader said the killing "showed that
Russia under Mr. Putin had reverted to the darkest tactics of its
Soviet past" and that "if the international community does not give
proper attention to what happened in Qatar," he said, "I am absolutely sure that these methods may be tried again in other countries, including Western countries."[22] It is not inconceivable that
the Kremlin could use its security services in the United States as
it has elsewhere. The trail of mysterious deaths, all of which happened to people who possessed information that the Kremlin did
not want made public, should not be ignored by Western countries
on the assumption that they are safe from these extreme measures.

---

[20] Jason Leopold et al., "Everyone Thinks He Was Whacked," BuzzFeed News, Jul. 28, 2017.
In recent years, members of Congress had called for Lesin to be investigated for money laun-
dering and sanctioned for human rights abuses. In July 2014, Senator Roger Wicker asked the
Department of Justice to look into whether Lesin had violated the Foreign Corrupt Practices
Act and anti-money laundering statutes, citing Lesin's acquisition of a luxury real estate empire
throughout Europe and the United States, including over $28 million in southern California
alone. Representatives Ileana Ros-Lehtinen and James McGovern wrote to President Obama in
March 2014 requesting that Lesin be sanctioned under the Sergei Magnitsky Rule of Law Accountability Act for having "personally threatened the then-owner of NTV television, Vladimir
Gunsinky, while Gusinky was being held at the Butyrskaya Prison in Moscow, demanding that
he transfer control of his media outlets (which had been critical of the government) to the state-
owned company Gazprom in return for dropping the charges." Under the terms reportedly proposed by Lesin, Gusinky was offered the option of selling NTV to Gazprom for $300 million (far
below its value) and a debt write-off, or sharing "a cell with prisoners infected with AIDS and
TB." Letter from Senator Roger Wicker, to Attorney General Eric Holder, Jul. 29, 2014; Letter
from Congresswoman Ros-Lehtinen to President Obama, Mar. 14, 2014; Arkady Ostrovsky, *The
Invention of Russia: The Journey from Gorbachev's Freedom to Putin's War,* Atlantic Books, at
275 (2015).
[21] Jason Leopold et al., "Everyone Thinks He Was Whacked," *BuzzFeed News,* Jul. 28, 2017.
[22] Steven Myers, "Qatar Court Convicts 2 Russians in Top Chechen's Death," *The New York
Times,* Jul. 1, 2004.

Appendix C: Russian Government's Olympic Cheating Scheme

At two World Championships, in 2011 and 2013, and at the Olympics in 2012, Russian athlete Maria Savinova beat American sprinter Alysia Montano for a spot on the medal stand.[1] However, investigations now show that Savinova's performance had been enhanced by a doping program directed by the Russian government. Other American athletes were also cheated, like Chaunté Lowe, who competed in the 2008 Olympic high jump, and moved from sixth place to third when, in 2016, the top three finishers—two Russians and one Ukrainian—were disqualified, eight years after they had stood on the podium and accepted their medals. Montano and Lowe are just two of many American athletes who the Russian state has cheated out of Olympic glory. Ms. Lowe believes she was robbed not just of the glory of the medal stand, but of the financial opportunity it would have brought: companies, looking to sponsor her, lost interest after she failed to medal, and, after her husband was laid off from his job in 2008, they lost their house to foreclosure.[2]

In 2014, the World Anti-Doping Agency (WADA), an independent international agency that sets anti-doping standards, launched an investigation into Russian doping after a German TV station aired a documentary titled "The Secrets of Doping: How Russia Makes its Winners." The documentary "alleged doping practices; corrupt practices around sample collection and results management; and other ineffective administration of anti-doping processes that implicate Russia, ... the accredited laboratory based in Moscow and the Russian Anti-Doping Agency (RUSADA)."[3] The WADA report, released in November 2015, mentions secret recordings of Savinova which "show that [she] has an in-depth knowledge of doping regimes, dosages, physiological effects of doping and new [performance-enhancing drugs]."[4] The report recommended a lifetime ban for Savinova and detailed the role of the FSB in the doping operation: it had set up extensive surveillance in Russia's main anti-doping laboratory in Moscow and had a significant presence at the testing laboratory in the Russian city of Sochi.[5] As one laboratory worker told WADA investigators, "[in Sochi] we had some guys pre-

[1] Chris Perez, "US Olympian Wants Medal She Had Stolen by Russian Dopers," *New York Post*, Nov. 9, 2015.
[2] Rebecca Ruiz, "Olympics History Rewritten: New Doping Tests Topple the Podium," *The New York Times*, Nov. 21, 2016.
[3] World Anti-Doping Agency, *The Independent Commission Report #1* (Nov. 9, 2015).
[4] *Ibid.* at 262.
[5] *Ibid.*

176

tending to be engineers in the lab but actually they were from the federal security service." [6]

After a disappointing performance by Russian athletes at the 2010 Winter Olympics, and having spent over $50 billion on infrastructure for the 2014 games in Sochi (with up to $30 billion of that allegedly stolen by businessmen and officials close to Putin, according to a report authored by murdered opposition leader Boris Nemtsov), Putin needed good results to prove to the Russian people that they needed his "strong hand at the helm." [7] For the Olympic Games in Sochi, therefore, it was not enough for the Russian athletes to have been doping in the months leading up to the competition—they would also take performance-enhancing drugs during the games.

At the testing lab in Sochi, photographs show how the FSB drilled a hole through the wall of the official urine sample collection room and concealed it behind a faux-wood cabinet. The hole led to a storage space that Russian anti-doping officials had converted into a hidden laboratory. From there, the urine samples were passed to an FSB officer, who took them to a nearby building, where he unsealed the supposedly tamper-proof bottles and returned them with the caps loosened. The bottles were then emptied and filled with clean urine that had been collected from the athletes before the Olympics. Up to 100 urine samples of Russian athletes were removed in this way, allowing them to continue to use performance-enhancing drugs throughout the 2014 Winter Olympics. Of the 33 medals Russia won during the 2014 Olympics, 11 were awarded to athletes whose names appear on a spreadsheet detailing the Russian government's doping operation.[8]

In December 2016, WADA released a second independent report that found that "[a]n institutional conspiracy existed across summer and winter sports athletes who participated with Russian officials within the Ministry of Sport and its infrastructure ... along with the FSB for the purposes of manipulating doping controls. The summer and winter sports athletes were not acting individually but within an organised infrastructure." Over 1,000 Russian athletes competing in the Olympics and Paralympics had been involved in the conspiracy.[9] In an interview for the 2016 documentary *Icarus*, the former head of Russia's anti-doping laboratory, Grigory Rodchenkov, estimated that of the 154 Russian medalists in the 2008 and 2012 Olympics, at least 70 cheated with performance enhancing drugs. He confirmed that Russia had "a state-wide systematic doping system in place to cheat the Olympics" and that Putin was aware of the program.[10] In remarks that were later retracted by the Russian government, the acting head of Russia's anti-doping agency admitted in 2016 that doping among Russian athletes was

[6] *Ibid.*
[7] Alissa de Carbonnel, "Billions Stolen in Sochi Olympics Preparations—Russian opposition," *Reuters*, May 30, 2013; Bo Petersson & Karina Vamling, *The Sochi Predicament: Contexts, Characteristics, and Challenges of the Olympic Winter Games in 2014*, Cambridge Scholars Publishing, at 22 (2013).
[8] Rebecca Ruiz et al., "Russian Doctor Explains How He Helped Beat Doping Tests at the Sochi Olympics," *The New York Times*, May 13, 2016.
[9] Professor Richard H. McLaren, *The Independent Person 2nd Report*, at 1, 5. (Dec. 2016).
[10] *Icarus*, Bryan Fogel, Director (2017).

"an institutional conspiracy." [11] Despite the tremendous amount of forensic evidence proving the conclusions of the WADA investigations, as well as the resulting decision by the IOC to ban Russia's official participation in the 2018 Winter Olympics, Putin has steadfastly denied the existence of a state-sanctioned doping system. [12]

The scale of Russia's cheating in the 2014 Winter Olympics led 17 of the world's leading anti-doping agencies to request that the International Olympic Committee (IOC) ban Russia from the 2018 Winter Olympics, noting that "a country's sport leaders and organizations should not be given credentials to the Olympics when they intentionally violate the rules and rob clean athletes." [13] In December 2017, Russia became "the first country in sporting history to be banned from sending athletes to an Olympic games for doping," when the IOC declared that athletes could not compete under the Russian flag, Russian officials could not attend the games, and Russia's uniform, flag, and anthem also could not appear anywhere at the 2018 games. [14] In response, Putin implied the ban was tied to his still-unannounced reelection campaign, saying "When will the Olympics take place? February, isn't it? And when is the presidential election? March. I suspect that all of this is done to create conditions on someone's behalf to provoke sport fans' and athletes' anger that the state allegedly had something to do with it." [15]

The Kremlin may have also ordered retribution against WADA and U.S. athletes, among others. Approximately ten months after the release of the first report, a group of hackers associated with Russia's military intelligence, commonly known as Fancy Bear or APT28, broke into WADA's databases. [16] The hackers released medical information about several U.S. athletes, including gymnast Simone Biles and tennis players Venus and Serena Williams. [17] Shortly thereafter, the same group of hackers stole emails from WADA officials and released selected conversations about Americans and other athletes. [18] In April 2017, Fancy Bear hackers reportedly breached the International Association of Athletics Federations (IAAF), which had voted to ban Russia from all international track and field events. [19]

After blowing the whistle on the scope of the Russian doping program, the former head of Russia's anti-doping lab, Dr. Rodchenkov now appears to be a Kremlin target. Rodchenkov fled to the United States after resigning from his post in the wake of the second

[11] Rebecca Ruiz, "Russians No Longer Dispute Olympic Doping Operation," *The New York Times*, Dec. 27, 2016.
[12] Marissa Payne, "Vladimir Putin Says 'Current Russian Anti-Doping System Has Failed,'" *The Washington Post*, Mar. 1, 2017.
[13] Sean Ingle, "Anti-Doping Agencies Call on IOC to Ban Russia from 2018 Winter Olympics," *The Guardian*, Sept. 14, 2017.
[14] Murad Ahmed and Max Seddon, "Russia Banned from Winter Olympics," *Financial Times*, Dec. 5, 2017; Press Release, International Olympic Committee, IOC Suspends Rusian NOC and Creates a Path for Clean Individual Athletes to Compete in Pyeongchang 2018 Under the Olympic Flag, Dec. 5. 2017.
[15] Neil MacFarquhar, "Russia Won't Keep Athletes Home, Putin Says After Olympic Ban," *The New York Times*, Dec. 6, 2017.
[16] Andy Greenberg, "Russian Hackers Get Bolder in Anti-Doping Agency Attack," *Wired*, Sept. 14, 2016. Fancy Bear/APT28 were also behind hacks that targeted the Democratic National Committee and the Clinton campaign in the 2016 U.S. presidential election. *Ibid.*
[17] *Ibid.*
[18] Sean Ingle, "Fancy Bears Hack Again With Attack on Senior Anti-Doping Officials," *The Guardian*, Nov. 25, 2016.
[19] Thomas Fox-Brewster, "Russia's Fancy Bear Hackers are Stealing Athlete Drug Data Again," *Forbes*, Apr. 3, 2017.

WADA report, where he is reportedly cooperating with federal investigators and the IOC. His whereabouts in the United States are unknown and the Russian government has announced that he will be arrested if he ever returns to Russia.[20] Rodchenkov's application for asylum in the United States is now complicated by the fact that Russian authorities charged him with drug trafficking (drug traffickers are not eligible for political asylum under U.S. law).[21] The charge and accompanying arrest warrant were announced on the same day that Rodchenkov had an asylum interview with U.S. immigration officials, leading his lawyer, a former federal prosecutor, to believe that Russian law enforcement authorities may have been tipped off, stating "that is a coincidence too remarkable to believe. It seems fairly clear they were trying to influence the immigration process."[22]

Putin has asserted, on live television, that Rodchenkov is "under the control of American special services" and asked "what are they doing with him there? Are they giving him some kind of substances so that he says what's required?"[23] According to the *Icarus* documentary and statements by Rodchenkov's lawyer, U.S. officials reportedly believe that Russian agents in the United States may be looking for Rodchenkov, and that "there may be a credible threat to his life."[24] Before he fled, Rodchenkov said that friends inside the Russian government warned him that the Kremlin was planning his "suicide."[25] Rodchenkov's lawyer believes that Russian officials are seeking to prevent him from providing further evidence and testimony regarding Russia's Olympic cheating, and asserts that Russian authorities "are lobbying U.S. government officials behind closed doors for his extradition back to Russia" and "if they succeeded, Dr. Rodchenkov would face death and torture at their hands."[26]

Other Russian officials involved in the doping scandal did not live long enough to tell their role in it. One former head of RUSADA, Nikita Kamaev, was fired from his post in the aftermath of the first WADA report. Around that time, Kamaev approached a newspaper with an offer to "write a book about the true story of sport pharmacology and doping in Russia since 1987 while being a young scientist working in a secret lab in the USSR Institute of Sports Medicine," saying that he had "the information and facts that have never been published."[27] Such a book might have invalidated hundreds of Olympic medals won by Russian athletes over decades if it could prove their participation in a state-sponsored

[20] Oleg Matsnev, "Russian Court Order Arrest of Doping Whistle-Blower Who Fled," *The New York Times*, Sept. 28, 2017.

[21] "WADA Informant Rodchenkov Faces Drug Trafficking Charges in Russia," *RT,* Dec. 12, 2017.

[22] Michael Isikoff, "As Putin Seethes Over Olympic Ban, Doping Whistleblower Fears For His Life," *Yahoo News*, Dec. 26, 2017.

[23] Des Bieler, "Vladimir Putin Suggests U.S. is Manipulating Key Whistleblower on Russian Doping," *The Washington Post*, Dec. 14, 2017.

[24] *Icarus*, Bryan Fogel, Director (2017); Michael Isikoff, "As Putin seethes over Olympic ban, doping whistleblower fears for his life," *Yahoo News*, Dec. 26, 2017.

[25] Grigory Rodchenkov, "Russia's Olympic Cheating, Unpunished," *The New York Times*, Sept. 22, 2017.

[26] Statement by Jim Walden, "Stop Russia's Retaliation Toward a Whistle-blower," *Walden Macht & Haran LLP,* Dec. 26, 2017, available at https://drive.google.com/drive/folders/1GdkmE4Uwjyt—75BrHodpOTN6-ADtnEF3?usp=sharing.

[27] "Late Russian Anti-Doping Agency Boss Was Set to Expose True Story," *Reuters*, Feb. 20, 2017.

doping program. Just a couple of months later, Kamaev was found dead from "a massive heart attack," even though colleagues said he had seemed healthy and never complained about his heart.[28] A few weeks earlier, the founding chairman of RUSADA, Vyacheslav Sinev, also died unexpectedly of "unknown causes."[29] The current head of RUSADA, Yuri Ganus, has expressed doubts that both men died of natural causes, saying, "it's clear that two people could not just die like this ... . I understand that there was a situation, and the entire anti-doping organization was disqualified, and in this regard, this is an extraordinary fact."[30] While Kamaev was fired by Putin and lost his life shortly thereafter, his superior, Vitaly Mutko, the Minister of Sport who oversaw the entire doping conspiracy, was promoted to Deputy Prime Minister.[31]

[28] "Russia Anti-Doping Ex-Chief Nikita Kamaev Dies," *BBC News*, Feb. 15, 2016.
[29] Andrew Kramer, "Nikita Kamayev, Ex-Head of Russian Antidoping Agency, Dies," *The New York Times*, Feb. 15, 2016; Michael Isikoff, "As Putin Seethes Over Olympic Ban, Doping Whistleblower Fears For His Life," *Yahoo News,* Dec. 26, 2017.
[30] "Members of the RUSADA Leadership Died 'Not Just So,'" *Pravada,* Sept. 20, 2017 (translated from Russian).
[31] Rebecca Ruiz, "Russia Sports Minister Promoted to Deputy Prime Minister," *The New York Times,* Oct. 19, 2016.

Appendix D: Russia's Security Services and Cyber Hackers

Russia's security services have worked with and provided protection to criminal hackers for decades, and, according to some experts, those same hackers are now responsible for nearly all of the theft of credit card information from U.S. consumers.[1] Despite a wealth of evidence, Putin has long denied any connection between Russia's security services and cyberattacks on foreign institutions, including the retaliatory hacks of WADA and the IAAF mentioned in Appendix C, which cybersecurity experts traced to hackers sponsored by the Russian government.[2] Various investigations have uncovered extensive proof that Russia's security services "maintain a sophisticated alliance with unofficial hackers," who are often offered a choice when facing charges for cybercrimes: go to prison, or work for the FSB.[3] Some scholars also believe that groups of unofficial, "patriotic hackers" are guided not by the security services, but by the Presidential Administration itself.[4]

One of Russia's oldest and most sophisticated cybercrime groups is known as the Russian Business Network (RBN). Before it went underground in 2007, RBN was a global hub that provided Internet services and was "linked to 60 percent of all cybercrime."[5] RBN is still involved in the full gamut of cybercrimes, including extortion, credit card theft, drug sales, weapons smuggling, human trafficking, prostitution, and child pornography.[6] Verisign, a major internet security company, has referred to the RBN as "the baddest of the bad," and many researchers describe RBN "as having the best malware, the best organization."[7] RBN is also rumored to have connections to powerful politicians in St. Petersburg and pos-

---

[1] Interview with Cybersecurity Expert, Sept. 2017; Kara Flook, "Russia and the Cyber Threat," *Critical Threats*, May 13, 2009, https://www.criticalthreats.org/analysis/russia-and-the-cyber-threat#—ftnref18. In 2016, more than 15 million U.S. consumers lost more than $16 billion due to identity theft or credit card fraud. Al Pascual et al., "2017 Identity Fraud: Securing the Connected Life," *Javelin*, Feb. 1, 2017.

[2] "APT28: At the Center of the Storm," FireEye, Jan. 11, 2017, https://www.fireeye.com/blog/threat-research/2017/01/apt28—at—the—center.html; "Fancy Bears: IAAF hacked and fears athletes' information compromised," *BBC*, Apr. 3, 2017.

[3] Andrei Soldatov & Irina Borogan, The New Nobility: The Restoration of Russia's Security State and the Enduring Legacy of the KGB, PublicAffairs, at 227 (2010); "APT28: At the Center of the Storm," FireEye, Jan. 11, 2017. https://www.fireeye.com/blog/threat-research/2017/01/apt28—at—the—center.html; Kara Flook, "Russia and the Cyber Threat," *Critical Threats*, May 13, 2009.

[4] Andrei Soldatov & Irina Borogan, *The New Nobility: The Restoration of Russia's Security State and the Enduring Legacy of the KGB*, PublicAffairs, at 223 (2010).

[5] Kara Flook, "Russia and the Cyber Threat," *Critical Threats*, May 13, 2009.

[6] Interview with Cybersecurity Expert, Sept. 2017.

[7] "A Walk on the Dark Side," *The Economist*, Aug. 30, 2007; Richard Stiennon, "Is Russia Poised to Retaliate Against Sanctions With Cyber Attacks?" *Security Current*, Aug. 7, 2014, https://www.securitycurrent.com/en/writers/richard-stiennon/is-russia-poised-to-retaliate-against-sanctions-with-cyber-attacks.

sibly now Moscow. In addition, one of its members is reportedly a former lieutenant colonel in the FSB.[8]

Cybersecurity experts have blamed Putin's government and the FSB for giving protection to the RBN,[9] who, according to Verisign, "feel they are strongly politically protected. They pay a huge amount of people."[10] Some analysts assert that the FSB's protection comes with a quid pro quo—when tasked, the RBN is expected to carry out the FSB's orders. In 2014, as the United States was considering sanctions against the Russian government for its illegal annexation of Crimea, one expert's sources told him there were indications that "the Kremlin will unleash the RBN if [U.S.] sanctions pass a certain threshold."[11]

According to the U.S. Department of Justice, FSB officials and hackers worked together to steal data from approximately 500 million Yahoo accounts—a cybercrime that cost the American company hundreds of millions of dollars.[12] Instead of working with U.S. officials to target the hackers, the FSB officials—who belonged to a unit that is the FBI's liaison on cybercrime in Russia—worked with the hackers to target U.S. officials.[13] They used the stolen account information to target Russian journalists critical of the Kremlin as well as American diplomatic officials, and gained access to the content of at least 6,500 accounts.[14] The case was just one of many that showed how Russian intelligence agencies "piggyback" on hackers' criminal operations as "a form of cheap intelligence gathering."[15]

The FSB also reportedly received piggyback rides from Evgeniy Bogachev, whom the FBI calls the "most wanted cybercriminal in the world," and who was sanctioned by the U.S. Treasury Department in December 2016 for engaging in "significant malicious cyber-enabled misappropriation of financial information for private financial gain."[16] Despite his most-wanted status in the United States and several other countries, Bogachev is living openly in a Russian resort town on the Black Sea, from where he reportedly works "under the supervision of a special unit of the FSB."[17] U.S. law enforcement has accused Bogachev of running a network of up to a million virus-infected computers, across multiple countries, which he has used to steal hundreds of millions of dollars.[18] Cybersecurity investigators noticed in 2011 that infected computers con-

---

[8] Kara Flook, "Russia and the Cyber Threat," *Critical Threats,* May 13, 2009. https://www.criticalthreats.org/analysis/russia-and-the-cyber-threat#—ftnref13

[9] Brian Krebs, "Wishing an (Un)Happy Birthday to the Storm Worm," *The Washington Post,* Jan. 17, 2008.

[10] "A Walk on the Dark Side," *The Economist,* Aug. 30, 2007.

[11] Richard Stiennon, "Is Russia Poised to Retaliate Against Sanctions With Cyber Attacks?" *Security Current,* Aug. 7, 2014.

[12] U.S. Department of Justice, U.S. Charges Russian FSB Officers and Their Criminal Conspirators for Hacking Yahoo and Million of Email Accounts (Mar. 2017); Ingrid Lunden, "After Data Breaches, Verizon Knocks $350M Off Yahoo Sale, Now Valued at $4.48B," *Tech Crunch,* Feb. 21, 2017.

[13] Aruna Viswanatha & Robert McMillan, "Two Russian Spies Charged in Massive Yahoo Hack," *The Wall Street Journal,* Mar. 15, 2017.

[14] *Ibid.*

[15] Michael Schwirtz, "U.S. Accuses Russian Email Spammer of Vast Network of Fraud," *The New York Times,* Apr. 10, 2017.

[16] Michael Schwirtz, "U.S. Accuses Russian Email Spammer of Vast Network of Fraud," *The New York Times,* Apr. 10, 2017; Press Release, U.S. Department of the Treasury, Treasury Sanctions Two Individuals for Malicious Cyber-Enabled Activities, Dec. 29, 2016.

[17] *Ibid.*

[18] *Ibid.*

trolled by his network were being mined for information related to political events. For example, after the U.S. government agreed to arm Syrian opposition groups, computers in Turkey that were part of Bogachev's zombie network began to receive search requests for terms like "arms delivery" and "Russian mercenary."[19] Later, searches related to Ukraine sought information on government security officials and even looked for documents that had the English phrase "Department of Defense." Given the stark difference from standard criminal searches on computers controlled by Bogachev and those searches, analysts believe that the purpose was espionage, and were likely a result of cooperation with Russian intelligence services.[20]

Bogachev also sold malware on the dark web, which often functions as an underground marketplace for cyber criminals. The New York Times has reported that some of the Russian hacker forums on the dark web explicitly state what kinds of cybercrime—such as bank fraud, drug sales, and counterfeiting—are permitted, with the sole exception that no targets can be in Russia or post-Soviet states. The rule among Russian hackers is "Don't work in the .RU" (.RU is the top-level country domain for Russia, meaning firms and banks in the country are off-limits), and breaking that rule results in a lifetime ban from many of the Russian hacker dark web forums.[21] One forum, for example, offered classes on how to steal credit cards, with "the strict rule that course participants do not target Russian credit cards."[22] The FBI has found that, instead of closing down these forums, the FSB has infiltrated them. FBI agents have even seen a Russian hacker they were investigating give a copy of his passport to a suspected Russian intelligence agent, implying that the state was likely either recruiting or protecting the hacker.[23]

Another notorious Russian hacker operating under the protection of the security services was Roman Seleznev, who targeted small businesses in U.S. cities like Washington, D.C., going after pizzerias, burrito shops, and bakeries. After U.S. law enforcement agents went to Moscow to present the FSB with evidence of Seleznev's crimes, his online presence vanished, suggesting that FSB officials had warned Seleznev that Americans were tracking him. U.S. prosecutors then concluded that "further coordination with the Russian government would jeopardize efforts to prosecute this case."[24]

A few years later, Seleznev re-emerged with the launch of a website that U.S. officials say "reinvented the stolen credit card market" and offered millions of stolen credit card numbers that could be searched and selected by customers based on credit card

[19] *Ibid.*
[20] *Ibid.*
[21] "America's Hunt for Russian Hackers: How FBI Agents Tracked Down Four of the World's Biggest Cyber-Criminals and Brought Them to Trial in the U.S.," *Meduza*, Sept. 19, 2017, https://meduza.io/en/feature/2017/09/19/america-s-hunt-for-russian-hackers; Michael Schwirtz, "U.S. Accuses Russian Email Spammer of Vast Network of Fraud," *The New York Times*, Apr. 10, 2017.
[22] John Simpson, "Russian Hackers Offer Courses in Credit-Card Theft on the Dark Web,"*The Times,* Jul. 19, 2017.
[23] Michael Schwirtz and Joseph Goldstein, "Russian Espionage Piggybacks on a Cybercriminal's Hacking," *The New York Times*, Mar. 12, 2017.
[24] Goldman, Adam & Matt Apuzzo. "U.S. Faces Tall Hurdles in Detaining or Deterring Russian Hackers." *The New York Times*, Dec. 15, 2016.

company and financial institution. Seleznev was careful to travel only to countries without extradition treaties with the United States, but State Department diplomats convinced officials in the Maldives, where he was vacationing, to detain and transfer him to U.S. custody. Russia's foreign ministry labeled the arrest an "abduction," though the Russian government's true cause for alarm might have been for different reasons; in intercepted emails, Seleznev reportedly claimed that the FSB knew about his identity and activities and was giving him protection.[25]

U.S. authorities found that Seleznev, while under the protection of Russia's security services, had breached point-of-sale systems (typically a cash register with a debit/credit card reader) at more than 500 U.S. businesses and had stolen millions of credit card numbers between 2009 and 2013, which he then bundled and sold on the dark web to buyers who used the card information for fraudulent purchases.[26] Another Russian hacker who stole credit card numbers, Dmitry Dokuchaev, reportedly had his prosecution in Russia for credit card fraud dismissed after he agreed to work for the FSB.[27] According to the U.S. Department of Justice, as an FSB officer Dokuchaev allegedly "protected, directed, facilitated, and paid criminal hackers" responsible for the breach of Yahoo customer data, which was also used to obtain credit card account information.[28] One expert asserts that hackers from Russia and Eastern Europe are now responsible for nearly 100 percent of all theft of consumers' payment card information at U.S. vendors' point-of-sale systems, and that 90 percent of that theft could be prevented by stopping only about 200 people, who are mostly hackers who got their start with the RBN in the late 1990s and act as force multipliers.[29]

Hackers from Russia and Eastern Europe often target point-of-sale systems at small U.S. businesses, such as restaurants, retailers, and car washes. And the buyers of that stolen information are mostly here in the United States.[30] Once hackers steal the credit card information from these vendors, they bundle it together with other stolen cards and sell or auction them off on underground websites. For example, police in New England spearheaded an investigation that found that 40 car washes across the country had been hacked at their point-of-sale systems, resulting in the theft of "countless" customer credit and debit cards. The information from those cards were then sold to U.S. buyers, who used it to re-encode gift cards and make fraudulent purchases of several thousands of dollars at stores such as Target. According to one of the detectives leading the case, all of the suspects using the fraudulent gift cards

[25] "America's Hunt for Russian Hackers: How FBI Agents Tracked Down Four of the World's Biggest Cyber-Criminals and Brought Them to Trial in the U.S.," Meduza, Sept. 19, 2017, https://meduza.io/en/feature/2017/09/19/america-s-hunt-for-russian-hackers.

[26] U.S. Department of Justice, "Russian Cyber-Criminal Sentenced to 27 Years in Prison for Hacking and Credit Card Fraud," Apr. 21, 2017. In April 2017, Seleznev was sentenced to 27 years in prison. Ibid.

[27] Andrew Kramer, "Hacker is a Villain to the United States, for Different Reasons," The New York Times, Mar. 15, 2017.

[28] U.S. Department of Justice, "U.S. Charges Russian FSB Officers and Their Criminal Conspirators for Hacking Yahoo and Millions of Email Accounts," Mar. 15, 2017.

[29] Interview with Cybersecurity Expert, Sept. 2017.

[30] Selena Larson, "Cybercriminals Can Take a Class on Stealing Credit Cards," CNN Tech, Jul. 19, 2017.

"are Blood gang members. And they're starting to work smarter, not harder."[31]

U.S. law enforcement officials and cybersecurity experts across the board have seen a large uptick in American street gangs using fraudulent purchases to fund their activities. According to the chief of the New York Police Department, "these gang members are tech-savvy."[32] As in the case above, stolen credit cards are used to buy gift cards and big-ticket items like large-screen televisions and iPads, which are then sold and the profits are used to fund weapon and drug purchases. In New York City in 2016, hundreds of gang members were arrested in possession of stolen credit card information, something that officials say "almost never happened" just five years ago, with "gangs using credit card fraud to finance their violent activity [becoming] more of a trend over the last five years."[33] In one case, 35 people affiliated with a Brooklyn street gang were "arrested for allegedly financing violent crimes with elaborate credit card fraud schemes."[35] The suspects reportedly purchased more than 750 credit card numbers from the dark web and used them to make purchases ranging from American Girl dolls to guns.[35]

Cyber hacking facilitated by Russian security services enables a host of illicit activity and inflicts cascading harm on U.S. consumers and businesses. The FSB provides hackers with immunity from domestic prosecution in exchange for the occasional use of their computer networks and hacking expertise for espionage or information operations. Under this protection, the Russian hackers' criminal activities include stealing the banking information of U.S. consumers with complete impunity and posting it for sale on the dark web. That information is increasingly purchased by U.S. street gangs, who use it to make fraudulent purchases that are, in turn, used to fund gang and other criminal activities. This sequence shows that the cyber hacking activities of the FSB, carried out with Putin's knowledge and approval and often in concert with criminal hackers, are harming the financial and physical security of Americans in the United States.

---

[31] "Card Wash: Card Breaches at Car Washes," *Krebs on Security*, June 23, 2014.
[32] Jonathan Dienst & David Paredes, "Violent Drug Gangs Increasingly turn to Credit Card Theft as Big Moneymaker," *NBC New York*, Feb. 7, 2017.
[33] *Ibid.*; Ida Siegal, "Brooklyn Gang Members Used Fake Credit Cards to Buy American Girl Dolls, Guns: Officials," *NBC New York*, Dec. 13, 2016.
[34] *Ibid.*
[35] *Ibid.*

Appendix E: Attacks and Harassment Against Human Rights Activists and Journalists Inside Russia

Human rights activists and independent journalists inside the Russian Federation have often become the victims of violent attacks and harassment on account of their work. While a state role in individual attacks is not always visible, the general impunity with which these attacks have occurred reflect the government's failure to uphold the rule of law and ensure justice for victims. This climate of impunity perpetuates an environment hospitable to further attacks.

For example, in July 2009, Natalia Estemirova, a well-known researcher with the Russian human rights group Memorial, who had worked extensively on documenting human rights abuses in the North Caucasus, was kidnapped by assailants in front of her home in Chechnya and her murdered body was later found in neighboring Ingushetia.[1] Authorities later claimed they killed the perpetrator in a shootout, but Estemirova's family and associates have long questioned the evidence supporting the official version of events.[2] No individuals have been convicted in connection with her killing. In February 2012, Memorial activist Philip Kostenko was beaten by two unknown assailants in a park, suffering a concussion and a broken leg, and was reportedly pressured by police while en route to the hospital to sign a document pledging not to file a police report.[3] In March 2016, two employees of the Committee for the Prevention of Torture, traveling with foreign journalists on a monitoring trip through Russia's North Caucasus, were hospitalized after being beaten by masked men wielding baseball bats, who later set their bus on fire.[4] The head of the Committee, Igor Kalyapin, was attacked a week later in the Chechen capital of Grozny, where local authorities investigated but never filed charges.[5]

The Committee to Protect Journalists (CPJ), a U.S.-based NGO that analyzes attacks on the press globally, cites at least 58 jour-

---

[1] "Russian Activist Natalia Estemirova Found Dead," *The Telegraph,* July 15, 2009.
[2] Eline Gordts, "Russia's Investigation of Opposition Murders Does Not Bode Well For Nemtsov Case," *Huffington Post,* Mar. 6, 2015.
[3] U.S. Department of State, *Country Reports on Human Rights Practices for 2012: Russia,* at 4.
[4] "Russia: Journalists, Activists Attacked in North Caucasus," *Human Rights Watch,* Mar. 9, 2016.
[5] U.S. Department of State, *Country Reports on Human Rights Practices for 2016: Russia,* at 6.

nalists killed in connection with their work in Russia since 1992.[6]
The murder in 2006 of *Novaya Gazeta* reporter Anna Politkovskaya
is particularly emblematic of the threats that journalists in Russia
face. Politkovskaya had written extensively on state corruption and
human rights abuses in Chechnya, and before her death, had ze-
roed in on the torture and killings perpetrated by then Chechen
prime minister Ramzan Kadyrov and his "Kadyrovtsy" personal security force. She had also written extensively on possible FSB connections with purported Chechen terrorists.[7] Politkovskaya had reportedly been threatened directly by Kadyrov when she interviewed
him in 2005, and before that was allegedly poisoned on a plane ride
to cover the Beslan terror attacks in North Ossetia in 2004 and detained by security forces during a 2002 visit to Chechnya.[8] After
she was murdered in the lobby of her apartment building on October 7, 2006, *The New York Times* noted that Putin "sought to play
down Ms. Politkovskaya's influence" by describing her reporting as
"extremely insignificant for political life in Russia" and saying her
death had caused more harm than her publications.[9] The investigation into her murder proceeded slowly, with a series of arrests, re-
leases, and retrials. Eight years after her death, five Chechen men
were convicted of killing Politkovskaya, with two receiving life sen-
tences.[10] A Moscow police officer pleaded guilty in 2012 to providing the murder weapon and surveilling the victim before her
death, receiving a reduced sentence in exchange for cooperating
with authorities. Nevertheless, many observers alleged that the
government's investigation of the murder stopped short of identifying—or punishing—the masterminds, and relatives of both
Politkovskaya and the Chechen defendants criticized the trial as
bogus.[11]

Additional examples of violent attacks against journalists in Russia include that of Mikhail Beketov, the editor of a local newspaper
in the Moscow suburb of Khimki, who was brutally attacked in
2008 by unknown assailants who left him with a crushed skull and
broken hands and legs; Beketov was left in a coma and required
a tracheotomy to breathe which left extensive scarring in his
throat.[12] Prior to the attack, Beketov had accused the Khimki
mayor of corruption in his decision to build a highway through a
forested area of the city, and he had been targeted for harassment
before, including his car being set on fire and the killing of his
dog.[13] Two years after the attack, no perpetrators had been ar-

[6] Committee to Protect Journalists, "58 Journalists Killed in Russia/Motive Confirmed," https://cpj.org/killed/europe/russia (visited Dec. 5, 2017).
[7] Scott Anderson, "None Dare Call It a Conspiracy," *GQ*, Mar. 30, 2017; Claire Bigg, "Politkovskaya Investigating Chechen Torture At Time of Death," *Radio Free Europe/Radio Liberty*, Oct. 9, 2006.
[8] Ben Roazen, "The Great Cost of Journalism in Vladimir Putin's Russia," *GQ*, Jan. 13, 2017; Committee to Protect Journalists, "Anna Politkovskaya," https://cpj.org/data/people/anna-politkovskaya (visited Dec. 12, 2017).
[9] Andrew Roth, "Prison for 5 in Murder of Journalists," *The New York Times*, June 9, 2014.
[10] Sergei L. Loiko, "Five Sentenced In Slaying of Russian Journalist Anna Politkovskaya," *Los Angeles Times*, June 9, 2014. Bizarrely, one of the suspected Chechen gunmen was shot in the leg in 2013 on a Moscow street, in what his lawyer alleged was an attempt to silence him. "Russia: Chechen Man on Trial in Killing Of Journalist Is Shot on Moscow Street," *Reuters*, Aug. 16, 2013.
[11] Sergei L. Loiko, "Five Sentenced In Slaying of Russian Journalist Anna Politkovskaya," *Los Angeles Times*, June 9, 2014.
[12] Committee to Protect Journalists, "Mikhail Beketov," https://cpj.org/killed/2013/mikhail-beketov.php (visited Dec. 12, 2017).
[13] "Russian Khimki Forest Journalist Mikhail Beketov Dies," *BBC News*, Apr. 9, 2013.

189

rested—rather, it was Beketov who was convicted of libel and ordered to pay damages to the Khimki mayor, though the verdict was later overturned. Beketov died in 2013 of choking that led to heart failure, which his colleagues asserted was directly related to the serious injuries he sustained in the Khimki attack.[14] In April 2017, veteran investigative journalist and co-founder of the *Novy Peterburg* newspaper, Nikolai Andrushchenko, died six weeks after he had been badly beaten by unknown assailants. His colleagues alleged the attack was related to his coverage of public corruption.[15]

Beyond violent attacks, criminal prosecutions have also been used to silence activists and Kremlin critics. In recent years, such prosecutions have targeted bloggers, filmmakers, and social media activists to signal that dissent is as risky online or in artistic contexts as it is over the air or in print. For example, blogger Alexey Kungurov was convicted in December 2016 of inciting terrorism and sentenced to two years in a penal colony.[16] His arrest came after he posted a piece that criticized the Russian military's actions in Syria.[17] Ukrainian filmmaker Oleg Sentsov, who had peacefully protested the Russian annexation of his native Crimea, was detained by Russian authorities in the occupied territory of Ukraine and transferred to Russia for trial on a range of terrorism-related charges. He was sentenced to 20 years imprisonment in August 2015.[18]

---

[14] Committee to Protect Journalists, "Mikhail Beketov," https://cpj.org/killed/2013/mikhail-beketov.php (visited Dec. 12, 2017).
[15] Jon Sharman, "Russian Journalist and Putin Critic Dies After Being Beaten Up by Strangers," *The Independent*, Apr. 19, 2017.
[16] PEN America, "Alexey Kungurov," https://pen.org/advocacy-case/alexey-kungurov (visited Dec. 12, 2017).
[17] *Ibid.*
[18] Sophia Kishkovsky, "Russia Gives Ukrainian Filmmaker Oleg Sentsov a 20-Year Sentence," *The New York Times*, Aug. 25, 2015.

Appendix F: Flawed Elections in the Russian Federation Since 1999

The conduct of democratic elections inside the Russian Federation has steadily deteriorated since Vladimir Putin came to power in 1999, as documented by repeated international election observation missions to the country. Coupled with the Russian government's growing efforts to suppress dissent broadly, the right of Russian citizens to choose their own government in free and fair elections has been increasingly stifled. After the upheaval of the 1990s and the beginning of the country's post-Communist transition, observers from the OSCE's Office of Democratic Institutions and Human Rights (ODIHR) described the December 1999 Duma elections as "significant progress for the consolidation of democracy in the Russian Federation" and noted a "competitive and pluralistic" process.[1] Barely three months later, after President Yeltsin had resigned and handed the reigns to Putin as acting president, the ODIHR observation mission expressed concerns over improper campaigning by state and regional officials and the limited field of candidates.[2] By 2003, ODIHR noted the Duma elections "failed to meet many OSCE and Council of Europe (COE) commitments for democratic elections" and called into question "Russia's fundamental willingness to meet European and international standards for democratic elections."[3] The assessment of the 2004 presidential election was equally bleak, finding that "a vibrant political discourse and meaningful pluralism were lacking" and citing problems with the secrecy of the ballot and the biased role of the state-controlled media.[4] There was no ODIHR assessment for the 2007 Duma elections, in which the United Russia party won a two-thirds constitutional majority, because the 70 would-be observers were denied visas, leaving them with insufficient time for meaningful election observation and leading ODIHR to scrap its mission.[5] Similarly, ODIHR said it could not observe the 2008 presidential election in Russia because of "limitations" placed by the government on

---

[1] The International Election Observation Mission—Russian Federation, 19 December 1999 Election of Deputies to the State Duma (Parliament), Preliminary Statement, Dec. 20, 1999 at 1.

[2] The International Election Observation Mission—Russian Federation, 26 March 2000 Election of President, Statement of Preliminary Findings & Conclusions, Mar. 27, 2000 at 1.

[3] The International Election Observation Mission—Russian Federation, 7 December 2003 State Duma Elections, Statement of Preliminary Findings and Conclusions, Dec. 8, 2003 at 1.

[4] The International Election Observation Mission—Russian Federation, 14 March 2004 Presidential Election in the Russian Federation, Statement of Preliminary Findings and Conclusions, Mar. 15, 2004 at 7-8.

[5] "Election Observers Unwelcome," *Spiegel Online*, Nov. 16, 2007.

the planned observer mission.[6] The U.S. State Department cited the Russian government's "unprecedented restrictions" on ODIHR and noted that international observers who did witness the poll deemed it unfair, given frequent abuses of administrative resources, a heavily biased media environment, and restrictive changes to the election code.[7]

The COE, the only outside body to field observers in the 2008 presidential election, heavily critiqued the election and lamented the absence of ODIHR observers. The COE called the 2008 poll "more of a plebiscite" than a genuine democratic exercise, citing the Kremlin's deliberate exclusion of the lone democratic challenger Mikhail Kasyanov, a former Prime Minister dismissed by Putin in 2004; the uneven media access favoring candidate (and Putin's preferred successor) Dmitry Medvedev; and the pressure placed by regional and local officials on public sector workers to vote for Medvedev.[8] While ODIHR has since conducted election observation missions in Russia, the OSCE has assessed that "the convergence of the State and the governing party" in elections fails to reflect genuine choice.[9]

---

[6] Organization for Security and Co-operation in Europe, "OSCE/ODIHR Regrets that Restrictions Force Cancellation of Election Observation Mission to Russian Federation," Feb. 7, 2008.
[7] U.S. Department of State, Country Reports on Human Rights Practices for 2008: Russia.
[8] Luke Harding, "Russia Election Not Free or Fair, Say Observers," The Guardian, Mar. 3, 2008.
[9] The International Election Observation Mission—Russian Federation, 4 December 2011 State Duma Elections, Statement of Preliminary Findings and Conclusions, Dec. 5, 2011 at 1.

Appendix G: Harsh Treatment of LGBT Individuals and Women in the Russian Federation

President Putin has fueled culture wars to draw a distinction between Russian "traditional values" and the purported decadence and corruption of the West. The results have been particularly acute in the state's treatment of private and domestic life, including of lesbian, gay, bisexual, and transgender (LGBT) individuals and women. A series of anti-LGBT laws introduced at regional levels in Russia in 2003 and 2006 and at the federal level in 2013 essentially prohibit the public mention of homosexuality, including "promoting non-traditional sexual relationships among minors" and drawing a "social equivalence between traditional and non-traditional sexual relationships."[1] Russia's anti-LGBT law also inspired copycat legislation that has been adopted or is pending in Lithuania, Belarus, Kyrgyzstan, and Moldova, and that was introduced but ultimately withdrawn or failed in Latvia, Ukraine, Armenia, and Kazakhstan.[2] In 2017, the European Court of Human Rights ruled that Russia's "gay propaganda" law, as it has often been called, was discriminatory and violated free expression.[3]

In the years since its passage, the gay propaganda law has fueled violent recriminations against LGBT activists in Russia. The Russian LGBT Network, an NGO, used Russian government data to calculate that 22 percent of all hate crimes in 2015 were directed at LGBT persons.[4] Press reports after the passage of the gay propaganda law cited harrowing examples of "homophobic vigilantism" in which "emboldened" right-wing groups would lure LGBT individuals to trick meetings via social media and then attack or humiliate them on camera.[5] One Russian LGBT activist noted that, of 20 such incidents his organization had tracked, only four were investigated and just one resulted in a court case.[6] More recently, reports emerged in early 2017 of a systematic campaign to round up and repress gay men in Chechnya, allegedly at the instruction of

---

[1] Sewell Chan, "Russia's 'Gay Propaganda' Laws Are Illegal, European Court Rules," *The New York Times*, June 20, 2017.
[2] Human Rights First, "Spread of Russian-Style Propaganda Laws: Fact Sheet" July 11, 2016.
[3] European Court of Human Rights, "Legislation in Russia Banning the Promotion of Homosexuality Breaches Freedom of Expression and is Discriminatory," June 20, 2017. Sewell Chan, "Russia's 'Gay Propaganda' Laws Are Illegal, European Court Rules," *The New York Times*, June 20, 2017.
[4] Russian LGBT Network, "22% of Hate Crimes In Russia Are Committed Against LGBT," https://www.lgbtnet.org/en/content/22-hate-crimes-russia-are-committed-against-lgbt (visited Dec. 31, 2017).
[5] Alec Luhn, "Russian Anti-Gay Law Prompts Rise in Homophobic Violence," *The Guardian*, Sept. 1, 2013.
[6] *Ibid.*

the powerful speaker of the Chechen parliament.[7] Some NGOs esti-
mate that as many as 200 individuals were detained in the campaign and subjected to various forms of torture, threatened with
exposure to their families and honor killings, and pressured to give
up the names of other gay men.[8]

The politicization of traditional family values in Russia has also
influenced the state's policies regarding the treatment of Russian
women. According to Russian government statistics from 2013,
Russian women are victims of crime in the home at disproportion-
ately high rates, while 97 percent of domestic violence cases do not
reach court.[9] Against this bleak backdrop, the parliamentarian who
introduced the original 2013 gay propaganda law also introduced a
law in 2017 dubbed the "slapping law" to reduce punishments for
spousal abuse to a misdemeanor and administrative offense.[10] The
law was adopted by a vote of 380 to 3 in the Duma and signed by
President Putin in February 2017, decriminalizing a first instance
of domestic violence if the victim is not seriously injured; some observers have noted its passage was hastened by support from the
Russian Orthodox Church.[11]

[7] Human Rights Watch, *They Have Long Arms and They Can Find Me: Anti-Gay Purge by Local Authorities in Russia's Chechen Republic*, at 1, 16, 19 (May 2017).
[8] Interviews by Committee Staff with U.S. NGOs.
[9] U.S. Department of State, *Country Reports on Human Rights Practices for 2016: Russia*, at 56.
[10] Sadie Levy Gale, "Russian Politician Behind Anti-Gay Law Wants to Decriminalise Domestic Violence," *Independent*, July 28, 2016.
[11] Tom Balmforth, "Russian Duma Approves Bill to Soften Penalty for Domestic Violence," *Radio Free Europe/Radio Free Liberty*, Jan. 27, 2017; Claire Sebastian & Antonia Mortensen, "Putin Signs Law Reducing Punishment for Domestic Battery," *CNN*, Feb. 7, 2017.

Appendix H: Disinformation Narratives, Themes, and Techniques

The Kremlin promotes a variety of anti-Western and pro-Russian "master narratives" across its propaganda platforms, both within Russia and abroad. Russian government propagandists subscribe to these narratives and follow them to craft and frame disinformation campaigns that advance the Kremlin's positions and interests. One study commissioned in 2012 identified several master narratives employed by Kremlin propagandists, including:

- *Savior of Europe:* Russia has been Europe's savior for over 200 years, ever since Alexander II stopped Napoleon's armies from dominating Europe in 1812. Russia also saved Europe from the Nazis, and Western nations tend to minimize this achievement. Russia should proudly assert its people's heroism to get the recognition it deserves and be admired as a great power.
- *Eurasian Bridge:* Russia was founded as a great civilization that acted as a bridge between East and West. The collapse of the Soviet Union, which went from the Baltic Sea to the Bering Strait, created a vacuum in a region that it is Russia's destiny to shape and lead. Russia has to advance its cultural, economic, and diplomatic relationships to forge a new regional union that can rival the other global powers.
- *Catching Up with Rivals:* In the 1990s, Russia tried to emulate the unfettered capitalism of the West, causing it to fall from its status as a global economic and cultural leader. Putin and Medvedev returned Russia to the path of prosperity and moved to modernize the economy beyond natural resources by harnessing the entrepreneurship and innovation of the Russian people. Russia must continue to follow this path toward a modern economy to remain strong and catch up to the other global powers.
- *Fortress Russia:* For centuries, Russia has been attacked on all fronts by imperial powers seeking to expand their borders, from Japanese fleets in the east to Nazi armies in the west. Now the United States, NATO, and Europe are conspiring to surround Russia and keep it from becoming an equal power. But Russia has and always will defend itself and will continue to hold its ground against aggressors that seek to weaken it.
- *Good Tsar:* Russia is at its best under the leadership of strong leaders like Peter the Great that bring order and stability. Western puppets like Boris Yeltsin were weak and let Russia descend into chaos during the 1990s. But after Putin came to power, order and stability returned. The Russian people should

place their trust in the Kremlin and be wary of its critics, who seek to return Russia to chaos.[1]

Within these master narratives there are numerous prominent themes, which are adaptable to current events. A GAO analysis of over 2,000 Russian disinformation stories in Europe from November 2015 to December 2016 identified several commonly used narratives.[2] The examples below show that some of these narratives are explicitly pro-Russia, while others do not mention Russia at all:

- *Western entities are Russophobic:* The West banned Russian athletes from the 2016 Olympic as part of its hybrid war against Russia, and the United States and NATO are preparing to destroy Russia after successfully causing the collapse of the Soviet Union.

- *Russia is a victim of the West, and Western media are anti-Russian or purposely spread disinformation and propaganda:* Media in the West falsely accuse the Russian government of spreading disinformation, supplying the missile that shot down Malaysian Airlines Flight 17, killing civilians in Syria, and murdering Alexander Litvinenko. The West is also trying to provoke Russia into starting a new war and falsely blames Russia for acts of aggression.

- *Russia is the world's protector:* Russian soldiers came to the aid of Crimea's Russian-speaking people when they were threatened by Ukrainian soldiers, and by annexing the peninsula Russia saved Crimea from war. In Syria, Russia's military intervention made terrorists agree to a truce.

- *Some Western entities support Russia or Russia's positions:* One in three Europeans consider Crimea a part of Russia and some European countries recognize Crimea as part of Russia. The U.S. media revered the outcomes of Russia's military intervention in Syria.

- *Russia's boundaries are not accurately reflected on maps, and Russia owns additional lands:* Ukraine has always been a part of Russia and the Baltic countries and Belarus are also part of Russia.

- *Russia has not violated international agreements or international law:* Russia did not annex Crimea—Crimea was returned to its native land as the result of a referendum. Russian military aircraft did not break any rules when they buzzed the U.S. warship Donald Cook.

- *Western entities are trying to destabilize other regions of the world:* The United States led a violent coup against Ukrainian President Viktor Yanukovych, created ISIS, and orchestrated the migrant crisis in Europe.

- *The Ukrainian government is illegitimate and violent:* The Ukrainian government came to power through a coup and is il-

---

[1] Monitor 360, *Master Narrative Country Report Russia* (Feb. 2012). Government Accountability Office, *U.S. Government Takes a Country-Specific Approach to Addressing Disinformation Overseas*, at 63 (May 2017).

[2] Government Accountability Office, *U.S. Government Takes a Country-Specific Approach to Addressing Disinformation Overseas*, at 67 (May 2017).

legitimate, and Nazis lead the Ukrainian government, which supports fascist policies and ideas.

- *EU and/or European governments are unable to manage the migration crisis or are manipulating the crisis for other purposes:* EU member states cannot protect their citizens from violent migrants, who are altering European culture. The EU is taking advantage of the migrant crisis to create an occupation army that will be authorized to take control of national borders without the permission of member states.
- *The West's values are evil, decadent, etc.:* The European Parliament promotes the gay movement in Europe and is trying to eliminate male and female gender identities. The sexual abuse of minors is a state-sponsored national tradition in Norway and the country's institution for the protection of children's rights supports this system.
- *The EU and/or European governments are American puppets:* The EU was created by the United States to take away sovereignty from European member states, and Germany facilitates U.S. hegemony over Europe.

Techniques

Russian government disinformation uses a wide variety of misleading propaganda techniques to persuade and convince audiences of its preferred narratives. The Center for European Policy Analysis has identified over 20 techniques commonly used by the Kremlin to spread disinformation.[3] Often, several of these techniques will be used in combination for a single article or story that promotes the Kremlin's narrative on a particular event. These techniques include:

- *Ping pong:* uses complementary websites to raise the profile of a story and get mainstream media to pick it up.
- *Misleading title:* uses facts or statements in a story that may be correct, but the title is misleading.
- *Zero proof:* provides no sources or proof to validate a story's facts or statements.
- *False visuals:* similar to false facts, but uses doctored visual productions to give extra weight to false facts or narratives.
- *Totum pro parte or "the whole for a part":* for example, using the opinion of just one academic or expert to portray the official position of a government.
- *Altering the quotation, source, or context:* facts and statements reported from other sources are different than the original. For example, a statement will be attributed to a different person than who actually said it or a quote is placed out of context to change its meaning.
- *Loaded words or metaphors:* obscures the facts behind an event by substituting accurate words with more abstract ones, for example saying that someone "died mysteriously" rather than "was poisoned." The Western press has also aided the Krem-

[3] Center for European Policy Analysis, "Techniques," http://infowar.cepa.org/Techniques (visited Dec. 31, 2017).

lin's narrative by using terms like "little green men" instead of "Russian troops" in Crimea, thereby maintaining a seed of doubt as to who they really were.

- *Ridiculing, discrediting, and diminution:* uses ad hominem attacks and mockery to sideline facts and statements that run counter to the Kremlin's narratives.
- *Whataboutism:* makes false equivalencies between two disconnected events to support the Kremlin's policies and promote its narrative. For example, comparing the annexation of Crimea to the invasion of Iraq.
- *Conspiracy theories:* use rumors and myths to anger, frighten, or disgust an audience. Examples include stories like "Latvia wants to send its Russian population to concentration camps," or "The United States created the Zika virus." Another version reverses the technique, by labeling factual stories as conspiracies.
- *Joining the bandwagon:* casts a certain view as being that of the majority of people, thereby giving it more credibility.
- *Drowning facts with emotion:* a form of the "appeal to emotion" fallacy, which drowns out facts by portraying a story in such a way as to maximize its emotional impact. The fake story of a Russian girl being sexually assaulted by Muslim immigrants in Germany is a good example, where, even though the story was proven to be false and widely discredited, it so inflamed people's emotions that they were distracted from the story's absence of facts.

Appendix I: Letter from Senator Cardin to European Ambassadors

The following letter requesting information on the Russian government's malign influence operations was sent to more than 40 ambassadors in Washington, D.C. who represent various European countries. Responses to this letter helped to inform the findings of this report.

June 13, 2017

DEAR AMBASSADOR, The U.S. intelligence community has assessed that the Russian government engaged in an influence campaign in 2016 aimed at the U.S. presidential election, including sponsoring and exploiting cyber intrusions and creating and spreading disinformation. As you know, there are several investigations underway to determine the scope and impact of this interference in our democratic process.

However, the Russian government's recent actions were not the first time it has sought to interfere in the elections of other states. Over many years, the Russian government has developed, refined, and deployed its toolkit for malign influence in Europe and elsewhere. We believe that these efforts, which seek to erode citizens' confidence in the credibility of democratic institutions, pose a grave threat to the national security interests of the United States and our allies and partners around the world.

The United States Senate Foreign Relations Committee minority staff, as part of our oversight responsibilities, is conducting a study of the Russian government's malign influence operations throughout Europe and other key countries around the world. To better understand the scope of this threat, we respectfully request any relevant information from your government.

Specifically, we are interested in information related to any of the following activities:

- Acquisitions made in your state in economic sectors such as energy, finance, infrastructure, media, and real estate by individuals or entities controlled, financed or affiliated with the Russian government, and who are known to or alleged to have engaged in corrupt practices.
- Dissemination of disinformation with the intent to influence and confuse the public debate on issues of national importance in your state, including attempts to libel or compromise leading political figures, civil society activists, and others who the Kremlin may have deemed a threat to its interests, by individ-

(199)

uals or entities controlled, financed or affiliated with the Russian government.

- Expansion of media organizations into your state's media markets, including TV, radio, and the internet by individuals or entities controlled, financed or affiliated with the Russian government.
- Funding, organizational assistance, or other support of any political parties, civil society groups, or other non-governmental organizations in your state by individuals or entities controlled, financed or affiliated with the Russian government.
- Attempts to infiltrate the computer systems of the government, political parties, civil society groups, non-governmental organizations, or private enterprises in your state by individuals or entities controlled, financed or affiliated with the Russian government, especially with the intent to steal and disseminate information to influence public debate.
- Any other information that may be relevant or helpful to our study.

Finally, we are also interested in learning about any countermeasures that your country has taken to prevent or respond to these malign influence activities.

We greatly appreciate your assistance in gathering this information, which will help inform our study and shape our recommendations for a strong, coordinated response with our allies and partners.

Sincerely,

BENJAMIN L. CARDIN,
Ranking Member.

○